RED ZONE

RED ZONE

China's Challenge
and Australia's Future

PETER HARTCHER

Published by Black Inc.,
an imprint of Schwartz Books Pty Ltd
Level 1, 221 Drummond Street
Carlton VIC 3053, Australia
enquiries@blackincbooks.com
www.blackincbooks.com

9781760642167 (paperback)
9781743821794 (ebook)

A catalogue record for this
book is available from the
NATIONAL
LIBRARY   National Library of Australia
OF AUSTRALIA

Cover design by Akiko Chan
Text design and typesetting by Typography Studio
Cover image: Bloomberg / Contributor / Getty

Printed in Australia by McPherson's Printing Group

MIX
Paper from
responsible sources
FSC
www.fsc.org   FSC® C001695

To Australia,
a life raft of liberty in a rising tide of tyranny

CONTENTS

Introduction   I.

1. Red Line   15.
2. Australia: Racist or Role Model?   26.
3. Let's All Get Rich Together   40.
4. What China Wants   50.
5. Taking the Flag   67.
6. Daggers in Your Smile   94.
7. The Big Fish and the Little Fish   113.
8. The Red Detachment of Women   116.
9. Lion Dance   122.
10. How Much Can a Communist Bear?   130.
11. "World in Great Disorder – Excellent Situation"   144.
12. What Does Xi Want?   157.
13. Make the Past Serve the Present   162.
14. The Fall and Rise of China   170.
15. Dragon in Your Living Room   180.
16. Paradox of Paranoia: Eleven Types of Pain   208.
17. Cyclops   226.
18. New Gold Mountain   238.
19. Not With a Bang   249.
20. Intelligence Test   261.

21. Dye Australia Red   271.
22. Can We Endure?   290.
23. Brace   301.

    Acknowledgements   341.
    Index   343.

INTRODUCTION

In one of the most enduring tales of humanity's long story, the Greek hero Odysseus is sailing home from victory in the Trojan War when his storm-tossed ship, thrown off course, finds itself upon a strange land. Hungry and thirsty after nine days in savage storms, Odysseus and his crew go ashore and soon find water and game. The captain then sends three of the crew ahead "to scout out who might live there – men like us perhaps, who live on bread". But the crew fail to return. Odysseus himself eventually goes in search and finds them "mingled among the natives, Lotus-eaters, Lotus-eaters who had no notion of killing my companions, not at all, they simply gave them the lotus to taste instead". Scholars today suggest that the lotus of Homer's Odyssey was actually the Egyptian blue lotus, the sacred narcotic water lily of the Nile. As Homer described, its effects were remarkable: "Any crewmen who ate the lotus, the honey-sweet fruit, lost all desire to send a message back, much less return." They forgot themselves – their mission, their homes, their families – "their only wish to linger there with the Lotus-eaters", as Homer tells the tale. Sensing danger, Odysseus drags them, in tears, back to the ship by force. He lashes them under the rowing benches and orders the rest of the crew to row hard for home.

Australia has spent years feasting on a metaphorical lotus. History and geography delivered the storm-tossed Australian economy onto the shore of a strange land, the once-mighty Middle Kingdom. Australia's political and business elites scouted ahead and discovered the sweet, opiatic seduction of effortless growth and easy profit. The elements came together with great serendipity: Canberra recognised the People's Republic of China in 1972; a year later, Australia was shocked to lose its privileged access to the British market when the UK joined the European Economic Community; five years after that, China made its epochal decision to enter the global market economy. China's economic rise was about to occur, and it would carry Australia with it.

The first Australian scouts were followed by more of their kind, who tasted the lotus and soon thought of little else. Just as Ancient Egyptian priests took the blue lotus to enter a euphoric trance that allowed them to commune with the gods, Australia's elites considered themselves a special priesthood with insight into the godlike beings who controlled the supply of the lotus: the chieftains of the Chinese Communist Party (CCP). Swooning in their enchanted haze, the scouts didn't stop to ask why they were chosen. They only called for the rest of the crew to follow. They didn't speak the local tongue, knew little of the land. They knew only one thing: the craving. The national dependency deepened.

Australian business and political leaders were the subjects of China's "foreign elite capture" policy. The New Zealand Sinologist Anne-Marie Brady, a leader in the scrutiny of Chinese global power and influence, describes this as a "comprehensive strategy to target foreign economic and political elites, in order to get them to promote China's foreign policy agenda within their own political system". The founder of modern China, Mao Zedong, described this as a policy to "make the foreign serve China". A great complacency took hold, not only in Australia but around the world. China grew to become the biggest trading partner of more than 120 nations. It has promised to invest in more than sixty countries under its Belt and Road initiative, the largest global infrastructure program since the Roman Empire.

Why was Odysseus so alarmed at the euphoric forgetfulness of his crew as they abandoned themselves to the lotus?

In 1990, then paramount leader Deng Xiaoping urged restraint on a China that was beginning to pulse with the possibilities of its own rising power. Deng urged his compatriots to "hide your brightness, bide your time". Xi Jinping has overturned this strategic maxim, which guided Chinese policy for almost a quarter-century under three presidents. He has declared that China is now "striving to achieve". This is a crystallising statement of China's transformation. It was a status quo power. It is now an ambitious one.

On taking power in 2012, Xi said that he was "laying the foundation for a future where we will win the initiative and have the dominant position". Xi and China's rulers had decided that the preparatory phase was over. They'd subdued the commercial and political classes in Australia and many other nations. China had built strength while the world was entranced by the lotus. And now it was time for China to exert its power.

Under Xi, China has seized maritime territories claimed by its neighbours, ignored an international court ruling that found this to be illegal, and fortified the territories with advanced weapons systems. Under Xi, China has imprisoned at least one million of its ethnic Uighur citizens in Xinjiang Province on the basis of their Muslim religion, denied that it had done so, but then conceded that it was a program of mass "re-education", a policy likened to apartheid and cultural genocide. Xi personally issued an internal instruction to show "no mercy".

Under Xi, China's program of international influence has been exposed for paying bribes to foreign officials, including US$1.2 million to the then president of the United Nations General Assembly, John Ashe. In Pacific nations that recognise Taiwan, not Beijing, as the sole legitimate government of China, China's officials have offered bribes of A$165,000 to politicians to get them to switch, according to the governor of Malaita Province in Solomon Islands, Daniel Suidani.

Canberra has reluctantly acknowledged these actions, making token protests over Beijing's breaches of international law, human rights and criminal law. But it has done nothing to change its posture, which closely resembles a kowtow. The lotus is too sweet, its effects too heady. Australia has been wilfully ignorant for a long time, long before Xi's term began, and remains so.

A Chinese diplomat working in China's Sydney consulate defected to Australia in 2005. Chen Yonglin, first secretary for political affairs, stated plainly at the time: "In accordance with their fixed strategic plans, the Communist Party of China had begun a structured effort to infiltrate Australia ... in a systematic way." Australia had been selected as a "weak link of the western camp". Xi had intensified and accelerated this agenda.

Anyone in Australia who criticised Beijing's policies was rebuked by the priesthood, China's apologists. They were warned sternly against "making China angry" and thereby "damaging the relationship". Australia has not been alone in this self-abasement in the face of Beijing's ambition. Even after Barack Obama accused China under Xi of using "sheer size and muscle to force countries into subordinate positions", he did nothing about it. The leader of the nation that established the post-war order was not prepared to defend it. More lotus, please.

Among the many countries intoxicated by the lotus are those that should be the greatest defenders of the Uighur Muslims in their hour of need. The Organisation of Islamic Cooperation – which includes Pakistan, Saudi Arabia, the UAE, Indonesia and Malaysia – issued a communique not to criticise China's mass repression, but to praise it. In 2019, the organisation said it "commends the efforts of the People's Republic of China in providing care to its Muslim citizens".

China's authorities have committed many more intrusions and offences against Australia, including the unpublicised kidnapping of Australian citizens from Australian soil by covert Chinese operatives. Their victims were taken secretly to China, never to return. This has been going on for over a decade, as reported by Zach Dorfman in the US journal *Foreign Policy* in March 2018.

Yet almost all governments have remained acquiescent. They overlook the mounting depredations by Beijing as they solicit trade and investment for their countries, as well as favours and special treatment for their elites. Who's to blame? China for offering the lotus, or foreign nations for forgetting themselves in their craving for it?

By 2019 Australia earned 38 per cent of all its overseas income from China. It was the most China-dependent developed country on the planet. The next biggest source of Australia's overseas revenue was Japan, generating 16 per cent. This economic dependence on one country was unmatched since its over-reliance on Britain. Australia had failed to learn the lesson of its recent history. Although it had been unable to rely on its so-called Mother Country, it believed it was prudent to depend on an authoritarian one-party state with a political system it did not comprehend. History was about to dispense the lesson once more.

Beijing has behaved badly. "The Communist party is in essence a secret society," wrote a Belgian Australian, the late Pierre Ryckmans, one of the most celebrated and incisive of twentieth-century Sinologists. "In its methods and mentality it presents a striking resemblance to an underworld mob. It fears daylight, feeds on deception and conspiracy, and rules by intimidation and terror."

Under Xi, Beijing has merely been extending its methods of keeping power at home to an unwary world. Or, as the former foreign affairs minister Qian Qichen put it in 1990: "Foreign policy is the extension of China's domestic policies." Xi has brought a new resolve and vastly more resources to the task. But Xi would not be succeeding without the quiescence of other powers. The Western world's business and political leaders have "sat in a sedan chair carried up the mountain by their Chinese partners", writes the prominent Chinese artist Ai Weiwei, a critic of the regime who's now living in self-imposed exile in Britain.

And a fine journey it was – crisp air, bright sun – as they reached the mountain's midpoint. But then the chair-carriers laid down their poles and began demanding a shift. They, too, sought the top position. The signal from the political centre changed from "don't pick fights" to "go for it".

Now what could the Western capitalists do? Walk back down the mountain? They hardly knew the way.

Ai says that "the Western system itself has been challenged". Its fundamental values have been tested, and it is failing. National governments and business elites have allowed their economic and commercial interests to anaesthetise them to considerations of sovereignty and humanity. Just as one of Xi's heroes, Karl Marx, would have anticipated: "The executive of the modern state is nothing but a committee for managing the common affairs of the whole bourgeoisie," Marx wrote in *The Communist Manifesto*. Western governments were the creatures of capital and would serve profit above all. Yet it's not a syndrome unique to the contemporary Western world. In the seventeenth century, India's Mughal princes invited Britain's East India Company to invest and trade in India. British merchants offered the prospect of greater riches and the Mughals wanted more. "Companies, it was thought, did not conquer, and therefore no threat had been detected," writes the Oxford historian Alex Von Tunzelmann. Invited in, the East India Company was not only a commercial force but an imperial one, soon asserting growing British sovereign power over India. The company was, in effect, the British empire in commercial guise. "The English have not taken India," Mohandas "Mahatma" Gandhi later wrote, "we have given it to them."

The Australian people grew concerned about Xi's underworld mob mentality long before the country's elites. Their consciousness was clear as they had never been invited to taste the lotus, which was reserved for political and commercial leaders. On the daily news, they saw Xi's regime grabbing territory illegally in the South China Sea, saw the brutal repression of

Uighurs in Xinjiang, saw Australian politicians mesmerised by the gains China offered. The people saw large-scale buying of Australian real estate by a country that does not reciprocate; they saw the absorption of Australian farmland and mineral prospects by a country that does not allow Australia to do the same in China; they saw the sale of the Port of Darwin to a country that would never sell a port to Australia. And they saw universities pandering to the Chinese market and CCP definitions of free speech. By 2016 the Australian people had drawn some hard conclusions about the policies of Xi's regime. At least eight in ten Australians were critical of China's human rights record, according to that year's Lowy Institute poll. The same proportion had a negative view of China's "military activities in our region". And six in ten were concerned about Chinese investment in Australia.

By contrast, the political class had to be shocked out of its fug of witless complicity. This was done not by an Antipodean Odysseus in an act of leadership by an Australian politician, although prime ministerial resolve was utterly essential. The shock was primarily administered by Beijing. "From 2015–16 risk started to overtake opportunity in the China relationship and Australia's security agencies recognised that," attests Rory Medcalf, head of the National Security College at the Australian National University, in an interview with me. "The difficulty was persuading the political class that this was their challenge to own."

The CCP's successful capture of former senator Sam Dastyari was impossible to ignore. This was revealed in late 2016, some months after the Lowy poll had been conducted, but it took over a year for him to be drummed out of the Senate in disgrace. There were three striking aspects to the Dastyari case.

First, it exposed how cheaply an Australian politician could be bought: Dastyari sold his policy views to a foreign power for hundreds of dollars in air tickets and thousands in legal costs. Second, it turned out he'd broken no law in doing so. Australia was wide open. Third, it showed the gaping disjunction between the people and the elites. It took a year of public anger and mounting pressure to force the Labor Party into removing the offender. And while the Turnbull Coalition government had lashed Dastyari for his conduct, the government took just as long to produce a bill that addressed this problem of national vulnerability.

"Dastyari unintentionally did the nation a favour," says Medcalf. "It was the point where the taboo on talking about this stuff was broken." Today, Turnbull says in an interview that "the greatest weapon China has isn't fleets or armies – it's renminbi and dollars, and Australian politicians are very wont to take it." Bit by bit, the political class has been forced to confront the reality of China's program to dominate Australia. To "take over", as the former national security adviser and former head of ASIO Duncan Lewis put it, "pulling the strings from offshore". It has become harder and harder for the priesthood to credibly defend China. Australia's leading apologists for Chinese authoritarianism have fallen silent one by one.

When Bill Birtles and Mike Smith, the last two Australian media correspondents working in China, were harassed out of the country in September 2020, even Bob Carr and Alexander Downer felt obliged to speak out. The two former foreign affairs ministers, one Labor and one Liberal, had tasted the lotus. Carr had been hand-picked by an agent of Chinese influence, Huang Xiangmo, to head a pro-Beijing think-tank at the University of

Technology Sydney. Downer had been recruited to the board of the local subsidiary of Huawei, China's national champion in telecommunications gear, before taking his post as Australia's high commissioner to London. Now, Carr and Downer were defending a free press and free speech and criticising Beijing's heavy-handedness. China had forced them to choose sides.

It's been argued that Birtles' and Smith's harassment was merely a "tit for tat" response to Australian provocation. On 26 June 2020, ASIO and the Australian Federal Police interviewed Chinese journalists in Canberra and seized their computers and phones as part of an investigation into foreign interference. But the actions of both governments were part of a longer chain of events. Beijing had shut out nineteen other Western correspondents in the year preceding the ASIO–AFP action, and had been refusing to issue a visa to ABC correspondent-in-waiting Sarah Ferguson for well over a year before the ASIO raid. Similarly, the correspondent-in-waiting for *The Sydney Morning Herald* and *The Age*, Eryk Bagshaw, had been waiting for more than half a year, his efforts at any kind of communication stonewalled.

The "tit for tat" claim is challenged further by the treatment of a former ABC correspondent in Beijing, Matthew Carney. In August 2018 the regime, not enjoying the ABC's coverage of China, blocked the ABC website, a distinction shared by dozens of other reputable media including the BBC, the CBC, Japan's *Nikkei*, France's *Le Monde*, Germany's *Der Spiegel*, *The Wall Street Journal* and *The New York Times*. Three weeks after the ABC had been blocked, Carney and his family were harassed into leaving China. Carney realised they had to flee when an interrogator at the Ministry of Public Security, on the pretext of a technical visa violation, threatened the liberty of his fourteen-year-old daughter: "I do have to inform you, Mr Carney, that we have a right to keep your daughter in an undisclosed location and I do have to inform you there would be other adults present." In Carney's account, made public in October 2020, he points out that the two years between his experience and that of Birtles and Smith "suggests there is more to [China's] actions against foreign journalists than tit-for-tat reprisals as the Chinese portray it".

Kevin Rudd has observed: "The reality is that the Chinese regime for press and its social media control has been tightening over the last seven years in a big way. This was clear almost in the first six months since Xi Jinping became Chinese leader. The writing has been on the wall for a long time that there will be a roll-back against foreign media coverage ... This is not specific to Australia, Germany or the United States. It's generic and it's become sharper and sharper."

If China's move against Birtles and Smith was tit for tat, it was also part of a pre-existing and concerted effort to reduce scrutiny by independent media and to phase out Australian bureaus, which had been reporting from Beijing continuously since the 1970s. It was a continuum of the Xi regime's intensification of repression, where "discourse control" is a high priority.

Australia has been forced to wean itself off the lotus, to remember itself. The convergence of Beijing's bad behaviour, Australian media coverage and public opinion meant that the country's elites had to defend the national interest above the interests of a foreign authoritarian power. Malcolm Turnbull was the first prime minister to take decisive action. In December 2017 he introduced a bill to prevent foreign interference. He referred to a famous line commonly attributed to Mao Zedong: "Modern China was founded in 1949 with these words: 'The Chinese people have stood up'. It was an assertion of sovereignty, it was an assertion of pride. And we stand up and so we say, 'The Australian people stand up'." The government said that the new law was not directed towards any one country, but Turnbull's rhetorical flourish made clear that it was, in fact, specifically targeting China.

The CCP mouthpiece *People's Daily* demanded that Turnbull change course and "reject political prejudices and paranoia". But that bill passed the parliament easily, crucially with bipartisan support from Labor, as have others brought by Turnbull's successor, Scott Morrison. The new posture on China was a national choice, not a partisan preference.

Australia has been emerging from its kowtow, the beginning of a much longer process. "We have to get Australians used to the fact that there will be a bad news story on the front page every day for the next ten years," says Medcalf, anticipating difficult times for Australia and the world in dealing with China's ambitions.

Xi has prepared his party for a vastly longer struggle. "The eventual demise of capitalism and the ultimate victory of socialism must be a long historical process," he told an internal CCP meeting shortly after taking power in 2012, according to a party journal released six years later. He echoed Deng Xiaoping's quote: "Consolidating and developing China's socialism will take dozens of generations."

Homer quoted Odysseus: "'Quick, no time to lose, embark in the racing ships!' – so none could eat the lotus, forget the voyage home. They swung aboard at once, they sat to the oars in ranks and in rhythm churned the water white with stroke on stroke." Odysseus was relieved to have escaped the land of the Lotus-eaters. But he and his crew were not safe yet.

Australia's pre-pandemic economic dependence on China had been an extraordinary 38 per cent. By mid-2020 it had grown to a breathtaking 48.8 per cent. Was Australia's declaration of independence real or illusory? What is domestic law against such leverage? Odysseus and his crew left the land of the Lotus-eaters, only to find themselves facing the Cyclops.

RED LINE

Malcolm Turnbull was troubled. The prime minister was considering banning Huawei, one of China's great companies and national champions, from the Australian continent. The telecommunications equipment maker also happened to be the biggest in the world in its industry, bigger than its US and Japanese rivals put together. Several countries had talked about banning it, but none had. The flagship company was to become an international acid test of nations' trust in China.

Australia was about to start building its 5G, or fifth generation, wifi network. Much more than a phone system with faster internet, 5G would enable the Internet of Things. Could Huawei be trusted to supply the country's central nervous system for a generation? Turnbull didn't think so. "One thing you know – if the Chinese Communist Party called on Huawei to act against Australia's interests, it would have to do it," he says in an interview with me. "Huawei says, 'Oh no, we would refuse.' That's laughable. They would have no option but to comply."

But the consequences of a ban? Turnbull knew that Beijing would seek to punish Australia. Of course, China allows no foreign firms to build its 5G network. But Beijing is not about reciprocity. It's about dominance. Xi Jinping had made it his personal mission to place Huawei at the centre of the global internet. He would later tell then US president Donald Trump that a ban on Huawei would "harm the overall bilateral relationship", according to Trump's former national security adviser, John Bolton. It was a remarkable elevation. Xi was putting the interests of one Chinese company at the centre of the world's most consequential great-power relationship. It was, evidently, an extraordinary priority for China.

Turnbull sought a middle path. Was there a way to accept Huawei into the system and somehow manage the risk? That's what Britain had done with Huawei in its 4G network. Turnbull's history showed no inherent hostility to the Chinese company. When Julia Gillard's Labor government banned Huawei in 2012 from supplying gear to the new National Broadband Network, Turnbull, as the shadow communications minister, promised to review the ban once in government. The Liberals ended up continuing Gillard's ban. But now Huawei – and the Beijing government – was pressing to enter the next frontier.

Turnbull spent months researching, talking to Trump and other leaders in late 2017 and early 2018. He repeatedly turned to Australia's top-secret electronic spy agency, the Australian Signals Directorate – equivalent to the US National Security Agency – for an expert verdict. Turnbull says, "I went back and forth with Mike Burgess [then head of the directorate and now ASIO's director-general of security], pressing him to find an effective means of mitigating the risk. I would have preferred to have all vendors available in Australia, but not at the expense of security." Burgess did come up with some mitigation measures. He and the ASD experts compiled a spreadsheet filled with hundreds of them. "We gave it a good red-hot go," a senior intelligence official involved in the process told me in an interview. But there was a catch.

Turnbull, said the intelligence official, "is a big believer in tech. His starting point was, 'Convince me that we can't manage the risks.' We worked extremely hard over eight, nine months, working it though." The signals intelligence experts started from the proposition that Huawei equipment could be used in Australia's 5G network. They posed themselves the question: how can we manage that risk effectively?

Burgess gathered his professional hackers from the ASD and asked them to play the red team, to put themselves in China's shoes. They were "the best and the brightest", said the official, drawn from the section that would be used to hack into networks overseas. They were told: "Let's game it. Apply what we would do if we had a vendor that was working for us." The telecommunications equipment vendor in question being Huawei, of course, the global leader in low-cost, high-grade telecoms gear.

A technologically sophisticated government already has the know-how to disrupt another country's 5G system. But if that government has sway over a 5G vendor in the country it wants to strike, explained the official, "you can get there quicker from flash to bang, with zero cost of entry". It could be done with a simple instruction to the company operating in the target nation's 5G system. And that would be a "serious problem" for the target country.

Because it would bring down a network? Yes, but it's more than that, said the senior Australian spy:

Here's the thing that most commentators get confused about with 5G, including some of our American friends. It's not about the interception of telephone calls. We've got that problem with 4G, we had it with 3G. It's not that 5G is just a faster mobile phone network. It has lower latency. [It's about] the speed at which boxes can talk to each other, and [at] higher density, so more devices can connect per square kilometre than ever before. It's machines talking to machines.

And if the 5G network stops working? "The sewerage pump stops working. Clean water doesn't come to you. You can imagine the social implications of that. Or the public transport network doesn't work. Or electric cars that are self-driving don't work. And that has implications for society, implications for the economy." For these reasons, the 5G network will be "number one on our critical infrastructure list" in need of protection once it's fully operational. Shutting down a 5G network at that point could throw the country into chaos.

So how would the Chinese government use Huawei to do such a thing? Putting himself in Beijing's shoes, the intelligence officer said: "If I want to understand how to break in, I don't have to break in. I just look at the blueprints – I understand the software, I know how it works. I know which engineering commands are there or what other commands are there for my purposes. That allows me to gain access, to switch things off, and that disrupts the country – elements of it, or the whole country. That's why you've got to be concerned."

Turnbull steeped himself in the detail. The prime minister was "very forensic in his questioning, he obviously did his own homework", related the senior spy. "Bought himself a book on 5G security, I kid you not. We had to buy the book and make sure we understood it. It was a good grilling. [He] actually took us out for a spin." The book, *A Comprehensive Guide to 5G Security*, is a dense, technical 474-page tome edited by experts in Finland, the US and Sweden.

As the Red Team of hackers worked through the risks, they compiled them in a spreadsheet. There were more than 300. Which meant that all 300-plus would need to be mitigated. Burgess and his staff brought the full compilation to Turnbull on big sheets of A3 paper and explained all the measures. They included having full and sole access to the source code, updates being done in Australia only, and full access to hardware schematics.

But even then, it would not be enough, they concluded. The devil was not only in the details – it was in the system design itself. And that was too hard to penetrate as outsiders. The senior intelligence officer explained: "It's the control of the design that gives you zero cost of entry. It's a lot harder to reverse-engineer to find the malign element. As opposed to talking to the designers and saying – as well as its legitimate function – if I give you this secret handshake, that requires you to turn it off. You can get there the hard way through trying to reverse-engineer it, or you can get there the zero-cost way by talking to the person who knows how it works. That's the differentiating factor."

On this basis, 5G components designed in China and made in a factory in China would pose a bigger risk than 5G components assembled in a factory in China but designed by Nokia in Finland or Ericsson in Sweden. In other words, it came down to strategic trust. The Commonwealth of Australia could rely on the Republic of Finland, home to Nokia, and the Kingdom of Sweden, Ericsson's domicile, but it could not trust the People's Republic of China to harbour only benign intentions.

What about simply limiting the deployment of Huawei's gear to less sensitive parts of the 5G network? This is exactly what Australia did with its 4G system. "Historically, we have protected the sensitive information and functions at the core of our telecommunications networks by confining our high-risk vendors to the edge of our networks," Burgess said in a 2018 speech. "But the distinction between core and edge collapses in 5G networks. That means that a potential threat anywhere in the network will be a threat to the whole network." Turnbull liked to summarise this in internal debates with the rhyme that "the core is no more". Burgess's final advice to Turnbull and his National Security Committee was that the risk could not be mitigated.

Turnbull examined the question with his ministers and public service chiefs in the cabinet's National Security Committee. If allowing Huawei into the system was a risk, a ban on it would carry risks of its own. Beijing had already damned Canberra for Turnbull's laws against foreign interference and espionage by ending annual visits by Chinese leaders and freezing ministerial contacts. It already had an embargo on political contacts with Australia. Now Australia would be uniquely exposed to Beijing's retribution if it were to be the first country in the world to designate Huawei as untouchable.

At this point, Peter Dutton intervened. The then Minister for Home Affairs had been involved in National Security Committee debates about Huawei over months, and he was growing concerned about Turnbull's resolve. In a recent interview, Dutton says:

Australia had been in [an] appeasement phase for a long time. We'd allowed dollars to cloud our judgment. We were on a knife edge, speaking frankly. Huawei was the tipping point. A number of us had pushed for years. The public was there [in supporting a tougher line], the advice to us and the intelligence was clear – why are we not responding?

I saw this as a momentous decision for the government because it would affect the wellbeing of the nation for a generation. 5G will control autonomous vehicles, it will be doing remote monitoring of medical devices. It would be unconscionable to allow it to be compromised.

Dutton approached the prime minister in the cabinet anteroom after a National Security Committee meeting on 27 June 2018, about six weeks before the government was due to make its final decision. "I said to him, 'This is a red line for me. We cannot allow Huawei into the network. I think the threat is only increasing, not mitigating.'" It was a threat to resign from the Turnbull cabinet. And that made it a leadership issue. Australia's political class was feverish for a decade indulging the apparently addictive craze of dumping prime ministers at the first opportunity. Dutton was the favourite prime ministerial candidate from the conservative faction of the Liberal Party, and was preparing to strike at his leader. Turnbull might not have needed any extra pressure, but Dutton says he wanted to be sure. Says Dutton: "While Malcolm arrived at the right decision, I think he was leaning towards a mitigation approach."

Turnbull had a different interpretation of their conversation. He recalled no mention of a "red line" nor any threat to resign. In a contemporaneous note in his diary provided to me, the then prime minister wrote: "Dutton came to see me to say that he could not accept any involvement of Huawei or ZTE in the 5G network, much muttering of how we have to be strong in the face of China. I reminded him that I had initiated the whole 5G review, that I had raised it with the US in DC, not vice versa, and had discussed it with Mike Pence, the intelligence community and, of course, with Trump. I emphasised we needed to work through this carefully not least because we need to coordinate with the US. He seemed okay at the end." Turnbull made no promises to Dutton, but the cabinet's National Security Committee decided to ban Huawei on 14 August.

The decision was made, the line drawn, but not announced for nine days. Turnbull played it cautiously. Australian diplomats informed Beijing of the ban days before the announcement. Turnbull phoned Trump the day before: "When I told Trump, he seemed a bit surprised." In the announcement itself, there was no mention of Huawei or of the smaller Chinese telecoms gear-maker ZTE, and no reference to China. Just a country-agnostic principle: Australia was now prohibiting "vendors who are likely to be subject to extrajudicial directions from a foreign government that conflict with Australian law". To keep it low-key, there was no press conference, just the statement.

Peter Dutton resigned anyway. After the Huawei decision had been made but before it had been announced, Turnbull decided that Dutton was about to challenge him for the prime ministership. Turnbull pre-empted him by calling a spill motion in the Liberal party room, which he won. Dutton then resigned from the ministry while he gathered strength for another assault in three days' time. It was at this moment, the eye of the storm, that the Turnbull government announced the Huawei decision. But this weighty moment got scant notice in the Australian media, consumed by yet another spin of the revolving door. The announcement was made on 23 August 2018, Turnbull's last full day as prime minister. He wasn't around for Beijing's reaction.

China's foreign ministry said that it was "gravely concerned" at Australia's "discriminatory measures". China's commerce ministry called it "the wrong decision" and warned of "a negative impact on the business interests of China and Australian companies". In theatrical crescendo, the Communist Party's *China Daily* newspaper denounced the decision as "poisonous to bilateral relations" and the *Global Times* said it was a "stab in the back" for Huawei.

By this time, Scott Morrison had come through the middle to defeat both Turnbull and Dutton to take the prime ministership. Dutton was reinstated as home affairs minister. In the secrecy of Turnbull's National Security Committee, Morrison as treasurer had teamed with Dutton to run the hardest line against Huawei. Dutton privately described Morrison as a "fellow traveller" on this decision. Morrison himself claimed its paternity in an interview with me: "I issued the statement" banning Huawei. "I was actually treasurer and acting Minister for Home Affairs at the time. It was actually my decision and my recommendation, along with Mitch Fifield", the Minister for Communications. Morrison had joint carriage of the legislation because of the treasurer's power over foreign investment, and Fifield because of his ministerial power over the telecommunications system. Of course, no cabinet decision is made without the endorsement of the prime minister. This is an example of the adage that success has many fathers, while failure is an orphan.

Australia was the first country to ban China from its 5G network, setting a precedent for others, including the US, Japan, India, New Zealand, Singapore, Denmark, Norway, the Czech Republic, Estonia, Poland and Vietnam. Britain had decided to accept Huawei, but then changed its mind in mid-2020. The Chinese-claimed island of Taiwan, which knows China more intimately than any other jurisdiction, also banned Huawei.

Most of these governments shut out Huawei by default rather than by declaration, achieving the same result but with less fanfare. Washington directed its noisy belligerence to Beijing, but Japan, New Zealand, Norway, Singapore and Vietnam appeared to merely choose other companies by chance, and India said nothing officially but circulated an internal direction to all government ministries to exclude Huawei from any tenders. These countries hoped to be less obvious targets for Xi Jinping's retaliation. Sweden was more direct. It's Post and Telecom Authority announced in October 2020 that it would ban Huawei and ZTE because the "influence of China's one-party state over the country's private sector brings with it strong incentives for privately owned companies to act in accordance with state goals and the communist party's national strategies".

Australia had some evidence for its decision. The Chinese Communist Party enacted the National Intelligence Law of 2017. This law unequivocally requires that "any organisation or citizen shall support, assist and cooperate with state intelligence work" and aid the national intelligence agencies to "carry out intelligence work at home and abroad". The weight of evidence only increased after the Turnbull government's announcement. Beijing has now taken further measures to co-opt China's private sector. By the end of 2018 more than 90 per cent of private businesses in China had established internal CCP cells to guide and monitor them, according to Beijing's official tally. And in 2020 Xi Jinping announced a policy that obliged private businesses to work with the party's United Front Work Department, which is responsible for mobilising Chinese populations abroad to serve Beijing's interests. Private companies are required to "unswervingly listen to and follow the steps of the party". Each of these measures explicitly adheres to the all-encompassing principle that Xi enshrined in the party's constitution in 2017: "Government, the military, society and schools, north, south, east and west – the party leads them all."

In this way the minutiae of Australian security and politics intersected with the great global geopolitics of our time. Morrison and Dutton now regrouped to prosecute Australia's resistance to the Chinese Communist Party's drive for dominance. And to brace for Xi's vengeance.

2

AUSTRALIA:
RACIST OR ROLE MODEL?

When Australia called for an international inquiry into the COVID-19 plague, there could be only one explanation: racism. China's government made the accusation, and immediately weaponised it. First, China's tourism ministry issued a travel warning on 5 June 2020 to tell its citizens there'd been a "significant increase" in racial abuse and violence in Australia. The ministry was correct, but what was the point of a travel advisory? A global pandemic was under way. Australia's borders were shut. The travel warning was a political threat against Australia's $11 billion income from Chinese tourism in a non-pandemic year. China's foreign ministry also took the opportunity to lecture Australia. Spokeswoman Hua Chunying said that China would like to "advise the Australian side to pay attention to the problems and take concrete measures to protect the security, rights and interests of Chinese nationals in Australia".

Next, China's education ministry joined in, warning students that Australia was both a health risk and a racist danger zone: "The spread of the new global COVID-19 outbreak has not been effectively controlled, and there are risks in international travel and open campuses. During the epidemic, there were multiple discriminatory incidents against Asians in Australia."

This proclamation threatened the overseas income stream of Australia's universities, which had become dependent on Chinese students for a third of their foreign earnings, another $11 billion in a non-pandemic year. The Australian dollar fell by 1 per cent on the day of the warning.

State-controlled media supplied colourful details of the racial violence. *Global Times* reported:

In March, a Chinese student from Hong Kong was punched in the face and injured for wearing a face mask, and a pair of Chinese students were attacked by local gang members in broad daylight in April. Chinese business owners were also targeted, finding racist slogans outside their shops and restaurants, or their properties being vandalised.

Even the most harmless activities were newly laden with dread: "Hanging out with friends and shopping could be dangerous." It carried a video in which a Chinese student in Australia said she had been offended when a taxi driver asked her, "Does bat taste good?" China Central Television claimed that Australia was host to "almost crazy discrimination and attacks against Asian ethnic groups".

Australian Sinologist John Fitzgerald, professor emeritus at Swinburne University of Technology, counted five Chinese ministries contributing to the punitive campaign against Australia: trade, education, tourism, foreign affairs and propaganda. Writing in *The Strategist*, he concluded that "a decision has been taken at the highest levels in Beijing" to apply pressure in an approach "wrapped in a communications strategy branding Australia an irredeemably racist country in thrall to US hegemony".

The most telling statement of Xi Jinping's intent was a *People's Daily* editorial on 28 April. Amusingly, in this editorial Beijing delivered a very serious accusation by targeting a very unserious proxy – *The Daily Telegraph*, a Murdoch-owned newspaper. The tabloid works hard to be controversial, priding itself on punchy puns and mischievous troublemaking. The *People's Daily* editorial singled out a *Tele* front-page triumph: a photoshopped image of China's red flag with a golden coronavirus superimposed on its five stars. The party newspaper headlined its editorial: "Provocation to human civilization must be rejected."

Fitzgerald noted that "someone near the top of the pyramid in Beijing decided to make an example of the rambunctious Sydney tabloid to signal an important message about Australia to every official, every business and every family in China". He explained that the editorial's by-line – Zhong Sheng, or "Voice of the Centre", meaning the central leadership – "is reserved for editorials signalling central party views on important international relations issues. It's fair to say it is the voice of Xi, one or two steps removed." Through this editorial, "Beijing notified the world of Australia's pariah status".

The CCP mouthpiece said: "*The Daily Telegraph* newspaper has exposed its narrow-minded psychology and dark intentions. The racist remarks about the novel coronavirus and the consequent racial discrimination, racial contradictions, and racial conflicts are all blatant provocations against modern civilization." John Fitzgerald set out the implication: "While Xi is running things, we can expect to hear much more about Australian racism, about Australian lapdogs dancing to American tunes, and about steering clear of Australia. The latest travel and education warnings over racism don't stand up to scrutiny because they don't have to. Our problem is not racism, it is Xi."

Australia does have a dreadful history of institutionalised racism. The Chinese Communist Party has a dreadful present of institutionalised racism. Australia has persistent problems of individuals with racist views. The Chinese Communist Party has persistent programs to impose racial persecution. Australia has been moving away from race-based official policy since it began dismantling the White Australia policy in the 1960s and 1970s. China has been moving towards an increasingly race-based definition of Chineseness. "From the mid-1980s onwards, the belated establishment of the dragon as a totemic animal for all Chinese has been coupled with the identification of 'Chinese-ness' as a set of physical characteristics," writes Barry Sautman, a professor of political science at Hong Kong University of Science and Technology. Specifically, "black hair, black eyes and yellow skin". He says that "racial nationalism in China serves mainly to reinforce the prevalence of what is euphemistically called 'Great Han chauvinism'". China has fifty-six officially recognised ethnic groups, but the Han make up 90 per cent of the total population. The non-Han nonetheless account for about 120 million people. Han chauvinism proclaims the inherent superiority of the Han over all others. While Chinese officialdom sometimes asserts the dragon as the emblem of all Chinese people, non-Han ethnic groups in China have their own traditional origin totems. The Mongols, for instance, have the wolf and the dog; the Tibetans the monkey; the Gaoshan the snake; the Li the cat; the Koreans the bear.

A closely associated theme in Han identity is the Yellow Emperor, the mythical Huang Di, supposedly born in 2704 BC.

In 1655 the first European mission to the Chinese court described the Chinese as having a white complexion, "equal to the Europeans". The concept of the Chinese as yellow-skinned was developed by the Chinese themselves. The great Yellow River and the Yellow Emperor meant that "the notion of a yellow race was a positive symbol of imperial nobility", as Frank Dikötter, a professor of history at Hong Kong University, has written. Yellow was the imperial colour. Many Han believe themselves to be the descendants of the Yellow Emperor. Chineseness, Dikötter points out, "is primarily defined as a matter of blood and descent: one does not become Chinese like one becomes Swiss or Dutch, since cultural integration (language) or political adoption (passport) are both excluded". And just as the dragon has been promoted as an icon of Chinese identity since the 1980s, "there has been a revival of the cult of the Yellow Emperor", says Sautman, "vigorously and officially elevated since the mid-1980s".

So when Xi Jinping took Donald Trump on a guided tour of Beijing's Forbidden City in 2017, his apparently casual explanation of Chinese civilisation was actually laden with meaning. As the leaders strolled through the ancient palace complex, with Melania Trump and Xi's wife, Peng Liyuan, Trump ventured that "I guess the oldest culture, they say, is Egypt," with 8000 years of history. His Chinese host countered that China was in a class of its own because, unlike Egypt, its civilisation was unbroken. We have the longest continuous civilisation in history, said Xi. "We have the same black hair and yellow skin that we inherited. We call ourselves descendants of the dragon." The US president replied with a laugh: "That's great."

Hong Kong columnist Lam Min Yat didn't think so. "According to President Xi, Chinese people = Descendants of Dragon =

Black hair and yellow skin. When Chinese people talk about 'Descendants of Dragon', they are actually talking about the Han ethnic group only," he wrote. "The Han Chinese usually think that they represent the Chinese nation. Chinese culture means Han culture. So, Chinese are with black hair and yellow skin. The other ethnic groups are invisible to them. This kind of Han chauvinism exists all over the Han-dominant China. President Xi is a good example of such Han chauvinism."

The Australian government discourages racism. Australia's anti-racist infrastructure includes a race discrimination commissioner, currently Chin Tan, anti-discrimination commissions at the state level and laws against racial discrimination and vilification. In contrast, the CCP enforces racial discrimination, with infrastructure including a network of detention camps for its Uighur minority that a member of the UN Committee on the Elimination of Racial Discrimination, Gay McDougall, said had turned the province of Xinjiang into "something resembling a massive internment camp". Credible reports describe programs of forced assimilation and systematic sterilisations of Uighurs. The US has officially classified Beijing's treatment of its Uighurs as "genocide". The parliaments of Canada and the Netherlands have voted to apply the same designation of "genocide". In an interview, the leading voice of the free Uighurs, Rebiya Kadeer, described one particular CCP practice: in Uighur families where the father is taken away to a detention camp, a Han Chinese man is imposed on the family as the head of the house – even though he is a stranger who does not speak their language, eat their food or worship their god.

"Australia definitely has problems with racism here, and there has been a surge of attacks and harassment against people of Asian appearance since COVID," says the Australia direc-tor at Human Rights Watch, Elaine Pearson. The advocacy network Asian Australian Alliance set up an online register to collect accounts of anti-Asian racism, including anonymous reports. From the start of the pandemic to September 2020, it collected "almost 500". The Lowy Institute polled Chinese Australians in November 2020 and found that 37 per cent said they'd been treated differently or less favourably in the past year because of their heritage. Thirty-one per cent said they'd been called offensive names. And 18 per cent reported being attacked physically or threatened with attack. Asked about the reasons for this hostility, 66 per cent cited the COVID-19 pandemic, and 52 per cent nominated the state of the bilat-eral relationship. Multiple answers were permitted. Obversely, 40 per cent said someone had expressed support for them in the past year because of their heritage. Beyond Australian Sin-ophobia, Indigenous Australians face entrenched problems of racism and disadvantage.

Nevertheless, Pearson points out that "every country has a problem with racism", and that a significant element is "whether it's government-led. We have issues of racism by some Austral-ians and maybe the government could be doing more to protect all Australians. But in China you have a systemic campaign to eliminate the religious and cultural rights of minorities. It's a question of whether you would take seriously any criticism from China. It's a bit rich coming from a country that systematically denies the rights of ethnic minorities."

*

When the CCP decided to impose a program of economic coercion in retaliation for Australia's push for a COVID-19 inquiry, it wasn't a surprise. The Chinese ambassador to Australia, Cheng Jingye, had already publicly threatened Australia with trade boycotts, thereby removing the veil from the veiled threats that China's diplomats have made for many years. President Xi Jinping told Australia's parliament in 2014 that the two countries should "be harmonious neighbours who stick together in both good times and bad times". But now that bad times had arrived in the form of a global pandemic and a global depression, it was threatening to make it worse by imposing sanctions. Cheng said that Australia's proposal for an international inquiry into the origins and handling of the pandemic was "dangerous" and demanded that the Morrison government drop the idea. "The Chinese public is frustrated, dismayed and disappointed with what Australia is doing now," he told *The Australian Financial Review*'s Andrew Tillett in an interview published on 26 April 2020.

> In the long term, for example, I think if the mood is going from bad to worse, people would think why we should go to such a country while it's not so friendly to China? The tourists may have second thoughts. Maybe the parents of the students would also think whether this place, which they find is not so friendly, even hostile, is the best place to send their kids to. So it's up to the public, the people to decide. And also, maybe the ordinary people will think why they should drink Australian wine or eat Australian beef. Why couldn't we do it differently?

So Cheng was asking us to believe that China's consumers, quite spontaneously, would declare a people's boycott of Australia. It was an attempt to deliver a thunderbolt threat, while keeping some plausible deniability. Of course, no such consumer boycott emerged. Instead, six weeks later the Chinese government started to impose the punishments Cheng had promised. Beijing issued the travel warning and the student warning, and then imposed the other sanctions on Cheng's list – on wine and beef. Beijing prohibited imports of Australian beef from specific abattoirs, purportedly because of mislabelling; it also announced an inquiry into imports of Australian wine, supposedly for dumping wine below the cost of production. It even added a bonus extra punishment – an 80 per cent tariff on imports of Australian barley. Combined, the Australian trade items subject to this coercion were worth around $25 billion in a non-COVID-19 year.

But China's authorities had a problem. They had frenetically opposed Australia's call for an international inquiry, but a month after Australia had proposed it, such an inquiry was endorsed unanimously by the World Health Assembly, with a record 137 nations co-sponsoring the motion. China was among them. True, the inquiry as finally agreed was not identical in every detail to the one Canberra suggested – the state-controlled *Global Times* said that Australia had suffered a "slap in the face" – but in substance the Australian idea had been embraced. The inquiry was a reality.

Xi still wanted to punish Australia for its cheek, ensuring an object lesson for other countries that might want to hold him to account for other transgressions. But Beijing could no longer use the inquiry proposal as its public rationale. This is when the accusation of racism emerged. It was a handy pretext. This is how China decided to brand Australia with that awful slur. "China can't play the race card, basically – look what's happening to the Uighurs and the Tibetans," says Elaine Pearson. And yet it did. If it gets away with it, it won't be because it's true.

Penny Wong's response to the accusation of Australia as racist? "First, racism does exist in our country, as it does around the world," says the Leader of the Opposition in the Senate and the shadow foreign affairs minister in a recent interview with me. "We should always act to uphold respect and fight prejudice and racism. And we do. Multiculturalism is an ongoing process and it's been a great success. We always have to work to strengthen it.

"Second, I think it's important to be clear about why it is that we assert what we do on the Uighurs in Xinjiang – because we support the UN Convention on Human Rights. And why we assert what we do on the South China Sea – it's not any preju- dice, it's a recognition of the importance of international law and stability and peace," she says. "And," says the Chinese-Malaysian Australian, "I'm very comfortable that I'm not racist."

Malcolm Turnbull, whose government imposed the Huawei ban and moved to protect Australia against CCP interference, has two grandchildren of Chinese heritage, as he has pointed out publicly on many occasions. Penny Wong was instrumen- tal in clinching Labor support for Turnbull's foreign interference bills. The argument that Wong or Turnbull made these decisions because they are racist is hardly credible. As Turnbull has said: "The proposition that someone whose granddaughter calls him 'Ye ye' is anti-Chinese is absurd."

Overwhelmingly, Australian people have a very favourable impression of Chinese people. More than eight in ten said that

Chinese people they'd met were a "positive influence", according to the Lowy Institute annual poll in 2016. Almost as many said the same of Chinese culture. Contrary to the accusations from Beijing's propaganda outlets and its apologists in Australia, Australia's attitude towards China is not based on a racist antagonism towards the Chinese. Incidentally, that was the same Lowy poll that found Australians were critical of China's government over its human rights policies and its military conduct in the region. It turns out that Australians are quite capable of telling the difference between a people and a regime.

Australians' high opinion of Chinese people is strongly influenced by the 1.3 million Chinese Australians who call Australia home. And Australia is happy to have them. "Can I say thank you to the Australian Chinese community," Prime Minister Scott Morrison said in February 2020. "You are magnificent." The Chinese community in Australia had been role models of responsibility in responding to the coronavirus. The Xi regime, on the other hand, was responsible for the coronavirus, its incubation and early spread. Again, Australians overwhelmingly can tell the difference.

The real reason for Beijing's politically tricked-up accusation of racism is not because Xi Jinping is interested in Australia as a case study in racial abuse. It is because Australia is increasingly regarded as a case study in how to stand up to China. In July 2020, a major US think-tank, the Center for Strategic and International Studies, published a report titled "Countering China's Influence Activities: Lessons from Australia". Its author, Dr Amy Searight, an Asia specialist, wrote that "although China's rise is felt all across the globe, perhaps no country has been as roiled politically by China's growing influence and political ambitions as Australia has over the past several years." She described Australia as a "'canary in the coalmine' – a cautionary tale about the ways in which China seeks to covertly influence and interfere with the political process in advanced democracies. It has also thrust Australia into a leading position as a country willing to take active steps to counter China's political interference and stand up to Chinese coercion."

Senior American officials concur. The topmost Asia policy official in the Pentagon in 2018, Randy Schriver, said in an interview that Australia has "woken up people in a lot of countries to take a look at Chinese activity within their own borders. I think Australia has done us a great service by publicising much of this activity and then taking action." John Bolton was the US national security adviser at the time Australia announced its Huawei ban and its foreign interference laws. "This is something Australia can take great credit for," he told me. "It was really Australia that pressed hard [on banning Huawei and ZTE]. Australia said to us, 'For God's sake, we have to move on this or China will be in our system and we'll never get it out.'" Indeed, when Turnbull phoned Trump to tell him about Australia's Huawei ban, Trump responded, "We're going to do that." Admiral Mike Rogers, head of both the US National Security Agency and US Cyber Command at the time, now looked to Australia's example: "The Australians had a good framework. I would encourage other nations to look at that. The US has not yet articulated a policy on 5G; Australia has," he told me in 2018.

America had been hesitating about Huawei. John Bolton said this was because Trump was still holding out hope for a mega trade deal with China. "He was prepared to trade Huawei away for the 'deal of the century'. Everything was on the table."

Trump ultimately gave up this hope, and swung from parleying with China to punishing it. The US banned Huawei from its 5G system when Trump signed an executive order in May 2019. It was nine months after Australia imposed its ban. Washington had already taken other steps to limit Huawei's reach inside the US, such as prohibiting it from federal government tenders. But, contrary to Beijing's claim that Canberra was merely following Washington, Australia was the first country to exclude the Chinese company from its 5G network, and then continued to urge the US and others to follow its lead.

In Britain, Bill Hayton – an Asia expert with the BBC and an associate at think-tank Chatham House – observes that "Australia is way out in front of the rest of the world in thinking about Chinese influence and operations. The quality of the debate is far higher than anything you see in Southeast Asia, and in the UK it has changed but mainly you have people banging on without knowing what they're talking about." The University of Canterbury's Professor Anne-Marie Brady attests that "everybody says Australia is ahead of everybody else – the overall trend looks to me that your politicians are pretty clear now, though you've got to remember there will be people resisting all along the way."

It is because Australia is in the vanguard that Xi – the first and the most formidable of those resisting along the way – has decided it must be stopped. Not because Australia is racist, but because it is a role model. "The reality," says Malcolm Turnbull, "is that the Chinese Communist Party does not believe in the Westphalian system, with all countries having equal rights. Their leaders say they do, but they don't." Beijing's real view of international relations, says Turnbull, is the famous statement by mighty

Athens to weaker Melos in the Melian Dialogue, according to Thucydides in his *History of the Peloponnesian War*. The question of doing "right" only applies in a negotiation between two equal powers, the Athenians explain. The Athenians then deliver the foundational Western definition of the doctrine of realism in international affairs: "The strong do what they can and the weak suffer what they must." "That's what we have to seek to avoid," concludes Turnbull. "We have to be able to maintain sovereignty."

The Athenians insist on dominance. The Melians only want to maintain their neutrality. But that is not enough for the Athenians; it does not constitute submission. The Athenian forces proceed to crush the Melians, enslave their women and children and replace their menfolk with Athenian settlers. The Chinese Communist Party put its own formulation of the Athenian principle of power at an international summit in 2010. In an unguarded moment, China's then foreign affairs minister, Yang Jiechi, told his Singaporean counterpart, George Yeo: "China is a big country and other countries are small countries, and that's just a fact." Yang was promoted to membership of the party's Politburo, its highest council, where he remains today.

The more power the CCP possesses, the greater the dominance it demands. And that's just a fact. If it's been that clear for that long, why did it take Australia – indeed, why did it take the world – so long to awaken?

3

LET'S ALL GET RICH TOGETHER

In 2010 an Australian businessman, Peter Mason, was sitting in his Sydney office when the phone rang. He didn't know that he was about to have a conversation with a spy he'd never met. It was a story he would be telling for years to come.

Australia's then director-general of security, the formal title of ASIO's chief, introduced himself. David Irvine proceeded to invite Mason to a one-on-one lunch. Mason is very well known in corporate Australia. After a career in investment banking, he chaired establishment institutions including David Jones, AMP and the Sydney Opera House Trust, and is on the board of Optus's parent company, Singtel. He wasn't hard up for a lunch invitation. But he'd never had anything to do with ASIO. He suspected it was a prank call.

"How will I know it's you at the restaurant?" Mason wanted to know? "

Because I'll be there to greet you," replied Irvine. "Trust me enough to come to lunch. And if I'm not there, you'll know it's not me."

Mason chuckled as he related the story to friends afterwards. "I was sceptical, but given the nature of the invitation, I said yes." As Mason took his seat at the lunch table, Irvine made his opening gambit: "So how is the transaction in Beijing going?" The AMP Society was in the midst of negotiating a large deal in China. But it was strictly confidential. "That got my attention," Mason recalled.

Irvine demonstrated his bona fides. He knew that Mason had been to Beijing recently. He knew that he'd stayed at the Westin Hotel. He even knew that the hotel had upgraded him to a corner room. "The Chinese were listening to you the whole time," Irvine told him. "And we were listening to them." He didn't reveal how.

Now he came to his point. Mason recounted: "ASIO wanted me to know that they were very nervous about China's infiltration of Australia's communication system." Specifically, they were concerned about the Chinese telecommunications equipment manufacturer Huawei. "And I should be aware as a director of Australian and international companies that it was a matter of sensitivity for Australia."

David Irvine has confirmed that he was issuing discreet alerts to large Australian firms at the time. "Quite early on ASIO found that it was in a position that it had to advise a number of major Australian companies that they had been compromised, most likely by China. We had a fair degree of certainty," he told me recently. "Huawei would have come up."

Australian companies had scant awareness of cyber espionage at the time. Where ASIO was able to detect cyber theft and cyber-intrusion, it quietly told the target firms. Often it was after the damage had been done. Victim companies sometimes accepted ASIO's advice; in that era of cyber innocence, others refused to believe that it was possible. ASIO had to convince them before they took any protective measures. ASIO sometimes gave companies pre-emptive warning. Irvine's lunch date with Peter Mason was one such alert. Irvine, now chair of the Foreign Investment Review Board, spent a lot of time briefing banks, mining companies and other major businesses in 2010. It would take longer for smaller companies to discover that their intellectual property had been stolen. As an official who was working in intelligence at the time observes, "They really only found evidence of that when duplicates of their products came out, coming mainly out of China."

The federal government itself acted on ASIO's warnings about Huawei. There were three phases. First, in 2010 the board of the NBN quietly decided that it would not accept any of Huawei's bids to take part in the creation of the national broadband network. This followed a briefing from Irvine and the then national security adviser, Duncan Lewis. Second, the NBN ban on Huawei was publicly confirmed by the Gillard government in 2012. Third was the Turnbull government's 2018 ban on Huawei and ZTE from constructing Australia's 5G network. "So the government's position of being very wary of Huawei was consistent, starting with the Rudd government in 2010, then Gillard and then Turnbull," said the intelligence official.

*

Peter Mason's encounter with Irvine occurred over ten years ago, which indicates that the informal system of quiet warnings and secret suasion was working. Prompting three questions. First, if Australia's authorities knew of the risk posed by Huawei and were able to counter it silently, why did they ultimately make a public declaration, which was bound to arouse complaints from

Beijing? Second, if a formally declared ban was indeed truly necessary, why wait till 2018? And third, if the intelligence agencies
had identified China as a hostile state that was already operating
against Australia in 2010, why did it take another seven or eight
years for Australia's members of parliament and the wider Australian public to get the message?

On the first question, the Gillard government was happy to
keep it quiet. It did not intend to announce shutting out Huawei
from the NBN. It was Huawei itself that revealed the information to reporters from *The Australian Financial Review*, who
duly reported in March 2012 that a government official had
told Huawei not to bother bidding on NBN tenders. The reason
given was a program of Chinese cyberattacks on Australian companies and governments. To check the story, the reporters went
to the government, which duly confirmed the ban. It was now
public, at Huawei's instigation.

Why? Because the Chinese firm wanted to use the disclosure
to pressure the Australian government into admitting it to the
NBN. It claimed discrimination. The *AFR* report said: "Huawei sources have also hinted that the Chinese government will
retaliate strongly against Australia if the ban on the company's
tenders is not lifted." It would be difficult for China to retaliate against something unknown. So Huawei chose to make it
known, setting Australia up for punishment.

On the second and third questions, the answer is broadly
the same: Australia did not want to confront reality. It was too
deeply committed to the dream, to the opioid temptation of
effortless, limitless profit, to the lotus flower of China's allure.
And too anxious about losing its supply of the sweet narcotic.

*

Standing to give the toast at a lunch in the chandeliered ball-room of a Sydney hotel, China's First Vice Premier raised his glass of wine to the hundreds of businesspeople before him. "Let's all get rich together!" exclaimed Zhu Rongji with a broad grin, to the delight of his audience. It was 1997, and it was not only the wine that was intoxicating.

Zhu was about to become premier of China, and China was about to become a full member of the global market system through admission to the World Trade Organization. The Soviet Union was a memory. It was difficult to reconcile Zhu's unabashed capitalist gloating with the name of the political group pursuing it, the Chinese Communist Party. Communism seemed such an anachronism. It was almost embarrassing to say the word. Zhu wore not a Mao suit but a business suit, talked more like Gordon Gekko than Karl Marx. The country's growth had been impressive. It was about to become explosive.

At the moment that the businesspeople in the room laughed and clinked glasses at the sheer audacity of Zhu's toast, China's economy was roughly twice the size of Australia's. Just as it had been when Canberra first extended diplomatic recognition to Beijing in 1972. The ratio – two to one – had not changed in a quarter-century. But by 2018, China's economy was nearly ten times the size of Australia's.

China's take-off was not unprecedented in its speed. Japan grew at similarly breakneck rates in its early decades after World War II. Nor was China's growth unprecedented in its duration. Japan's post-war boom ran about as long. What set China apart was sheer scale. At 1.4 billion people, China contains almost a fifth of humanity. Taken together, the speed, duration and scale of the transformation was truly one of the wonders of the modern world.

Two specifics can help us appreciate the abstract. First, China used more cement between 2011 and 2013 than the United States used in the entire twentieth century. "It's a statistic so mind-blowing that it stunned Bill Gates and inspired haiku," wrote a *Washington Post* reporter. Second, China's growth lifted 850 million people out of absolute poverty in the four decades to 2013. That was the population of planet Earth until the nineteenth century. The World Bank observes that, of all the people in the world who managed to escape poverty in the last four decades, seven of every ten were Chinese. It describes this as "unprecedented in scope and scale". Or, in the words of China's government, "a miracle in the development of mankind".

Zhu's toast was no delusion. Along the way, Australia and China did get rich together. China displaced all other trading partners to become Australia's biggest export market. In 2019 China bought a third of everything that Australia sold to the world. That was double the share of the next biggest market, Japan. The last time Australia was so dependent on one country for its income was in the 1950s, when it was a client state of Britain. For a sense of China's preponderance, consider this: pre-pandemic, Australia's revenue from Chinese tourists was more valuable than the entirety of Australia's exports to the United Kingdom.

Still, as valuable as tourism and other services trades are to Australia, they pale in comparison to the resources business. The sale of rocks accounted for 53 cents in every dollar of total Australian sales to China in 2019. That was mostly iron ore, but included coal, bauxite and other ores. Add other raw materials, such as gas and wool and beef and barley and lobsters, and almost three-quarters of Australia's total exports to pre-pandemic China were raw products, feeding the Chinese industrial machine as well as its banquet tables and households.

China's appetites are so voracious that it doesn't just wait to see what Australian exporters might offer to sell. An industry of citizen exporters sprang up to satisfy its needs, filling their shopping trolleys with Australian baby formula, vitamins and skincare products and then mailing them to increasingly discerning retail customers in China. Pre-pandemic, this trade was operated by around 150,000 Chinese students and tourists and other residents in Australia, known as *daigou*, a term that translates as "buy on behalf of". Its estimated sales were $2.5 billion a year, according to a company that helps service the *daigou*, AuMake. Sales that corporate Australia was too slow or too complacent to pursue are made by enterprising individual Chinese. Even sailors with the Chinese navy joined the rush. The crews of three Chinese naval ships on a port visit to Sydney in June 2019 were photographed carting vanloads of baby formula onto their warships to take home.

"China remains the premier growth opportunity for many Australian companies despite a slowing economy and increased regulatory risk," Stewart Oldfield of market intelligence firm Field Research wrote in *The Australian Financial Review* in mid-2019.

> Australia–China trade has continued to grow strongly over the past two years despite tensions. Two-way goods trade expanded by 17.5 per cent in 2018, five times faster than global trade growth, topping $192 billion … Australian-listed company exposure to China goes well beyond its traditional strengths in iron ore and coal and these days includes infant

formula, education and employment services, pharmaceuti-
cals, fruit, wine and tourism.

There are many tales of woe, but a company or industry that
successfully catches the China market updraft feels like it's gone
from climbing the stairs to zooming skywards in a high-speed
elevator. Wine, for instance. A decade ago, Australia sold three
million cases to China a year, worth $120 million. By the end of
2019, it had risen to 17 million cases, fetching $1.1 billion and dis-
placing the French wine industry as the biggest supplier to China.

The Reserve Bank of Australia has "more staff looking at China
than any other single overseas economy", according to its governor,
Philip Lowe, even though the United States is still by far the larger
of the two. So why devote more resources to studying China?
Partly because of the opportunities. Casting ahead to 2030, the
Australian Treasury forecasts that the total size of the US economy
will be US$24 trillion. Which sounds impressive until you see that
it projects China's to be US$42 trillion, 175 per cent the size of
America's.

Of course, it is merely a forecast. Many over the past twenty
years did falsely predict a collapse of China's economy, but most
have been so worn down by being so wrong for so long that they
have given up. That does not mean a Chinese economic shock is
impossible. As he prepared to retire in 2017, China's then central
bank chief, Zhou Xiaochuan, stunned markets with the blunt-
ness of a warning that "we should particularly defend against"
a "sharp correction, what we call a 'Minsky moment'". A sudden collapse in asset prices like real estate and shares, in other
words. China has not repealed the laws of economics but has
managed to navigate them successfully for far longer than most

Western analysts would have credited. And this is another reason that Australia's Reserve Bank devotes more resources to China-watching – because of the risks. "Among the largest economic risks that Australia faces is something going wrong in China," said the governor. Or, as business commentator Robert Gott-liebsen put it: "We are incredibly dependent on China – in some ways we are a state of China."

And a final reason is because of the peculiarities. Lowe mentioned some of these, foremost that Australia and China have "different political systems". And the differences need extra effort to comprehend, he said.

Indeed, although Zhu Rongji was a pivotal economic reformer in China and presented himself to his rapturous Australian audience as an arch-capitalist, he was always committed to the Chinese Communist Party's iron rule and relentless repression. It was Zhu who opened the way for a much wider play of market forces in China's economy. He reformed China's lumbering state-owned enterprises and modernised its financial system. This was "reform", the first half of the "reform and opening" mantra at the centre of China's growth policy, authored by the breakthrough leader Deng Xiaoping. And it was Zhu who presided over China's entrance to the World Trade Organization – the "opening" that powered China's historic rise.

But while Zhu, also known as the Iron Premier, was effective as an economic liberaliser, he was a political conservative. "Zhu's success in establishing central coordination over explosive local growth was a remarkable achievement," Orville Schell and John Delury wrote in their book *Wealth and Power*. "Yet he never sought to touch the radioactive core of the new economic reactor bequeathed him by Deng – the political system. Perhaps he had learned a lesson from the fate of his predecessor Zhao Ziyang, still under house arrest."

The former premier Zhao never managed to emerge from his confinement. His sin was to favour political liberalisation. His cardinal sin was to oppose Deng's order to massacre the students protesting peacefully in Tiananmen Square in 1989. Deng removed him from office and while he was never charged with any offence, he was never allowed his liberty. He died after fifteen years of house arrest in a state-provided home that had once been home to the hairdresser of the empress dowager in the final years of the Qing dynasty, China's last. The house was close to Zhu's office, the former premier a prisoner just a stone's throw from the workplace of the serving premier, a standing warning to Zhu of the risks of attempting political reform.

Yet when Zhu spoke to democratic audiences, he would keep alive the great Western fantasy: that China's liberal enlightenment was on its way. Not in a direct mimicry of Western systems, but liberalising nonetheless: "We're not afraid of democracy," he told US reporters in 1999, but needed time "to gradually do better and gradually turn China into a country that is completely under the rule of law". He was reassuring the West, part of a party-wide effort to buy the democratic world's cooperation while China pursued breakneck development to match and surpass the US. China was hiding its brightness, biding its time, just as Deng had instructed. Until Xi Jinping declared the wait to be over.

For Australia, a country with enormous exposure to a great power with a fundamentally different system, the essential starting point is to ask: what does China want from the world? And, specifically, what does China want from Australia?

4

WHAT CHINA WANTS

For Joe Hockey, the realisation hit while he was sitting in a traditional thatched hut in Bali. After only two days as Australia's treasurer, he was utterly unprepared for his meeting with China's finance minister. It was September 2013, and Hockey was representing Australia at a meeting of the twenty-one Asia-Pacific Economic Cooperation countries. Chinese officials had shuttled back and forth to the hut for hours finessing every detail, but when Lou Jiwei strode in, sat down opposite Hockey and blithely lit a cigarette, it wasn't detail that concerned him. "So," Lou opened by saying, "why won't you let me buy Rio Tinto?"

Rio is one of the world's great mining companies. It draws high-quality iron ore, bauxite, diamonds, gold, copper and uranium from its mines in Australia, Canada, Mongolia and elsewhere. Although it's only part-Australian, with dual headquarters in London and Melbourne, it is one of Australia's most valuable corporate assets. In 2008 China made a bid through a state-owned firm to buy 15 per cent of the company. Beijing was anxious to lock down the raw materials to feed its vast industrial appetites. The global financial crisis was underway, so it was going cheap. The Rudd government approved the sale, but made clear that 15 per cent was the maximum stake for a state-owned foreign investor. Now, five years on, Lou Jiwei wanted to revisit the limit.

"That's fine," Hockey parried, once he'd recovered from his surprise. "As long as you'll let Qantas buy China Southern", a state-owned airline, the biggest in Asia. Lou didn't like that idea. He tried another angle: "All I want," he told Hockey through an interpreter, "is to buy 15 per cent of your top 200 listed companies." The Australian treasurer's response was to laugh at the brazenness of the proposal. If granted, it would make the Chinese government the biggest single investor in corporate Australia. In many companies it would make the Chinese government the most influential shareholder. And, overall, it would give the Chinese government unmatched sway over the conduct of companies, industries, banks, financial markets, regulators and governments.

When the brash former head of China's sovereign wealth fund saw that this wasn't going to be accepted, he put another idea to Hockey. Lou suggested Chinese buyers could take major stakes in Australia's big banks. Hockey didn't countenance this, either. Rather than allow Lou to work through a list of options for acquiring broad ownership of Australia's corporate crown jewels, Hockey suggested they move on to a "more meaningful" topic.

The encounter stunned Hockey. It revealed several important aspects of the Chinese government's intent and conduct. First, Lou put aside any pretence that state-owned companies act independently of the Chinese Communist Party. It was clear that he expected to direct the behaviour of Chinese state-owned firms. Second, Lou's proposals were a naked play to use the resources of the Chinese system to buy the maximum possible ownership, and, with that, the maximum possible power and influence over Australia. There was nothing said about investment returns or business profitability. Lou was interested in ownership for its own sake. Third was the sheer brazenness of the bid. It revealed towering arrogance and raw hubris. What did China want from Australia? As much power and influence over its economy as it could possibly get. It's possible that Lou had no real expectation that such an abrupt and ambitious bid would be considered seriously. If so, we can only assume that he hoped to awe the new Australian treasurer with his power. In the event, a Chinese state-owned firm did manage to buy a slice of Rio, its coalmining business. Yancoal bought full ownership of Coal & Allied from Rio for $3.5 billion in 2017.

*

For Stephen Conroy, it hit in a phone call from someone he'd thought was on his side. Conroy, then a Labor senator and Victorian powerbroker, was the shadow defence minister. He took a call from the general secretary of the NSW Labor Party, Kaila Murnain. It was 17 June 2016, and a federal election was due in just fourteen days. "Steve, if you don't change your China position, we are going to lose $400,000" in a promised political donation, she told him, according to the account that a shocked Conroy gave to many of his colleagues at the time. The timing gave it extra potency. The sudden loss of such a big pledge so close to an election could punch a hole in the party's final ad campaign, maybe even a decisive one. He added his interpretation: "This is serious when they can manipulate us two weeks out from an election."

For a political party, that is a huge sum. The public hearings of the NSW Independent Commission Against Corruption in 2019 revealed that NSW Labor was prepared to break the law and engage in elaborate cover-ups to get its hands on a donation one-quarter as big during a state campaign. After the hearings, Murnain lost her job over that scandal. Curiously, it was the same donor, the property tycoon and billionaire Huang Xiangmo, behind both offers, according to evidence to ICAC on the state campaign and according to multiple Labor sources on the federal. For the record, he has denied being the donor on either occasion.

A donation of $400,000 would have been among the biggest donations from any individual in Australian political history. Huang was a permanent resident of Australia and lived in a $12.8-million home in Sydney's Mosman, which he's since been forced to abandon. The Australian government cancelled his visa and declared him persona non grata after ASIO found him to be a covert agent of influence for the CCP.

The "China position" that was so upsetting that Huang would offer $400,000 to change it? The previous day, Conroy had debated the defence minister, Marise Payne, at the National Press Club as part of the election campaign. In the course of debate, Conroy declared that a Labor government would take a firmer stand in resisting Chinese encroachments on its neighbours' territorial claims in the hotly contested South China Sea: "The Turnbull government has hidden behind ambiguous language," said Conroy. "We believe our defence force should be authorised to conduct freedom-of-navigation operations consistent with international law."

Conroy refused to alter his position. Murnain's reaction? "Ms Murnain is said to have been seen in Labor head office cursing about losing 'hundreds of thousands' of dollars worth of donations after Victorian Stephen Conroy made utterances on Labor's policy on the South China Sea," according to a report in *The Australian*.

What Huang failed to buy in the wholesale market, he decided to shop for in the retail market instead. He quickly organised for another Labor senator, Sam Dastyari, to declare a more Beijing-friendly position. Dastyari wasn't a relevant front-bencher, so his words wouldn't carry the same weight, but he was a Labor powerbroker nonetheless, with solid influence in the NSW Right faction, which was often at odds with Conroy's faction in the Victorian Right. Better to have at least some of the federal Opposition spouting your favoured policy than none at all.

That same day, Dastyari called a press conference and, standing side by side with Huang, said that "the South China Sea is China's own affair", and that Australia should "respect China's decision". Only Chinese-language media were invited. When challenged by Australian reporters over his reputed comments, Dastyari denied them. Until an audio recording emerged. Dastyari had been a cheerful recipient of Huang's cash for some time. A key point here: he had disclosed the money he'd taken from Huang. It was all legal. Property developers, such as Huang, are prohibited from giving money at the state level, but not at the federal. Dastyari was drummed out of federal parliament in disgrace, not for accepting Huang's money but for dissembling over the favours he was doing for him. It might have been legal, but it certainly created the perception of corruption.

The first lesson from this episode is how cheap it is to buy Australian politics. When Huang Xiangmo wanted to have a bit of a flutter, he gambled hundreds of millions of dollars a year at one casino alone. We know from a 2015 leaked internal email from Melbourne's Crown Casino that Huang put nearly $800 million through its tables in one year. By comparison, the donations Huang offered political parties to change policy, and potentially compromise themselves, were mere pocket change. It exposes an extremely uneven contest. A desperate, low-rent political system has grave difficulty resisting the temptations offered by an extraordinarily well-funded influence-seeking operation. To illustrate, someone with Huang's play-money allowance could donate ten times the combined advertising spend of both major parties at the 2019 election and still have half a billion dollars in his pocket to splash on Crown Casino's games of chance. And Huang was just one covert agent of influence, according to ASIO.

Second, this incident jolted Australia into realising how little it knew of the Chinese government's covert influence campaign. When I first disclosed that Labor had been offered $400,000 to change its policy on the South China Sea, my colleague Nick McKenzie, an investigative reporter for *The Age* and *The Sydney Morning Herald*, was alarmed. It was the impetus, he says, for his decision to pursue a major 2017 investigation of China's influence operations in Australia. The series, in conjunction with the ABC's Chris Uhlmann and *Four Corners*, was a key moment in waking Australia up to the operation. And we only received this warning because Conroy refused the offer and let his colleagues know about it. How many other such proposals have been made and silently accepted? In truth, we have no idea and no systemic way of finding out.

The intelligence agency whose primary job is to guard against foreign interference, ASIO, has only a limited idea. Covert foreign intrusion into the heart of Australian politics is "something we need to be very, very careful about", the former head of ASIO, Duncan Lewis, says in an interview. Lewis retired from the role in 2019. "One spectacular case in New South Wales was Sam Dastyari. It's quite clear to me that any person in political office is potentially a target. I'm not trying to create paranoia, but there does need to be a level of sensible awareness. When people talked about [how to define foreign interference in] our political system, I used to get the comment, 'We will know it if we see it.' But not necessarily. Not if it's being done properly. There would be some I don't know about."

The Australian system is wide open in two critical ways. First, because "federally, Australia has some of the most lax political donations laws in the developed world", in the words of a senior lecturer in politics at the University of New South Wales, Lindy Edwards. The political donation laws are "full of holes that can be exploited to hide where parties' incomes are really coming from". She calculates that the major parties disclose transparently only 10 to 20 per cent of their true incomes as donations. And, second, because Australia has no federal anti-corruption commission. The system is dark, and there is no agency whose job it is to shine a light.

*

For three top leaders of the Labor Party in 2017 – Penny Wong, Bill Shorten and Richard Marles – it hit them in a meeting with a top Chinese official. Meng Jianzhu was visiting Sydney in April that year and asked to meet the Opposition leader. Meng was a member of the Politburo, meaning that he was one of the twenty-five most senior members of the Chinese Communist Party. Shorten invited Wong, Labor's foreign affairs spokesperson, and Marles, defence spokesperson, to the meeting at the Commonwealth Parliamentary Offices in Bligh Street.

Beijing's biggest priority at the time was to get Australia to approve an extradition treaty. The Chinese government argued that corrupt officials were fleeing and hiding in Australia. Beijing wanted the ability to extract them to face charges in China.

It was true that officials had fled in the face of Xi's vast and zealous anti-corruption campaign. In six years of Xi's campaign to catch "tigers and flies" – major figures as well as minor ones – the party and state authorities punished 1.5 million people, many of whom were purged from the party, meaning an end to privilege and the onset of hardship. Of these, 58,000 were prosecuted in the court system and two sentenced to death. Among them were some of the very biggest creatures in the Chinese jungle, including cabinet-level officials, top party bosses and two dozen senior generals. According to China's media, one general had collected so much ill-gotten cash, gold and antiques that it took ten army transport trucks to remove it all. The other key aspect of the campaign that's been commonly observed by China-watchers is that while probably most of the people accused were indeed guilty of corruption, everyone accused was certainly guilty of belonging to the wrong political faction.

It was just such a treaty that pitched Hong Kong into the convulsive street protests of 2019. As the people of Hong Kong well know, there is no rule of law in mainland China, only rule by politics. There is no independent judiciary, so there can be no guarantee of fairness. Millions marched against Hong Kong's proposed treaty with Beijing. They did not want to allow the CCP easy reach into the city, to pluck people out and disappear them into China's prosecution and prison system.

But in 2017 Australia's government supported the idea of an extradition treaty with the People's Republic of China and had already negotiated the text. It just needed parliamentary approval. Meng, in charge of all law enforcement in China as secretary of the Central Political and Legal Affairs Commission, wanted to get Labor on board to ensure smooth passage. But when he met some resistance from the Labor trio, Meng shocked them. He threatened them.

"It would be a shame if Chinese government representatives had to tell the Chinese community in Australia that Labor did not support the relationship between Australia and China," he said, according to a report by *The Australian*'s Primrose Riordan and later confirmed by participants independently. It was a threat to mobilise the 1.2 million ethnic Chinese people living in Australia against Labor.

The threat was counterproductive. Meng had shown the Labor leadership the ugly face of political coercion. It alarmed them. It confirmed Labor's concerns about exposing people in Australia to the CCP's reach. Labor's position only hardened. "I decline to change my position," Shorten replied, according to people present at the meeting. Labor opposed the extradition treaty. The treaty was now a dead letter. Meng reached retirement age later that same year and no longer holds office.

There are three key elements of the incident. First, a top member of the Chinese leadership thought it acceptable to threaten an Australian political party with political reprisal. Second, he was prepared to intervene directly in Australian domestic politics, using the power of the Chinese state to favour one party against another to get his way. These two facts offend the principle of non-interference in another sovereign country, a principle that the Chinese government always preaches, but is revealed here as not practising. Third, he represented the Chinese ethnic population of Australia as a national political asset of China that can be mobilised by Chinese government representatives. This presumption is false: some ethnic Chinese residents of Australia do give higher allegiance to their country of origin than to their country of residence, but a great many do not. Meng, and any Chinese mainland official who lays claim to their loyalty, does all Chinese Australians great harm.

This assertion that Beijing somehow has the ultimate claim on all ethnic Chinese peoples' loyalties is based on a racist premise. It's this: it doesn't matter where you were born, where you live, where you want your children to grow up, where you choose to invest your life and your loyalty, which country gives you citizenship; you are ethnic Chinese, and your race transcends all else – including your own free will. That immutable predetermination is the very definition of racism.

The Chinese Communist Party doesn't present this as a matter of choice. It's not a question of Chinese Australians feeling residual affection for China, which would be quite natural. It's a matter of compulsion according to official policy. There are some 60 million ethnic Chinese living in about 180 countries worldwide. Of these, about 80 per cent are citizens of the countries that they live in. But a teaching manual published by the party's United Front Work Department, the CCP department that organises Chinese populations overseas to covertly serve its strategic interests, states: "The unity of Chinese at home requires the unity of the sons and daughters of Chinese abroad." It exhorts its cadres to emphasise "flesh and blood" ties to the motherland. The manual, titled *China United Front Course Book*, isn't in general circulation but was obtained by London's *Financial Times* in 2017. The claim to enforced racial loyalty is supplemented with instruction on how it should be aided by "providing funding or other resources to selected overseas Chinese groups and individuals deemed valuable to Beijing's cause", in the words of the *FT*. This undercuts the standing and trust that the entire Chinese Australian population enjoys in Australia. When an immigrant decides to take up citizenship, he or she gives this oath: "I pledge my loyalty to Australia and its people, whose democratic beliefs I share, whose rights and liberties I respect, and whose laws I will uphold and obey." In laying claim to the eternal soul of every ethnic Chinese person, Meng and the party he represents seek to make every Australian Chinese person who has taken this vow into a liar at best and a traitor at worst.

*

For Feng Chongyi, it hit when he saw the advertisements for a pair of concerts. They were billed as "Red Songs" to celebrate Chairman Mao Zedong. One concert was to be held in Sydney Town Hall and another in Melbourne Town Hall. They were scheduled for September 2016, to mark the fortieth anniversary of the death of the founder of the People's Republic of China. The problem, of course, is that the leader known as the "Great Helmsman" was also a great purveyor of death.

"It immediately caught our attention," says Feng, an associate professor of Chinese studies at the University of Technology Sydney. "The idea of a Mao concert would be controversial even in China itself because it's a symbol of the Cultural Revolution, which reminds people of the nightmare of horrible suffering and persecution. Especially for the people who came to Australia to escape persecution in China." After Mao's disastrous Great Leap Forward created a man-made famine that killed anywhere from 18 million to 56 million people, he recovered political control with the violent purge known as the Cultural Revolution, which killed millions more. In engineering these great convulsions, Mao was responsible for more deaths than any other leader in history.

But the glorification of Mao in the great civic gathering places of Australia's two principal cities didn't seem to strike anyone outside the Chinese community as odd. The two town halls took the bookings as if they were school choirs or stand-up comedy. Would they have so readily booked concerts glorifying the lives of Stalin or Mussolini or Pol Pot or modern history's other brutal dictators? Australia has long boasted of being close to China, but this is just one indication that if there is any closeness it has come without any real comprehension.

So who would stage such events? Two groups calling themselves cultural associations which are, according to Feng, "organisations of the United Front". Feng says that there are at least 300 United Front associations in Sydney alone, and hundreds more in other Australian cities. They can be community groups, "patriotic" associations, business chambers, student associations or hometown groups. The Australian Council for the Promotion of Peaceful Reunification of China is a prominent one. Others include the Chinese Students and Scholars Associations on university campuses, the China–Australia Entrepreneurs Association and the Australian Guangdong Chamber of Commerce.

Christina Wang, the chief executive of the International Cultural Exchange Association, which made the bookings, denied any links with the Chinese government and said all key organisers had been in Australia for decades. "We are artists, we just want to put on a good display of song and dance," she said.

The Mao concerts illuminated the deep schism in the Australian Chinese communities between a pro-Beijing group and a pro-Australian group. "A divide has emerged broadly between two camps: naturalised Australians who migrated in the 1980s and '90s with the spectre of the Tiananmen Square crackdown of 1989 fresh in their memories, and more recent émigrés who have been enriched by China's economic miracle of the past two decades and are emboldened by their country's rise as a major international power," wrote Philip Wen, former Beijing correspondent for *The Age* and *The Sydney Morning Herald*.

Feng and friends quickly organised a coalition, the Australian Values Alliance, to object to the Red Songs concerts. "We are here to protect our Australian values. We choose to live in this country so we need to protect our home," said spokesman John Hugh. The alliance planned demonstrations outside the two town halls.

The concerts were cancelled amid concerns for public safety and poor control of the ticketing system, with many tickets handed out for free. "We don't want there to be a split in the Chinese community," Wang commented. "If this does cause a divide, we are willing to abandon the performances."

With 1.2 million Chinese Australians, or one in twenty of the population, this schism in the community is something Australia probably should understand, at least a little. Professor Feng isn't imagining the hand of the United Front in the Chinese diaspora. It's been hiding in plain view. Indeed, Xi Jinping has called the United Front Work Department one of China's "three magic weapons", together with party-building and armed struggle. He was quoting Mao. Mao described the relationship between the three in 1939, when he was still leading the Communists as a guerilla revolutionary force: "The party is the heroic warrior wielding the two weapons, the united front and the armed struggle, to storm and shatter the enemy's positions."

Xi reinvigorated and enlarged the department after its previous director was arrested in the anti-corruption purge. In 2015, at the annual conference of the United Front Work Department, Xi called on the department to emphasise three new areas of work: overseas Chinese students, representative individuals in new media, and the young generation of entrepreneurs and businesspeople. "From the party's Politburo Standing Committee down to its grassroots committees, united front work involves thousands of members, social organisations, and fronts," write two Western experts on the subject, American Peter Mattis and Australian Alex Joske. "Wherever the party is found, be it a government ministry or a party committee in a joint venture, the united front system is likely to be operating." That includes China's embassies and consulates.

Something as minor as the cancellation of the two concerts celebrating Mao was, in fact, an important victory, according to Feng. "I'm very happy about it. This is regarded as the first victory, that a performance of Red culture has been blocked overseas. It's had an impact on Chinese communities around the world."

In 2018, the United Front Work Department was strengthened when work on religious groups, ethnic minorities and the Chinese diaspora was explicitly placed under its control, and it was formally given control of three State Council (cabinet equivalent) agencies responsible for work in those areas: the Overseas Chinese Affairs Office, the State Administration for Religious Affairs, and the State Ethnic Affairs Commission.

In Australia, the United Front Work Department has had much more to work with in recent years. "With mainland Chinese migration sharply increasing in recent years, state-backed political astroturfing has become more pronounced, from pro-Beijing South China Sea demonstrations in Melbourne and

Sydney, to mobilising cheering, flag-waving crowds to drown out Free Tibet and Falun Gong demonstrators during President Xi Jinping's visit in 2014," Philip Wen explained. What are the alignments among the 1.2 million Chinese Australians? Feng, who migrated from China to Australia in 1995, says, "My judgment is that [the] anti-Communist[s] are in a very tiny minority, and die-hard Communist supporters are also a tiny minority, and the vast majority are in between, wavering."

*

For John Garnaut, it hit when he was interviewing a Chinese billionaire in a mock castle. Garnaut was the Beijing correspondent for *The Age* and *The Sydney Morning Herald* when he managed to get the first Australian media interview with the elusive Chau Chak Wing.

The billionaire property developer and chair of the Kingold Group had been given Australian citizenship. His wife and two of his three children lived in Sydney, but he preferred to live in his home base in the thriving southern Chinese city of Guangzhou, just north of Hong Kong. It was here that he built a mansion with a tower of Australian sandstone, nicknamed his "castle". The castle sat atop a hill surrounded by an enormous complex of plush villas and apartments, complete with the estate's own clubs, schools and golf course, all built by Chau, master of all he surveyed. It would emerge years later that ASIO reportedly suspected Chau, like Huang Xiangmo, to be a covert agent of Chinese government influence. ASIO has neither confirmed nor denied these reports. Chau denies that he is any such thing, and he has never been charged with any wrongdoing.

Sitting down to interview him in his mansion, Garnaut wanted to know about Chau's donations to Australian political parties. Chau was a generous political donor. Even then, in 2009, he'd already given $2 million. That made him the biggest overseas-based donor to the Australian political system. Chau's answer to why he'd been so generous was diplomatic: "I am very happy as a citizen to play my role of participant in the democratic process," he said through an interpreter. But Alexander Downer's answer to why Chau might have given $30,000 to his 2007 re-election committee was hilarious: "Perhaps he just found me incredibly interesting and rather amusing."

Chau's political donations paled in comparison to his donations to two universities. He agreed to give $20 million towards a new Frank Gehry–designed building for the business faculty at UTS, famously built in the likeness of a giant crumpled brown paper bag, plus $5 million for a scholarship fund. And another $15 million for the Chau Chak Wing Museum at the University of Sydney. And those donations were nothing compared to the price he paid James Packer in 2015 for his house in Sydney's Vaucluse. Seventy million dollars. Without actually setting foot inside it.

Even more impressive than Chau's access to money is his access to power. When Xi Jinping travelled to Australia as vice premier in 2010 and invested an unusually long time in getting to know the then prime minister, Kevin Rudd, Chau travelled with him. He has been seen travelling with Xi on other occasions since. China has many billionaires, but very few enjoy such intimacy with the president.

It was Chau's treatment of Garnaut that truly impressed the reporter. In writing up the 2009 interview, Garnaut said that Chau had offered to pay airfares and hotel bills for the reporter and his assistant. Offer declined. Chau sent his chauffeur and black Bentley to pick him up from the airport. Offer accepted. Garnaut later said that Chau had given him a gift bag containing three expensive bottles of French wine at the end of the interview. And another three to his assistant. And followed up with another four later, ten altogether. The wine, which they donated to a charity auction, fetched some $7000. It didn't stop there. Chau also offered to host the reporter and his family for a holiday at his resort, according to Garnaut. For free. Offer declined. And even offered him a reporting job in which he'd be free to write whatever he wanted. Chau owned a number of newspapers in China and Australia. That offer, too, was declined. The offers were so lavish and so insistent, Garnaut decided, that Chau must have been seeking more than just a soft interview. He believed he was being wooed as part of a larger Chau influence-building effort.

When Chau later sued Garnaut for defamation, Garnaut told the court that he felt Chau had been trying to snare him in a "reciprocity trap" as part of a "web of patronage". Chau told the court he didn't recall giving Garnaut wine. The job offer had been a joke. And he couldn't be sure that the John Garnaut in the courtroom before him was the same person who'd interviewed him years earlier. Chau, incidentally, won the defamation case.

But by then Garnaut had quit his reporting job and gone to work for the then prime minister, Malcolm Turnbull. It was a move with consequences well beyond Garnaut's career. Garnaut had decided that Australia had to wake up to the Chinese Communist Party's plans for the country. That it was his mission to assist the awakening. And that he could better help as an official than as a journalist.

5

TAKING THE FLAG

When Australia's parliament is in session, an outsized national flag hangs in the House of Representatives. But the one on display on 28 June 2018 was quietly souvenired by a member of parliament, who took it home.

It wasn't a dare or a prank. It was Anthony Byrne's way of having a memento of an important moment in Australian lawmaking. Most Australians haven't heard of Byrne, although he's been in federal parliament for more than twenty years. Which is fine by him. His unusual position in Australian politics requires he avoid the limelight. Byrne is the Labor Party's unofficial ambassador to Australia's intelligence agencies. He has maintained a closeness to Australia's spy central that is unique for a politician without formal ministerial office. Byrne is an Opposition backbencher, representing a Labor seat in outer Melbourne. You could call him the shadow minister for the shadows.

Byrne took the flag to celebrate the passing of a pair of bills designed to bring Chinese Communist Party interference in Australia under some sort of control. They were the National Security Legislation Amendment (Espionage and Foreign Interference) Bill 2018 – shorthanded to EFI – and the Foreign Influence Transparency Scheme Bill 2018, known as FITS. "I thought it was an existential threat to Australia, and the passage of the bills was a defining moment, as defining as John Curtin's 1942 'turn to America' moment," Byrne told me, speaking of the then Labor prime minister's appeal to the US for help in defending Australia from Japanese invasion in World War II.

And Byrne went to great lengths to help the bills pass. As the opposing side of politics is happy to acknowledge: "Anthony Byrne deserves the Order of Australia for his work on these laws," according to the attorney-general responsible for them, Christian Porter. Which is rare praise for an Opposition MP dealing with a government initiative. What was going on?

*

Of course, chief credit for the laws has to go to then prime minister Malcolm Turnbull for initiating the bills. And he's happy to take it, in inimitable Turnbull style. When told that Byrne had likened the laws' importance to Curtin's famous wartime speech, Turnbull demurred but pointed out: "I used to sleep in the Curtin bedroom at The Lodge," the official Canberra residence of the prime minister.

These Australian politicians, Labor and Liberal, are not the only ones who thought it an important moment. So did Beijing. Two years later, the Chinese government placed those laws at number three on their hit list of fourteen most-hated Australian decisions, ones they wanted reversed. Beijing described them as "foreign interference legislation, viewed as targeting China and without any evidence". The two higher-rated grievances were against Australian decisions to block some Chinese investment proposals, and the ban on Huawei.

The EFI and FITS bills were indeed a threshold act in Australia's national life, the first decisive action in open defiance of Beijing. The laws implicitly accuse the Chinese Communist Party of covertly undermining Australian democracy in the "grey zone" of political warfare so favoured by Beijing. And they explicitly began the process of standing against it. "We woke up from our slumber just in time," says Byrne. The head of the ANU's National Security College, Rory Medcalf, says that Australia was an inadvertent role model: "We didn't set out to be the leader, just to do what we needed to do. But we ended up being the role model."

Against considerable resistance from a system grown fond of Chinese money, and knowing they should expect a backlash from Beijing, the two major political parties managed to cohere in a case study of bipartisanship in the face of an external danger. Democracy's critics argue that such systems are too fragmented, too feeble, that the dedication to democracy that prevailed against fascism in World War II would not be found in the leading democracies today. "In an autocracy, one person has his way," said the English philosopher Celia Green. "In an aristocracy, a few people have their way. In a democracy, no one has his way." Yet, in this instance at least, the two main parties combined to make sure the national interest got its way. But only just. Their coherence almost dissolved into tribal argument and politicisation. In fact, it did.

But before the breakdown reached the media, bipartisanship was put back together with a dramatic public shaming, a private threat from the prime minister, and a remarkable episode of cooperation across party lines. All to the drumbeat of warnings from ASIO about "unprecedented" levels of foreign interference and revelations of covert CCP payments, manipulations and intrusions into Australian politics, universities and society.

From the outset Turnbull had to confront a deep complacency in the government and in big business. Government departments maintained the status quo; political parties were more interested in soliciting Chinese funds than in defending Australian sovereignty; companies were captivated by China's promise of easy profits. Even the intelligence and law enforcement agencies were initially hesitant. As Minister for Home Affairs, Peter Dutton was responsible for ASIO and the Australian Federal Police. He said in an interview that the heads of these two agencies up until September 2019, Duncan Lewis and Andrew Colvin, "had done very well but there needed to be a new approach".

It was risky to confront China. There were few volunteers to disturb the stupor. Turnbull went for the "break glass in case of emergency" option. He brought in an outsider, John Garnaut, the journalist and former China correspondent. As another prime minister of a previous generation had brought in another Garnaut to break an earlier Australian complacency and shape a new agenda for a new era.

*

Bob Hawke was halfway through the wrenching, decade-long project to transform Australia. There was pain in the process as factory after factory shut down. It was hard for many to see a happy ending. But Hawke never lost sight of the vision splendid. It was to be a great gift to the country, a gift that still gives today.

Hawke described the Australia he came to lead as having "walked down the gentle path to economic mediocrity". With his treasurer, Paul Keating, Hawke stripped away the tariff protection, opened Australia to the world and rejuvenated an exhausted economy. Together with some consolidation by the Howard–Costello governments that followed, it set the country up for the twenty-eight years of unbroken expansion that it enjoyed until the COVID-19 pandemic struck. That long boom was the root source of every job, every opportunity and every new government benefit since. It's been called Australia's "Third Golden Age", following the commodities boom to 1890 and the immediate post-war boom.

After five years of tough dislocation, Hawke wanted to reinvigorate the reform program. He hit on the idea of showing the people a vision of the future, to give the project a clearer purpose, an encouragement to persist. And to keep the people voting Labor, naturally. He turned to Ross Garnaut to conjure it. Garnaut was perfect for the purpose. He was a distinguished economics professor at the Australian National University. He had served as Hawke's economic adviser. Hawke had then appointed him ambassador to Beijing at a time of great Chinese reform and opening. Now, in 1988, he commissioned Garnaut to write a report that would "encourage community discussion and debate" on "Australia's place in the region" and how to go about "adapting our country to realise more fully its almost unbounded economic potential".

Ross Garnaut's report was titled *Australia and the Northeast Asian Ascendancy*, but universally was known as the Garnaut Report. It embraced South Korea, Japan and Taiwan, but at the centre of the opportunity sat China. The report was to be released in 1989. Unhappily, that was the year Beijing unleashed its army against the unarmed student protesters in Tiananmen Square. Hawke's tearful speech in response to the massacre is remembered for its raw humanity: "When all those who had not managed to get away were either dead or wounded, foot soldiers went through the square bayonetting or shooting anybody who was still alive," he said, as his voice quavered and caught. "They had orders that nobody in the square be spared. And children and young girls were slaughtered," he said, as tears began coursing down his face. "Thousands have been killed or injured, the victims of a leadership that seems determined to hold onto the reins of power at any cost. At awful human cost." He announced that all Chinese students living in Australia at the time would have their visas extended, and some 42,000 ultimately were granted permanent residency. His emotions were real and his tears authentic, but he was also a hard-headed leader who would not allow sentimentality to interrupt his plans for the nation. He launched Ross Garnaut's report on how Australia could best take advantage of China's coming boom five months after the massacre.

How did Hawke reconcile his repugnance at China's leaders with his decision to pursue intensified relations? "China remains unquestionably one of the key countries in the Asia-Pacific and it is in all our interests that the decade of openness and reform is not lost irretrievably to the Chinese people or to the region." So he portrayed increased trade as a benefit to China's people, as well as to Australia's. And the prime minister hinted that Australia's engagement with China could exert a moral influence: "A very important element of Garnaut's analysis is that we carry into our relations with Northeast Asia many positive and influential assets. These include – I name only a few of the most important – our proud, vigorous and deeply entrenched democratic traditions, our standards of human rights, our multicultural tolerance, our principles of free trade unionism." These mainstays of principled engagement remain relevant.

Garnaut's report was a major news event at the time and did exactly what Hawke had hoped. Australia internationalised its economy to take advantage of the China boom to follow, and intensified its political relationship for the same reason. The export of Australian values was less successful than the export of Australian iron ore and meat, however. Democracy, human rights, multicultural tolerance and free trade unionism remain dockside, marooned at our ports, with no buyers in Beijing.

Twenty-six years later, another Australian prime minister commissioned another Garnaut to write another report centred on China. But where Bob Hawke asked Ross Garnaut to write about the opportunity presented by China, Malcolm Turnbull assigned John Garnaut to write about the threat. Two generations of the same family, each responding to their country's needs of the day, each of their lives entwined with the restless relationship between the Middle Kingdom and the Great Southern Land. Ross, in his report, had anticipated a time when China would become the strategic equal of the United States. "This was always going to be a hard time, when it becomes clear that China is, or soon will be, the world's largest economy, with great geo-strategic weight," he says today in an interview. "While China's political shape as it became a developed economy has always been uncertain, the Statue of Liberty was unlikely to be amongst the possibilities. There was always going to be systemic competition between a rich China and the US-led West."

He could not have anticipated in 1989 that his then fifteen-year-old son would be the one commissioned to advise the Australian government on how the country should protect itself from some of Beijing's most pernicious covert efforts to win it over as part of that competition.

When Hawke sent his father to be Australia's ambassador to Beijing, John Garnaut went with him. He was twelve years old. When John had the opportunity to return to Beijing as a foreign correspondent for *The Sydney Morning Herald* and *The Age* in 2007 after two decades away, he was thrilled. He'd been writing about economics in Australia and now was going to be writing about the most exciting economic story in the world. John Garnaut had fond memories of China and great hopes for its future. "I came to China thinking I knew something about the place," he later wrote. He described himself as a "China optimist". The romance slowly wore off as reality set in. "In those days, I had a simple aspiration: to tell Chinese stories through Chinese voices. I thought Western media focused on the negative, ignoring the progress being made." When he came across the story of two cousins who had survived a coalmine collapse in September 2007, he "thought it was just the kind of uplifting adventure story I was seeking". When he delved, he discovered that the Meng cousins had been left for dead by their bosses, knowingly trapped beneath the surface in the collapsed mine. When their colleagues had moved to rescue the pair, the local Communist Party chief had ordered them locked up to prevent a rescue. It turned out that the mine was illegal. Better to let the Mengs die than concede the existence of an unauthorised mine. When the cousins did manage to dig their way out, half-dead, after six days, they were chased out of town. "It proved to be my first lesson in the brutality of power without accountability," John reflected later.

Another revelation came when he was covering the aftermath of an earthquake in Sichuan province in 2008. Stepping through the corpses and destruction of a ruined town, Garnaut came across a survivor, hanging upside down, with his pelvis crushed between two boulders. "He was alive and had the strength to speak. I told him that if he was brave enough to hang on, the rescue team would come for him," he recounted. "That proved to be a lie. On the highway above, battalions of People's Liberation Army soldiers sat in trucks, eating watermelons and occasionally staging mock-rescues for the benefit of the camera teams that were beaming propaganda footage across the country."

And in writing about one farcical scene, John Garnaut conveyed to readers the difficulty of avoiding being compromised by the party. A cadre had handed him a farewell gift of a leather satchel, and when he reached inside he found a red envelope addressed to his youngest son. He tried to hand the cash envelope back in the street outside his hotel, failed, and instead tossed it into his would-be benefactor's Audi. Garnaut then ran into his hotel, pursued by one of the cadre's aides. As the journalist retreated into the hotel lift, the determined donor tossed the red envelope in behind him. "I banged the open button, just in time, and threw it back after him. It skidded Frisbee-style along the marble, directly through his legs. Success! I slumped against the wall of the elevator as it rose to the eighteenth floor. But then I thought of my two other children, and reached back into the bag. Sure enough, there were two more red envelopes. When I returned to the ground floor, the Audi was gone. But the original red envelope was still there, its ten crisp $100 bills untouched in the middle of the hotel lobby – a silent, red memento of how much I still had left to learn."

But it was his encounter with Chau Chak Wing that led John Garnaut to investigate the Chinese government's efforts to increase its influence on Australia. The further he looked, the more alarmed he became. On his return to Australia he set aside plans to write a book and went to work for the prime minister.

Chinese party-state interference in Australia already had come to Malcolm Turnbull's attention. He'd taken some steps. He'd asked ASIO's Duncan Lewis to brief the national secretaries of the major political parties on the risks of accepting political donations from suspected foreign agents, including Huang Xiangmo and others. But asking a political campaigner under pressure to refuse money is like asking the ocean to refuse rain. No matter how much you have, there's always room for more liquidity.

When John Garnaut joined his staff in 2015, Turnbull gave him security clearance to access all the materials he needed across the various agencies of the federal government to lead the writing of a classified report into Chinese influence operations in Australia. While the report remains classified, its contents alarmed the government sufficiently that it produced two new pieces of legislation to counter Chinese covert intrusions: the EFI and the FITS. The first broadens the definition of espionage to include attacks on critical infrastructure such as electricity or telecommunications and interference with Australian democratic rights using violence or intimidation, and increases the penalty for lying in applications for government security clearances. The second requires anyone acting on behalf of a foreign government to put their name on a public register.

Turnbull presented the legislation to the parliament on the afternoon of 7 December 2017. It was the same day that, after a long and tortuous plebiscite, same-sex marriage was legalised by a vote of the parliament. So the foreign interference bills got scant media attention. They would have been a major story on almost any other day. The prime minister told the parliament: "When the director-general of ASIO, Duncan Lewis, says the threat from espionage and foreign interference is 'unprecedented', then we know that we must act. The director-general is telling us that the threat we face today is greater than when Soviet agents penetrated the federal government during World War II and the early years of the Cold War."

Turnbull issued a warning to Beijing: "If you are acting to further the interests of a foreign state in ways that are clandestine or deceptive then we will shine light upon your actions and, where necessary, we will shut you down. It means that if you use inducements or threats to manipulate a political process or public debate then we will unleash the full force of powerful new laws and defend our values and democratic institutions. And it means that foreign actors who would do us harm are now on notice: we will not tolerate covert, coercive or corrupting behaviour in our country." How do we know this was directed at Beijing? Because of the prime minister's next words: "Media reports have suggested that the Chinese Communist Party has been working to covertly interfere with our media, our universities and even the decisions of elected representatives right here in this building. We take these reports very seriously." He also cited Russia and North Korea, but this was, above all, a China story.

John Garnaut would later write for the American journal *Foreign Affairs*: "Australia is the canary in the coal mine of

Chinese Communist Party interference . . . Nobody knows what happens when a mid-sized, open, multicultural nation stands its ground against a rising authoritarian superpower that accounts for one in every three of its export dollars."

A few months later, in July 2018, the chief executive of Donald Trump's successful presidential election campaign, Steve Bannon, used the same metaphor. Australia was the "canary in the mineshaft", he said in an interview. "Australia is at the forefront of the geopolitical contest of our time." But Bannon thought that Australia was losing. Chinese investment had bought control of Australia's economy and was in the process of buying control of its political system, he assessed. "Because of Australia's example, it will not happen here in the US," said Bannon. "It will not be allowed to happen. People are woke." Trump had just announced the first tariffs on China's sales to the United States. The trade war had begun three days before Bannon's comments, and he was exultant. "I can't emphasise Friday night enough – it was the day that President Trump stood up for the American worker."

Others applied different metaphors. To the commander of the US Pacific Command, Admiral Harry Harris, Australia was "the tip of the spear" in the West's efforts to fight back against China's encroachments. That was one of the reasons Harris wanted to be appointed US ambassador to Australia. Donald Trump duly named him to the post in early 2018, only to quickly countermand himself and dispatch Harris to serve as US ambassador to South Korea instead. To a Chinese mainland academic, Australia was a pioneer, and not in a good way. Australia had played a "pioneering role in an anti-China campaign", according to Chen Hong, director of Australian studies at East China

University during a visit to Australia in 2019 organised by the Chinese embassy. "The two-way exchanges have been going very well until 2017, when Australia launched this attack on China," he said. "If other countries follow suit, that is going to be recognised as extremely unfriendly. I think the responsibility is totally on the Australian side," Chen said. "China always promotes friendship." Despite some improvements under Scott Morrison, Australia–China relations had entered a freeze, "which in Chinese means a very cold period". It turned out to be a chilly phase for Chen himself. Chen, a frequent visitor to Australia, had his visa revoked in 2020 on advice from ASIO that he posed a risk to national security.

Ross Garnaut showed Australia how to open itself to the China opportunity. A generation later, John Garnaut showed Australia how to protect itself against the China threat. Or, at least, one important dimension of it. Was it that the Garnauts, father and son, were so different? They weren't running personal projects or freelancing for their own amusement. Each was responding to the needs of the government of the day as prime ministers sought advice on the problems of the time. Was it that Australia had changed so much? Hawke was Labor and Turnbull Liberal, but both their governments were centrist. Both pursued agendas to internationalise Australia to trade, to investment, to the Asia-Pacific, to the world. Both sought more intense relationships with China. Hawke opened the iron ore trade with China, for instance. Turnbull's government legislated the China–Australia Free Trade Agreement.

It was not that one Garnaut was so profoundly different to the other or that Australia had changed so radically. It was China that had transformed. The scale of its economy, the resources of its government, the ambition of its leaders, the confidence of its officials had surged. There is no better evidence than Xi Jinping's overturning of Deng's strategic maxim. Deng's injunction that China "hide and bide" had given way to Xi's era of "striving to achieve".

Attesting to its peaceful intent, China for decades liked to point out that it had never maintained an overseas military base. Until it opened one in the African nation of Djibouti in 2017. Beijing always insisted that it was a country that respected international law. Until it rode roughshod over its neighbours' claims and built islands and military bases on contested areas of the South China Sea, flagrantly disregarding a finding by the Permanent Court of Arbitration in The Hague that it had "no historical rights". And Beijing still maintains that it does not spy or intrude on Australia. Although ASIO's then chief, Duncan Lewis, said in 2018 that foreign interference in Australia was "unprecedented", and said in 2019 that it posed an "existential threat" to the state. While at ASIO he was careful not to single out China. But in an interview immediately after retiring, he said that while it was not only China that preoccupied the Australian authorities, it was "overwhelmingly" China.

What had *not* changed was the foundational psychology of the Chinese Communist Party. By the late 1920s the party was a covert, guerilla, revolutionary movement. After it succeeded in seizing power, it created the machinery of state and now operates one of the world's greatest powers. But the party's thinking and behaviour is still strongly influenced by the mentality of the covert, guerilla, revolutionary movement of the 1920s.

John Garnaut's classified report to Turnbull armed the prime minister with the evidence he needed. He used it to begin the breaking of one consensus, but it would take years for a new one to fully form. In the meantime, he decided to act. Garnaut's work, though presented in scrupulously technocratic terms, showed that the Chinese Communist Party was waging sustained, well-organised campaigns to infiltrate Australian politics at all levels; to penetrate Australia's research labs, universities, companies, defence contractors and political parties, to strip them of their best work and most valuable secrets; to intimidate and smother critics in universities; to subvert and threaten Australia's intelligence services; to manipulate and mobilise the Chinese Australian community through the United Front Work Department to serve the party's agenda.

Turnbull had the benefit of other work too, including ASIO briefings and a report he'd commissioned from the attorney-general's department on the CCP's intrusion and interference. Turnbull wrote in his memoir, *A Bigger Picture*, of how the party used its United Front Work Department to "advance support for China's objectives in the Australian community generally and in the Australian Chinese community in particular. A number of prominent Chinese businessmen were working closely with the UFWD and their agenda included co-opting Australian politicians and opinion leaders. The road to doing this was, of course, money: political donations for both major parties and commercial opportunities as well. There was so much financial incentive to get on well with China; it was, as they say in the classics, 'win win'."

The prime minister and his ministers developed the EFI and the FITS to try to complicate the CCP's efforts on two fronts: direct Chinese government espionage being carried out against Australia by the official organs of the Chinese system, and the indirect influence-building activities carried out by others acting on their behalf. But governments rarely have the luxury of controlling both houses of parliament. Since 1949, governments have had majorities in the Senate for around just one-fifth of the time. Turnbull faced the usual situation and would have to persuade Labor or the crossbench to get the bills through the upper house. He had two factors in his favour, however. One was the atmospherics – the Sam Dastyari atmospherics in particular. The NSW Labor senator and party powerbroker, after being compromised by Huang Xiangmo, was going through his inexorable decline and fall as the government was preparing the bills and tabling them in the parliament. As Dastyari would ruefully reflect later: "I shouldn't have been [Labor's] bagman when I was a serving Australian senator." That scandal put political pressure on the Labor Party to support the government's proposed laws.

Second was the fact that the bills related to national security. The two main parties customarily try to deal with defence and national security matters on a bipartisan basis. The specific mechanism for this is a parliamentary committee, the Parliamentary Joint Committee on Intelligence and Security, or PJCIS. It has eleven members. The government of the day nominates six members, the opposition five. It's responsible for sensitive and sometimes classified matters. It tries to be, and generally succeeds in being, sensible, effective and low-key. And to produce bipartisan recommendations on bills before they reach parliament, clearing the way for their approval without quibble.

The chair at the time, and until December 2020, was the Liberals' Andrew Hastie, who'd left school hoping to become a journalist but ended up as a captain in the SAS before entering parliament. The deputy was Labor's Anthony Byrne, who'd grown up on the Kalgoorlie goldfields learning at the School of the Air, later running the Anxiety Disorders Foundation of Australia before going into politics. Following standard procedure, the committee took the two bills for scrutiny. Turnbull pressed it to come out with its bipartisan recommendation as soon as possible.

But the bills got bogged in the committee. The government had drafted them poorly. They needed a lot more work. Turnbull agreed to a redrafting, recognising that the bills were too woolly-worded. He and former attorney-general Christian Porter, the minister responsible, sat down and together revised the foreign interference bill to more sharply focus on foreign governments and the political parties and entities they controlled. They also tried to meet the demands emerging from the PJCIS. The prime minister told Porter in early 2018 that he wanted the bills through the committee, with a bipartisan recommendation, and legislated by the parliament within four months. Turnbull had enjoyed his rhetorical flourish in the House when first presenting the bills in December 2017 – "we will shut you down" – aimed at Beijing. It would be embarrassing if he weren't able to get them through his own country's parliament.

When little happened, Turnbull started to suspect that there was more than just committee work holding it up. He was right. Labor had been engaging in a go-slow. "There were a lot of people who didn't want it to happen," says Byrne. "Why would you want to see your major trading partner as a country that could be an existential threat to you?" In internal debates, Labor MPs and senators argued that the bills were "unnecessary, xenophobic, an overreaction, just political, and at the time these arguments had some weight. It was significant enough to potentially derail the bills," according to Byrne.

The resistance wasn't only among sitting MPs and senators. In his memoir, Turnbull complained that while he was trying to get the bills passed, university heads were critical publicly – he cites Michael Spence, then vice chancellor of Sydney University, accusing Turnbull of "Sinophobic blatherings". Turnbull wrote: "Added to the list of regular critics are former politicians like Paul Keating, Bob Carr and our own Andrew Robb, and former diplomats like Geoff Raby. While they would disavow that it has any influence, all nonetheless have commercial interests in remaining on the very best terms with Beijing. And, of course, many politicians and their parties rely on generous donations from Chinese business figures. Nobody wants to have a row with China, but far too many Australians aren't particularly fussed how high a price we pay to avoid one." The Labor leader, Bill Shorten, seemed ambiguous. In the past, the Liberals had overreached on national security matters to try to show Labor as "weak". He suspected that this could be another example.

China's ambassador to Australia intervened publicly in April to try to deter the government. Typically of Xi's regime, he issued a threat against Australia. "Trading ties could be damaged if the situation is not repaired," Cheng Jingye told the media.

Committee chair Andrew Hastie, seeing a logjam forming, decided to detonate it. He would use parliamentary privilege – an ancient Westminster right to allow legislators to speak freely, unhindered by defamation laws – to name billionaire Australian businessman Chau Chak Wing. He would shame Chau as a suspected agent of party influence who'd allegedly bribed a top UN official. Hastie had discovered his explosive material when he and some of the committee members travelled to the US in April 2018. In Washington DC they met US counterparts and were briefed by the CIA and the FBI. The committee also had a special interest in calling on the US Attorney's Office for New York's southern district. It was here that Hastie found his bombshell. The special interest? This was the office that had prosecuted Chinese Communist Party agents for a notorious case: the alleged bribery of the president of the United Nations General Assembly, John Ashe. Chau says he would not have paid money to Ashe if he'd known it was not to an official United Nations account. He has never been charged with any criminal offence.

Chau already was suing *The Sydney Morning Herald* and *The Age* for naming him as an alleged source of the corrupt funds paid to Ashe. The paper's former Beijing correspondent who'd broken the story was none other than John Garnaut. Chau went on to win the defamation case. Because the newspapers lost, no other media dared name him as an alleged source of the money. They feared the same fate: a costly court ruling against them. Which would mean that Chau's alleged involvement in the bribery case would never be mentioned again. But if a member of parliament were to name him under privilege, the matter would be open for reporting by all media.

In the Ashe case, a US court jailed Australian-American-Chinese Sheri Yan for twenty months in 2016. Celebrated as "queen of the Australian-China social scene", Yan had been working for Ashe at the UN. She pleaded guilty to bribery. She'd been the go-between, funnelling over A$1 million in bribes to the UNGA president, chiefly from three Chinese businessmen who were seeking influence and favours. Chau hadn't been named in the US proceedings. A property developer identified only as CC-3 was cited in a court deposition as the source of US$200,000 of the corrupt money paid to Ashe. Garnaut had named Chau as CC-3, for co-conspirator number three.

Now, on an evening in May, Andrew Hastie took to the floor of House to take up the story. In the minute before he dropped his bombshell, he sent text messages to Turnbull, Porter and Dutton as a courtesy to let them know what he was about to do, but deliberately giving them no time to try to stop him. "Today I raise a matter before the House that is of great importance to the Australian people," Hastie began. "It is a matter that poses a threat to our democratic tradition, particularly the freedom of the press, and our national sovereignty."

He mentioned his trip to the US: "During discussions with US authorities I confirmed the long-suspected identity of CC-3. It is now my duty to inform the House and the Australian people that CC-3 is Dr Chau Chak Wing, the same man who co-conspired to bribe the president of the United Nations General Assembly, John Ashe, the same man with extensive contacts in the Chinese Communist Party, including the United Front. I share it with the House because I believe it to be in the national interest. My duty first and foremost is to the Australian people and to the preservation of the ideals and democratic traditions of our Commonwealth. That tradition includes a free press."

Chau's lawyer said later that his client was very "disappointed that an elected representative would use the cover of parliamentary privilege to repeat old claims and attack his reputation just weeks before some of these matters are tested in court" in a defamation case. He pointed out that Chau had not been charged with any offence and said that made Hastie's attack "all the more extraordinary". Chau said that he didn't know his US$200,000 payment had gone into an unofficial UN account.

The story dominated the morning news. Hastie was running around Lake Burley Griffin at 7 a.m. when Turnbull called. "He was grumpy," Hastie later related to colleagues. "I'd knocked the government's budget off the front pages. And he was legitimately concerned about intel leaking into public via the parliament." Hastie told his leader that he'd confirmed CC-3's identity with the lawyers of the US Attorney's Office for New York's southern district. It hadn't come from an intelligence agency; he hadn't leaked any intel. Hastie had even taken the precaution of letting a contact of his at ASIO know of his speech two days in advance. No objections had been raised. "My motivation is to get this bloody legislation moving," Hastie said.

Hastie was also troubled that Chau was successfully using the defamation laws to shut the media up and suppress debate. Hastie wanted to use the parliament to argue exactly why foreign interference laws were needed. Chau had donated $4 million to both the Labor and Liberal parties since 2004, as well as $45 million to universities, making him one of the biggest donors in the land. It's an uncomfortable fact that neither side of politics likes to be reminded of. Turnbull had changed the political donations laws to ban foreigners from making payments to politicians. But Chau was an Australian citizen. Hastie knew he'd make himself unpopular with colleagues naming Chau under privilege.

And even more unpopular with some in Labor. Bill Shorten and his attack dog Mark Dreyfus pounced to try to score a political point. They hoped to wound Hastie as payback for Dastyari's downfall. And to pose as defenders of the China relationship in the process. In Question Time, Shorten challenged Turnbull with the accusation that Hastie had used sensitive FBI intelligence in his unveiling of Chau. He insinuated that this was a breach of US trust and would harm Canberra's intelligence ties with Washington. Turnbull told the House it wasn't so.

A Liberal senator who'd been in the US briefings with Hastie confirmed as much to me. Senator David Fawcett was in the room when Hastie had confirmed Chau was CC-3. "It was not classified, it was not the FBI, and Andrew made it clear that the information could be used publicly and they were fine with that." The chargé d'affaires at the US embassy at the time, James Carouso, commented: "The bottom line is that we have lost no confidence in our ability to work with the parliament, or with Mr Hastie as chair of the parliamentary committee. Nothing has changed. There are more important issues."

Indeed. Just a week earlier, the Chinese air force landed nuclear-capable heavy bombers on a disputed island in the South China Sea's Paracel group for the first time. Three weeks earlier it had installed anti-ship and anti-air cruise missiles on disputed territory in the Spratlys, islands that Xi Jinping has promised China would not militarise. Islands for which China's claim has "no basis in law", according to the international tribunal in The Hague. At the same time that Shorten and Dreyfus were pretending to be outraged at Hastie, ASIO's Duncan Lewis was telling a parliamentary committee that "the grim reality is that there are more foreign intelligence officers today than during the Cold War, and they have more ways of attacking us".

Some in Labor, including Byrne, cheered Hastie. Labor's Michael Danby publicly congratulated Hastie for "having the guts to stand up and do that". And the public's verdict was overwhelming. Hastie has said that his office was inundated with hundreds of calls and emails of congratulations and encouragement. Between 500 and 1000, his staff estimated. The office phone had rung nonstop for three days. It was the greatest upwelling of support he'd had on any issue.

Hastie had discovered the two Australian views of China's regime: the elite view and the people's view. The elites had been the subject of Beijing's lavish attention for decades. The free trips, the generous donations, the well-paid jobs and undemanding board appointments for politicians after they'd left parliament, the warm cocoon of support and generosity that enveloped "friends of China". Beyond parliament, Hastie was privately reprimanded for his speech by more than a few establishment figures. He prefers not to name them, except to say that they are eminent Australians who've been beneficiaries of the same generosity, receiving support for themselves, their institutions or their favoured causes. Hastie himself had been the beneficiary of a $10,000 campaign contribution from Huang Xiangmo for the 2016 election. Huang had paid a larger sum to the federal Liberal office, which then parcelled it out to individual politicians. Because Huang used "cut outs" to disguise the payment's origins, Hastie initially didn't know the donor's true identity. He was only told when he asked to whom he should write a "thank you" note. He kept the money for about a year but returned it when the Dastyari affair blew up and he realised the risks.

As NZ Sinologist Anne-Marie Brady has explained in her extensive study of party methods of elite capture, "the CCP's political use of 'friendship' is not the same as having a real, genuine friendship for the Chinese people and love of China. Being a 'friend of China' is effectively a job description. The politicising of 'friendship' was invented by the Soviets and it was a tool of their foreign policy too. But the CCP perfected it and made it their own."

Although some were outraged by Hastie's declaration in parliament, the Australian people, on the other hand, had cooled towards the Chinese regime as they witnessed the party-state's behaviour, in Australia and abroad. The public had become concerned that Australia was accommodating an overbearing autocracy, and were wondering why their leaders weren't taking a firmer stance. Hastie was showered with brickbats in the parliament, but given bouquets by the people.

The episode only firmed Turnbull's resolve. He soon decided he'd give Shorten an ultimatum, and phoned the Labor leader. "If we don't get these bills out of [the] committee with a bipartisan recommendation, I will re-list it for debate in the House." Turnbull says that he got a broad reassurance from Shorten. But Anthony Byrne was worried that his leader wasn't taking the prime minister seriously. He told Shorten, "If you think this guy is mucking around, he's not – this is happening." The laws would become politicised and Labor would be on the losing side of the argument. "He'll put the bills in the parliament and wreck Labor."

If the proposals had become politicised, with Labor rejecting them, three things would have happened. First, about one-third of the population would instantly have opposed the bills on the basis of tribal identification. Second, if they'd managed to pass the parliament with the support of the Senate crossbenchers, they would have remained controversial, with the possibility of a future Labor government repealing them. Third, it would have opened a pathway for the Chinese party-state to play one Australian political party off against another. It would have weakened the national position and strengthened Beijing's bargaining position immeasurably.

Not satisfied with Shorten's response, Byrne then did three things. First, he brought in what he's called the "break glass in case of emergency" solution: Penny Wong. Byrne said that Wong "played a decisive role in the end" in delivering a workable Labor position in those climactic couple of days. The Labor leader in the Senate approved of the intent of the bills. She liked the key element of the foreign influence bill, the proposed transparency register: anyone working for a foreign power would have to declare the fact, but nothing more. There's no penalty or stigma, but failure to declare yourself carries a penalty of up to five years' jail. "I call it the Al Capone legislation," Wong told me, after the notorious Chicago mobster who couldn't be prosecuted successfully for his many nefarious crimes and multiple murders but in the end was caught for tax evasion. "You can get them for failure to register so you don't have to get them for foreign interference." Wong established with Byrne the parameters of Labor's negotiating position: where it could compromise, and where it would not.

Second, Byrne took the initiative of going to Turnbull to plead for more time. He needed to get an extra couple of days for the committee to arrive at a consensus. As Question Time broke up and members left the chamber, Byrne buttonholed the prime minister in a hallway. He found Turnbull impatient. Labor MPs had been deliberately stonewalling the bill, Turnbull told him. "You are fucking us on this bill and I've had enough," he said, according to Byrne's recollection. The Labor MP said he'd give his personal guarantee that the committee would reach a consensus if Turnbull agreed to two more days. Byrne told me the argument he put to Turnbull: "You might fuck us politically if you introduce the legislation. But if you do, you will wreck the essential bipartisan consensus that this parliament needs for the legislation to work and not to be altered in future. This is foundational legislation. You know it. I know it. It has to be bipartisan." In a 2021 interview, Turnbull didn't recall the conversation but acknowledged that Byrne always sought to be constructive on national security matters. Byrne says the prime minister agreed to the two days, and Turnbull doesn't differ in his account.

Third, Byrne and Dreyfus went to see Christian Porter. They found him open to compromise but wary. The meeting concluded without any formal agreement. Byrne later went back to see Porter separately. He filled Porter in on his discussion with Turnbull. They both agreed that it was essential to craft amendments that would be supported by both parties.

With the clock ticking, they sat down to write them. "It was extraordinary," said Byrne. "To get consensus I was sitting with Porter in his office as he literally rewrote the bills by hand", the Liberal attorney-general agreeing terms with a Labor backbencher. For his part, Porter said that Byrne's efforts were "heroic". The bills won the bipartisan recommendation of the PJCIS and sailed through both houses of parliament without any partisan debate. And into the statute books. As a matter of national choice, not partisan argument.

The process of collaboration improved the bills immensely. Mark Dreyfus gave some examples. "Unamended, these bills would have threatened journalists with severe criminal penalties for reporting on matters in the national security space that might have embarrassed the government," he told the House. "They would have imposed enormous administrative burdens on charities across our country – and even on those who supported them – backed up by criminal sanctions for non-compliance. These laws would have required any Australian academic engaged in joint work with an overseas university or academic to register as a foreign agent, again, on pain of criminal prosecution if they did not. Clearly, these outcomes would have been completely unacceptable to most Australians."

Anthony Byrne was relieved and proud of the outcome. In commending the bills to the House, he conveyed his view of the situation's gravity by quoting John Curtin's 1942 radio broadcast to the people of America. With the Imperial Japanese forces threatening invasion, Curtin said: "Be assured of the calibre of our national character. This war may see the end of much that we have painfully and slowly built in our 150 years of existence. But even though all of it go, there will still be Australians fighting on Australian soil until the turning point be reached, and we will advance over blackened ruins, through blasted and fire-swept cities, across scorched plains, until we drive the enemy into the sea."

But, of course, creating a new law is one thing; enforcing it is another. In this case, one prime minister created the new laws, but their enforcement fell to another. The revolving door of the Australian prime ministership turned yet again. Turnbull was gone within two months of the FITS and EFI bills passing. When Scott Morrison replaced him, it seemed for a while that the bills would be orphans, with no one to care for them and effectively implement them. Because nothing much happened.

6

DAGGERS IN YOUR SMILE

The great and the good appear before the National Press Club in Canberra every week. But this particular performance was met with special anticipation. Authoritarian regimes don't enjoy submitting themselves to the impertinence of journalists. They never do it in any meaningful way at home, and they avoid it abroad. The Chinese embassy had had a longstanding invitation from Australia's premier journalistic forum, but it'd been fourteen years since any Chinese official had agreed to speak there. No representative of Xi Jinping's regime had accepted. But on 26 August 2020, Wang Xining was about to change that.

The deputy ambassador of the People's Republic spoke of the need for mutual respect between Australia and China. Confident, courtly, shaven-headed and speaking very competent English, the former censor of foreign correspondents in Beijing faced a roomful of correspondents and a national TV audience. "Respect will anchor our relationship in the torrent of differences," he said. "Let the sun shine in our relationship." He smiled frequently.

Reporters pointed out that Chinese government ministers had refused to return phone calls from their Australian counterparts for months. Was that respectful? Wang evaded the question on the first two attempts. On the third, he answered: "I don't think we have received any requests for a phone call." He immediately added that he was speaking on behalf of China's embassy in Canberra, not all parts of the Chinese government, giving him a technical way out. But he did emphasise: "There is no block." "And if we receive a request, it will be done in a very diplomatic way."

What the reporters in the room didn't know was that Xi's government had rejected an Australian minister's request for a phone conversation that very morning. The agriculture minister, David Littleproud, had formally asked twice to speak with his Chinese equivalent, Han Changfu. Littleproud made his first approach through the Australian embassy in Beijing on 13 May. He wrote a letter to Han nine days later about Beijing placing tariffs on Australian barley. He wrote another letter to Han on 20 August asking for a phone conversation to discuss broader matters of agricultural trade. That letter noted Beijing's decision to investigate Australian wine, a possible prelude to imposing trade penalties on the billion-dollar-a-year export trade. It also proposed holding the regular high-level dialogue on phytosanitary standards in agriculture trade and a meeting of the Australia–China Joint Agricultural Commission. Littleproud received only silence.

On the morning of Wang's appearance at the press club, Chinese officials finally responded – 105 days after Littleproud's first request for a phone call. They said that Littleproud's request to speak was rejected. A text message sent to Australia's embassy in Beijing said that it was "still not appropriate to discuss this". The message was relayed to Canberra the next day. A very diplomatic way indeed.

In case Littleproud was asked about Wang's comments during parliamentary question time, his department drafted an answer for him. If asked, the minister would have stated the dates and details of his requests – and the rejections. This would have revealed Wang's evasiveness. But no one asked the question.

Australia's trade minister, Simon Birmingham, had made his own requests to speak to his Chinese counterpart, Zhong Shan. By the time Wang took to the podium, Birmingham had formally written twice to Zhong, seeking a phone call. Officials acting on Birmingham's behalf had also contacted Chinese authorities another six times to ask for such a phone call, or to follow up on requests for one. Is it possible that all of those approaches were conducted directly through Beijing, bypassing the Chinese embassy in Canberra? No, it's not. Those contacts included at least two face-to-face meetings between Department of Foreign Affairs and Trade officers in Canberra, making requests on behalf of Birmingham, and Chinese embassy officials, according to authoritative sources. As Beijing added more and more Australian export items to the punishment list – after barley it was beef, then tourism, university education, thermal coal for making electricity and coking coal for making steel, followed by cotton – Birmingham made more and more requests to speak with Zhong. By late October 2020, Australia's trade minister and his officials had made at least thirteen requests and follow-ups in six months. All were rebuffed, ignored or put off.

The foreign affairs minister, Marise Payne, had made about half a dozen requests to communicate with her Chinese counterpart, Wang Yi, by the time of Wang's address. Most of the requests were made by letter but one was through a direct phone call to Wang's office, according to government sources. And, once again, multiple requests were made on Payne's behalf by Australian diplomats in Canberra during meetings with the Chinese embassy. All of Payne's approaches were ignored. Wang wasn't merely being evasive. He was flat-out lying.

What else was happening unseen between the two nations while Wang conducted his propaganda exercise for the cameras? Escalating cyber-attacks, for one thing. Eight days after Wang's appearance, Australia's then defence minister, Linda Reynolds, announced that the country was being subjected to cyber-attacks of growing scale and intensity: "This type of activity really does blur what we previously understood to be peace and war, which is what we call that grey zone in between," she said. She revealed that the Australian Cyber Security Centre had received 59,806 reports of cyber-attacks in the year before 30 June 2020, or one every 8.8 minutes. Some attacks were committed by opportunistic cyber criminals trying to steal or defraud their way to profits, she said. And "there are sophisticated and very well-resourced state-based actors who are seeking to interfere in our nation in this grey zone in any opportunistic way that they can". This reference to "sophisticated . . . state-based actors" is code for China. The situation had intensified since June, she said, when Prime Minister Scott Morrison had issued a national alert. At the time, Morrison had said, "Australian organisations are currently being targeted by a sophisticated state-based cyber actor." The attacks were widespread, affecting "all levels of government, industry, political organisations, education, health, essential service providers and operators of other critical infrastructure". If Morrison's announcement was intended to warn Beijing off, it had the opposite effect. Linda Reynolds updated the situation: "I can assure you all today that that threat has not diminished since then – in fact, it has increased."

However, for those in Wang's audience at the press club, the most bitter secret that the diplomat concealed was a clandestine detention that had taken place in Beijing days earlier.

Wang appeared before the assembled Australian journalists knowing that his government's agents had seized a respected Australian business journalist, Cheng Lei. Not on suspicion of any real crime; it was a political act. The arrest would not be public knowledge for another five days. Cheng, an Australian citizen, was a presenter on the state-owned China Global Television Network. As the BBC reported, "Ms Cheng suddenly disappeared from screens and ceased all contact with friends and family. Her profile and interviews were wiped from CGTN's website." Better known in China and the US than at home, Cheng Lei, forty-five, migrated to Australia with her family at the age of ten. She returned to China as an adult to work for the US financial news channel CNBC, then for CGTN. Her two children still lived in Australia with her parents while she pursued her TV career. The Chinese government later revealed that she was being held in an undisclosed location under "residential surveillance", a category used to detain people without charge for up to six months. She was suspected of "criminal activity endangering China's national security", according to the authorities, with no detail provided. This is a catch-all so broad as to convey nothing except that someone powerful wanted her locked up.

Cheng was the second Australian writer or journalist to be detained in China in twenty months. Dr "Henry" Yang Hengjun was grabbed under the same "national security" catch-all in January 2019. A former public servant for various Chinese government ministries, including foreign affairs, he moved to Sydney, where he wrote spy novels and pro-democracy blog posts, before relocating to the US. Agents arrested him during a trip to China. After seven months in detention, he was charged with spying. Foreign affairs minister Marise Payne said she was "very concerned and disappointed" at news of the arrest. "There is no basis for any allegation Dr Yang was spying for the Australian government." It later emerged that he was being held in isolation, interrogated daily while shackled to a chair. The real reason for Yang's detention appears to be that he advocated for democracy and against authoritarianism. Similarly, it seems that Cheng Lei's real offence was to criticise China's authoritarianism on her Facebook page.

At another time, these acts of political free speech might not have been enough to sweep their authors up into the regime's punitive apparatus. But Xi's regime had moved into a heightened phase of repression at home and of domination abroad. The Chinese and Australian governments had entered a new era of confrontation. Australia had stood up, and China was seeking to make it bow down again. And Wang's offer of sunshine? Receiving a diplomatic overture from Wang was like receiving flowers from the Mafia. No wonder he smiled so much. It was a piece of Orwellian diplomatic theatre. The eminent Australian Sinologist Geremie Barmé thinks this comparison unfair. "It's an insult to the Mafia," he says. "Because the Mafia has Omertà while the Chinese Communist Party has no code of honour." Barmé cites an old Chinese proverb, "Within your smile, there are daggers", as another way of capturing the same concept. "Because the people you are dealing with need to know that behind these overtures there are threats."

Wang also gave Beijing's fullest explanation yet for its public campaign of stepped-up trade coercion against Australia. The Chinese people felt betrayed by the Morrison government's proposal for an international inquiry into the origins and handling of the COVID-19 virus. "This shocking news of a proposal", he said, "coming from Australia, which is supposed to be a good friend of China", had created a sense of betrayal that he equated with Brutus's stabbing of Julius Caesar. He quoted the famous line from Shakespeare's play, when the king sees his loyal friend among the assassins: "Et tu, Brute?" Australian ministers had named Wuhan as the point of origin of the pandemic. "And they did not pinpoint any other places as a possible origin, possible source. So China, we believe, was singled out for the review." And he invoked the standby accusation that Australia "hurts the feelings of the Chinese people".

This was the same official who complained loudly when Australia closed its border to China. As the pandemic spread like wildfire from China to the rest of the world and the Morrison government – acting on the advice of the chief medical officer – decided to protect the country, Wang called the border closure an "overreaction". He said that China was "not happy" with the decision and said Australia should pay compensation to the Chinese students who'd been inconvenienced. Australia was hardly alone, with many other nations also blocking entry to travellers from China, among them New Zealand, the US, Indonesia, India, Taiwan, Indonesia, Japan, South Korea and Israel. Even the Chinese city of Hong Kong cut off arrivals from the Chinese mainland. And of course, China had already closed its own borders to prevent reinfection from abroad. Beijing announced its ban on foreigners six days before Australia closed its border to China. In other words, Wang denied that Australia had the right to control its own borders. By Wang's logic, China was free to close its border but Australia was not; China was entitled to spread COVID-19 but Australia was not entitled to protect itself. Was this his definition of mutual respect? He had wanted

Australia to let the pandemic in, risking the health of its people and its economy; now he was calling for Australia to let sunshine in to lighten the relationship.

Did he expect to be taken seriously? The Australian media did take him seriously. Reporting of the National Press Club event played it straight, with coverage that quoted his key points and main themes, his claims, his overtures, his denials. It was a professional effort, standard treatment by Australian media. As a practised polemicist and propagandist who'd worked with Western media for years, Wang knew this was the sort of treatment he could expect. It was a world away from the way the media are required to behave in China. No filters were applied, ideological or political; nothing was censored; none of the reporters was a "plant" from the government; none delivered a hostile diatribe against the speaker.

In the People's Republic, the media have always operated under the strict control of the Chinese Communist Party – it's long been called the CCP's "tongue and throat". But in the Xi Jinping era, that control has intensified. In a tour of three newsrooms in 2016, Xi said that all media, including commercial tabloids, had to be edited "in the right direction" – in reporting not only domestic events, but also social news, international news, even entertainment. Xi claimed that the party's media, which comprises all of the biggest outlets, including the *People's Daily*, China Central Television (CCTV) and the Xinhua News Agency, "must love the party, protect the party, and closely align themselves with the party leadership in thought, politics and action". And, in his most notable flourish, "they must have the party as their surname", he added. When Xi, who is CCTV'S national president by virtue of his position as CCP general secretary, sat in the presenter's seat in front of the cameras as part of his visit to the broadcaster, a message flashed across viewers' TV screens: "CCTV's surname is 'The Party'. Absolutely loyal. Ready for your inspection."

A professor of political philosophy at Nanjing University, Gu Su, commented: "The party is exerting stricter control over media and they will play more roles in spreading ideological thoughts, party policies and party approved mainstream values." Willy Wo-Lap Lam of the Chinese University of Hong Kong observed: "This is a very heavy-handed ideological campaign to drive home the point of total loyalty to the party core."

Note that whether it's Xi or a commentator talking about what the media disseminate, the first item in the list is always ideology. Or ideas. Or thoughts. One of the translations of the Chinese expression for propaganda is "thought work". This is not mere marketing or public relations, putting lipstick on pigs. This is the manipulation of whether you are thinking about pigs, whether pigs are animals, whether they are good or bad, even whether you have the vocabulary to name the animal you think might be a pig to start with. And what you think about pigs is no trivial point. In George Orwell's 1945 allegory of communist society, *Animal Farm*, the pigs held power and directed the other animals because "with their superior knowledge it was natural that they should assume the leadership". Yet what is supposedly "natural" in one political system is alien in another.

Ideology and thought – *yishixingtai* – is the overarching realm in which the party seeks to establish its domain. This is not just a domestic effort. Xi's predecessor, Hu Jintao, said in 2003 that "creating a favourable international public opinion environment" was important for "China's national security and social stability".

In the same year, the People's Liberation Army added "media warfare" to its officially designated political goals. "Their view of national security involves pre-emption in the world of ideas," says Peter Mattis, a fellow at Jamestown Foundation in Washington and a former CIA analyst. So, for instance, CCTV created its international service, China Global Television Network, inspired by the success of Al Jazeera, the international news network run by Qatar's government.

In 2009, still in the pre-Xi era, Beijing decided to invest US$6.5 billion to amplify its voice in the world. For scale, that was a greater sum than the entire annual economic output of fifty-one nations at the time. It was a major effort to develop a defensive censorship-based approach into the massive exportation of propaganda disguised as news media, trying to influence the global climate of ideas. Today, China spends about US$10 billion a year on extending its "soft power" worldwide, a sum that includes its media budgets but other endeavours too, such as Confucius Institutes, Confucius Classrooms, the sponsoring of cultural festivals, films, books, exchange programs, the subsidising of foreign students studying in China, the hosting of conferences, foreign aid, and the training of foreign officials in China, according to an estimate by US Sinologist David Shambaugh of George Washington University.

President Xi in 2013 said that ideology and thought work was the primary line of defence for the party's grip on power. "The dissolution of a regime often begins in the field of ideas," he told an internal party meeting. In apparent reference to the collapse of the Soviet Union, he continued: "After the *yishixingtai* line of defence has been breached, other lines of defence will be difficult to hold." The party must "resolutely engage in propaganda".

Today, CGTN broadcasts a free-to-air satellite service to over 100 countries, in English, Arabic, French, Spanish and Russian. It is an arm of the Central Committee of the Chinese Communist Party, and is registered in the US as an agent of influence of a foreign power. A *New York Times* piece in 2019 on the network's US service caught some of its distinguishing features: "It broadcasts forced confessions to American audiences. It avoids subjects that displease Beijing. It cuts away when wind musses the hair of Xi Jinping, the Chinese president."

In Australia, CGTN is broadcast in English on the Foxtel cable TV service. And when the ABC ended its shortwave radio broadcasting into the Pacific region in 2017, China Radio International took over its frequencies and started telling the CCP's version of the news. The ABC reported that, according to Graeme Smith of the ANU, Chinese-language radio in Australia has been bought up by China Radio International or its affiliated companies across most major Australian cities. "They have effectively monopolised the Chinese-language airwaves" in Australia, he said. China analyst and linguist Alex Joske, formerly with the Australia Strategic Policy Institute, says that all Chinese-language print media in Australia are controlled, directly or indirectly, by the party – with two exceptions, *The Epoch Times* and *Vision Times*, which are both published by Falun Gong, the Chinese religious group banned in China.

The Chinese metaphor for using other countries' media to distribute its propaganda abroad is "borrowing the boat to go out to the sea". The rest of the world has been obliging in loaning – or selling – its media boats to the CCP. And in 2020 Xi's regime formally asked the media of nearly 100 other nations to join Beijing's efforts. "The Belt and Road News Network issued an open letter to its alliance members of 205 media outlets from 98 countries around the world, calling on them to give the message of unity and support to the public, tell stories of how countries fight together by looking over for and helping each other, and give the warm message of unity and strength," the *People's Daily* reported in May. The party mouthpiece said that media in the partner nations should tell positive stories of China's management of COVID-19. Through the Belt and Road initiative, Xi is laying down much more than rail lines and highways; he is seeking to extend the priority network for the party's primary line of defence – ideology and thought work – across the world.

When Wang Xining stood before the National Press Club, he spoke English but performed in a language that Australia is not equipped to decipher – a small but important part of Beijing's global campaign to "resolutely engage in propaganda". For instance, Wang told his audience: "China is committed to building socialist democracy and rule of law, deepening reform and opening-up, strengthening legal establishment, improving governance system and capability, and imposing strict disciplines within the party." Sounds impressive at first glance, right? Take another look. That sentence contains six main concepts. Let's decode each briefly.

First, the party's idea of "socialist democracy" is neither socialist nor democratic. As for socialist, the International Monetary Fund reported in 2018: "China has moved from being a moderately unequal country in 1990 to being one of the most unequal countries." As for democracy, the annual Varieties of Democracy report compiled at Sweden's Gothenburg University ranks 179 nations in order of their liberal democratic freedom. China comes in at number 174, in the same league as Syria, Yemen and

Saudi Arabia. The party calls it "socialist democracy" to convey that China's Communist Party prizes a collective approach – it's about the collective wellbeing, not individual liberties. And it's true that the party monitors public opinion intimately and often tries to address concerns, seeking to pre-empt any mass outbreak of dissent. But, as scholar Fu Zhengyuan has said, "the fact that the shepherd may take notice of the baying of his sheep does not make sheep participants in decision making".

Second, "rule of law" is the antithesis of "rule by man". The United Nations explains the concept: "The rule of law is a principle of governance in which all persons, institutions and entities, public and private, including the State itself, are accountable to laws that are publicly promulgated, equally enforced and independently adjudicated." China's paramount leader during the late 1970s and the 1980s, Deng Xiaoping, said: "What the old China has left us with is a tradition of feudal autocracy, rather than a tradition of democracy and rule of law." And it suits the party very well to persist with a neo-feudal autocracy. There is no rule of law in China. There is only rule by the party. The 2017 Party Congress said it plainly: "east, west, north, south – the party leads everything". And as long as Xi Jinping controls the party, there is only rule by Xi. "After decades of collective leadership, Xi Jinping is taking China back to personalistic leadership," says Susan Shirk, a Sinologist at the University of California, San Diego. "By the end of his first five-year term, Xi had consolidated greater personal power than Jiang [Zemin] or Hu [Jintao] had ever held ... Xi's hold on the People's Liberation Army is even more complete than his hold on the CCP and the government."

Third, Wang boasted of China's "deepening reform and opening up", which is a reference to years of promises from Xi to allow the market a greater influence over the allocation of resources in the economy. The China Dashboard is a project that monitors China's economic reform progress. It's run by the Asia Society Policy Institute, headed by Kevin Rudd, and the US Rhodium Group's Dan Rosen. Rudd and Rosen examined their dashboard and concluded in September 2020:

> Long-promised changes detailed at the beginning of the Xi era haven't materialised. Though Beijing talks about "market allocation" efficiency, it isn't guided by what mainstream economists would call market principles. The Chinese economy is instead a system of state capitalism in which the arbiter is an uncontestable political authority.

Fourth is "strengthening legal establishment". Willy Wo-Lap Lam of the Chinese University of Hong Kong points out that Chinese courts today are more manipulated and opaque than they were forty years ago. For instance, long segments of the trial of the notorious Gang of Four were broadcast on national TV in 1980–81. The Gang of Four, led by Mao's widow, Jiang Qing, was a powerful clique in Mao's later years that wielded authority during the sweeping chaos and murder of the Cultural Revolution. Deng Xiaoping used a kangaroo court to discredit them as he consolidated power. In that trial, the Chinese public could hear an emotional Jiang angrily challenge the authority of the court, the law and Deng himself. But when Xi has used the courts to purge political enemies, such as former commerce minister Bo Xilai, the public was not allowed to know of Bo's protestations of innocence. Party-run media proclaimed that a live microblog feed from the courtroom was proof of the transparency of

China's justice system. But Lam points out that statements by Bo in his own defence were censored, such as when he denied that he wanted to be China's premier or "China's Putin". Or when he protested that his trial was "unjust and unfair", as he was stripped of all assets and sentenced to life imprisonment for corruption. Wang's claim of "strengthening legal establishment" is also at odds with Xi's mass arrests of human rights lawyers, defence attorneys and even eminent constitutional scholars. What Wang meant, in effect, was the strengthening the party's unchallengeable dominance over the judicial and legal systems.

"Improving governance system and capability", Wang's fifth concept, was introduced by Xi Jinping in 2013. It sounds dull; in truth, it's anything but. It's a plan to bring China closer to totalitarianism – the thorough entrenchment of the party as the permanent and inevitable nerve system for the control of every muscle and fibre of the Chinese system.

You'll notice that journalistic writings about Chinese authorities sometimes refer to the Chinese government, and sometimes to the Chinese Communist Party. This is a distinction that seems to make sense: the government refers to the system of state institutions and administration peopled by civil servants, while the party inhabits the political leadership and directs the government from the top. In a democracy, the political leadership comes and goes with elections, but the organs of the state remain. In China, however, great effort has gone into enmeshing the two so that they are inseparable. The party leadership want to fuse the two to make sure that its power over the organs of the state cannot be reduced or diluted. Which is why Sinologists generally don't write of the party and the state as separate entities, but instead refer to the "party-state". There have been debates within China over the years over whether to allow a separation, a decentralisation, to make the system more flexible and adaptable. Some decentralisation did occur, in ebbs and flows. Xi is determined to end such flirtations.

"Improving governance system and capability" is Xi's program for tightening this inseparability even further. "Strengthening the Party's comprehensive leadership at all costs is central to Xi's institutional reform," writes Baogang Guo of Dalton State College in the US state of Georgia. "Its goal is to reverse the trend of political decentralisation and improve the effectiveness of central policy coordination. Xi gives a new meaning to unified party leadership. He states the Party will 'set the purpose for the whole nation, provide coordination and integration that are critically important [for] a nation as vast and diverse as China, and effectively mobilize resources to achieve developmental goals.'"

Guo continues: "Additionally, the party leadership is considered absolute in two areas: one is the army, and the other is political and legal work. The first concerns the control of 'guns', and the second, the power of the 'knife'." Xi in 2019 listed 100 areas of governance that were to be overhauled to cement this fusion of party and state. Guo even has a new name for this achievement – "partocracy". He explains it as a system that ensures the "primacy of the Party is above the supremacy of the law".

Finally, Wang spoke of "imposing strict disciplines within the party". One of the features of Xi's rule has been his vast and unrelenting purges, his "anti-corruption" campaigns. Willy Lam says that Xi's program to catch corrupt "tigers and flies" in the party-state apparatus – the big predators as well as the mere insects – may be "the single most notable achievement" of his administration. By October 2018, Xi's regime had investigated more than 2.7 million officials and punished more than 1.5 million people. Among them were seven national-level leaders, including Bo Xilai. And two dozen generals. According to official data, at least two officials received the death penalty.

The campaign is a purge of the corrupt, but a politically selective one. No allies of Xi and his faction were among the victims. One indicator: proposals for politically neutral anti-corruption measures have stalled. A so-called "sunshine" law requiring uniform disclosure of officials' asset holdings, for instance, was abandoned. People close to Xi – such as his older sister, Qi Qiaoqiao – who were reported by Western media to have accumulated unexplained riches have remained conspicuously untouched by the anti-corruption drive. The billionaire real estate tycoon Ren Zhiqiang was untroubled by the campaign until he criticised Xi Jinping's handling of the COVID-19 plague. In an essay, Ren described Xi as "a clown stripped naked who insisted on continuing being emperor". Ren was quickly expelled from the party for "vilifying the image of party and country". A lightning investigation into his affairs found him guilty of corruption and he was sentenced to eighteen years' jail. As Deng Yuwen, former editor of a Communist Party newspaper, put it: "The core goal of cleaning up the political and legal system is also to obey Xi in everything."

At the National Press Club, China's deputy ambassador spoke the language of the Chinese Communist Party, the most durable and successful authoritarian political movement of modern history, the only regime on the planet that has presided over a vast and thriving internet economy while strictly controlling all political discussion within it, walling it off from the outside world and censoring anything deemed politically sensitive.

"Political language," said that shrewd analyst of totalitarianism George Orwell, "is designed to make lies sound truthful and murder respectable, and to give an appearance of solidity to pure wind." Orwell was speaking of English, and only barely lived long enough to see the foundation of the People's Republic of China. But he would have appreciated the party's creation of an alternative reality through its mastery of management and manipulation of political language.

Perry Link, an expert in Chinese linguistics, explains how China has long had two ways of speaking, according to topic – there's ordinary talk for "buying fish in the market, asking your sister-in-law to pass the soy sauce, or shouting at a child to get out of the rain". And then there's "official talk" used in classrooms and newspapers, formal meetings and welcomes to foreign dignitaries. Official talk was "only shuffling words that had been drained of the ideals and principles they had originally represented", Link writes in his book *An Anatomy of Chinese*. The distinction between the two sharpened dangerously in the late Mao era: "During the Great Leap Forward, people had to speak of 'great bountiful harvests' at the same time that the largest famine in world history was unfolding", for instance. And failure to adhere to such "official talk" could be deadly.

In such a world, it's much easier to comprehend apparent contradictions, daggers within smiles, blackmail within bouquets. A fiction author and literature professor in the early twentieth century, Wu Zuxiang, gave this explanation of how to interpret "official talk": "There is truth in Chinese newspapers, but you have to know how to find it. This often means reading upside down. If they say great strides have been made against corruption in Henan, you know that corruption is especially bad in Henan.

If they say dozens of police were hurt in a clash with students, you know hundreds of students were injured if not killed."

Wang Xining gave Australia a taste of China's "official talk" – approved propaganda laden with blatant falsehoods and dire threats, packaged to seem straightforwardly constructive. Dangerous climate change loomed; the talk was of sunshine. If Australia failed to understand the message, whose fault was that?

7

THE BIG FISH
AND THE LITTLE FISH

The big fish is swimming along contentedly one morning when he passes two little fish.

"Good morning," say the little fish, greeting the big fish.

"Good morning," he replies. "Isn't the water lovely today?"

Once he's gone, one of the little fish turns to the other and asks: "What's water?"

Humans operate in a climate of ideas, shaped by language – whether we recognise it or not. Those who control the climate of ideas and the words to express them control the contours of our thoughts, which, in turn, define our scope for action. Mao Zedong understood this – and so does Xi Jinping. The first of Mao's three "magic weapons" to ensure the party's success was ideology. President Xi has revived the cult of Mao and Maoism. After an earlier trend to allow some limited criticism of Mao's dire blunders, Xi has banned any such criticism as "historical nihilism". As part of this revival, he has also restated Mao's formulation, saying that the party's first "magic weapon" is its ideology.

Ideology is a "set of ideas, beliefs and opinions about the nature of people and society, providing a framework for a theory about how people should live", according to the Brockhampton *Dictionary of Ideas*. "A nation's ideology is reflected in the political system it creates." China's political system is utterly different from that of any democracy. And most democracies are deeply entwined with China. Some, Australia in particular, have allowed themselves to become economically dependent on China, without any real comprehension of the system or the climate of ideas that sustains it. Perhaps earlier familiarity would have been helpful, but better late than never. The bad news is that democracies in general and Australia in particular are starting from a very poor level of comprehension. The good news is that because Xi is persisting with Mao's core ideology from a century ago, it is largely a known quantity.

Xi is generally rated as the most powerful of China's leaders since Mao. "There is, unfortunately, no indication that Xi is using his extra powers to promote novel ideas about reform," says Willy Wo-Lap Lam. "There seems to be a severe deficit in ideas about how to ring in the new. On the one hand, there is a refusal to admit and recognise past mistakes." These include the massacre of students in Tiananmen Square in 1989, the shocking man-made famine under Mao's Great Leap Forward, and the violence and social scarring of Mao's Cultural Revolution. The party's enduring failure is its unwillingness to put in place any checks or balances to prevent similar horrors happening again. However, "even more devastating is the Xi administration's refusal to consider solutions that smack of 'international norms'", says Lam. "Xi's solution is a kind of narcissistic self-perfectionism." The evidence for this is Xi's own words. He has called on the party to "purify itself and to seek self-perfection, self-renewal and self-resuscitation".

Xi's conservatism and rigidity is based on fear, observes Lam. It's a result of his "paranoia about the sudden implosion of the

Party or the obliteration of the mandate of heaven", the fate that befell the Communist Party of the Soviet Union. Or, as Xi Jinping himself has put it: "We must ensure that our red heaven and earth will never change their colour." As a result, says Willy Lam, any reform in Xi's China is bound to be "reform within a birdcage". Or a fish tank.

8

THE RED DETACHMENT
OF WOMEN

They are beguiling, these women of the revolution. They look fierce, strong and dangerous as they aim their rifles in tight formation, yet they are beautiful and lithe as they pirouette and arabesque their way across the stage. They wear the uniform of the People's Liberation Army, yet their legs are bare in bermuda shorts, racy for their day. How to make sense of them?

The Red Detachment of Women was a project of Jiang Qing, the wife of Chairman Mao Zedong. It was one of the eight permitted "model dramas" of the revolution. It was first performed in 1964 in Beijing, but now brilliantly executed in Melbourne. They are performing ballet, but they are delivering propaganda. "Wall-to-wall with Communist cheese", in the words of one reviewer, Anne-Marie Peard. "It's a two-hour long propaganda poster with pointe shoes. All it's missing is Mao's face and a Little Red Book."

Victoria's premier, Daniel Andrews, announced the ballet's Australian debut in 2017 as a "coup". The protesters outside the theatre thought it a takeover of a different kind. About 100 members of the Chinese Australian community carried banners and handed out leaflets. "The well-dressed opening night crowd filed in, past protesters shouting, 'Fascist ballet!' and 'Go back to China!'," reports Peard, writing for aussietheatre.com.au.

Set during China's Civil War of the 1920s and '30s, it tells the tale of a slave girl who flees her violently abusive owner, an evil landlord. She returns with the Red Detachment to deliver vengeance. The evil landlord is defended by soldiers of the nationalist Kuomintang but the Red Detachment, naturally, is victorious. The evil landlord, of course, is slain.

The slave girl is honoured by being appointed political commissar of the detachment, the representative of the Chinese Communist Party. The commissar's job is to ensure the political loyalty of the troops. The army, then as now, belongs to the party, not to the Chinese state. Mao famously said: "Every Communist must grasp the truth, 'Political power grows out of the barrel of a gun.' Our principle is that the Party commands the gun, and the gun must never be allowed to command the Party."

The protesters, members of the Australian Values Alliance – the same group that successfully shut down the Red Songs concert in Sydney in 2016 – denounced the show as a glorification of a totalitarian despot who oversaw the deaths of some 40 to 50 million Chinese people. And the audience? The reviewer for *Daily Review*, Maxim Boon, found it to be "a chilling reminder of the power and purpose of disinformation". But he was aghast that the Melbourne audience had a very different reaction: they loved it.

The situation was so perverse it reminded Boon of Mel Brooks's comedy *The Producers*. In the movie, a couple of con men need to stage a theatrical failure that's guaranteed to lose money, so they create a new musical – "Springtime for Hitler: A Gay Romp with Eva and Adolf at Berchtesgaden". Boon takes up the story:

It's a show they believe so tasteless, offensive and ideologically repulsive that audiences will be sent running. Much to their astonishment, it actually ends up being a box office smash hit. Watching National Ballet of China's production of *The Red Detachment of Women*, the headline event of the Arts Centre Melbourne's Asia-Topa Festival, I couldn't help but feel the same striking sense of disbelief as the audience warmly applauded.

The Chinese Australian protesters outside were offended and angry at the politics; the theatregoing patrons inside were delighted at the spectacle "without the faintest hint of cognisance". Boon, who today is classical music critic for *The Age* newspaper, was flabbergasted. The Arts Centre Melbourne wouldn't have staged a show glorifying Stalin's Soviet Union or Hitler's Third Reich. How could it fail to see that Mao's Communist Party was every bit as objectionable? In the eyes of another reviewer, Antonia Finnane, a professor of Chinese history at Melbourne University, the performance "seems more in keeping with North Korea than with contemporary China, entertaining but somehow absurd until the finale, when a line of soldiers advances towards the audience with rifles, to the tune of 'Forward March'".

Finnane points out that the story is set on Hainan, an island province in China's tropical south. Hainan houses China's most important naval base, including an underwater submarine base with tunnels that allow its fast-attack and nuclear-powered ballistic missile-armed submarines to leave and return without being observed. China's navy would soon overtake the US's to become the biggest in the world. Hainan is also the biggest island in the South China Sea, that roiling locus of Chinese territorial grabs. "A Melbourne audience might well wonder: is it simply a coincidence that in precisely the period that China has been ratcheting up its claims on the South China Sea, the National Ballet Company of China has been performing *The Red Detachment of Women* on one international stage after another?" poses Finnane.

In 2018, the People's Liberation Army Air Force sent one of its long-range strategic bombers, the H-6K, to touch down on Woody Island in the contested Paracel Islands. From the newly built base there, or in the equally contested Spratlys, the H-6K could strike anywhere in Southeast Asia, or indeed Japan, South Korea or the US base in Guam. The party's military now challenges other nations' military ships and planes that approach the armed territories it has built to straddle the South China Sea, the world's most important commercial artery. The commercial shipping lanes through the South China Sea are Australia's lifeline, its principal channel for earning a living in the world.

Mao himself attended the premiere of *The Red Detachment* in 1964. The "Great Helmsman" was building a powerful propaganda-ideological-political-military dictatorship, the foundation of the most enduring and successful authoritarian regimes in modern history. *The Red Detachment of Women* was a nationalistic accompaniment to one of its breakthrough moments: it debuted some two weeks before China's first nuclear weapon test. In 2017 the ballet accompanied another breakthrough moment: the party's conquest over US hegemony in the Pacific, over the international law of the sea, over the claims of five neighbouring states. Those who understood the meaning and power of the Melbourne performance of *The Red Detachment* were the Chinese Australian protesters, the Sinologists, the expert reviewers and, of course, the Chinese government officials and advocates who'd organised its staging. The enraptured audiences were unwittingly committing what Maxim Boon describes as "the normalisation and reverence of State-sanctioned propaganda, even when it takes the guise of a pleasant night out at the theatre". It was indeed a "coup", but perhaps not as Daniel Andrews had meant it. The great bulk of the audience was simply not equipped to comprehend the beguiling spectacle in front of them.

*

When Australia proposed an international inquiry into COVID-19 in April 2020, it wasn't just Beijing that expressed opposition; some of Australia's more China-dependent businesspeople took Beijing's side. Kerry Stokes, the billionaire founder of Seven West Media, wanted the Australian government to heed the party's "anger". Stokes took space on the front page of *The West Australian*, which he happens to own, to argue: "If we're going to go into the biggest debt we've had in our life and then simultaneously poke our biggest provider of income in the eye it's not necessarily the smartest thing you can do." He also defended the Wuhan wet markets, the apparent origin of the virus, as an essential food source.

Stokes' newspaper reported him saying: "If Beijing's anger is not quelled it could have catastrophic consequences for the economy." The made-in-China pandemic had plunged the world into the deepest downturn since the Great Depression and was killing hundreds of thousands of people around the world, but, according to Stokes, China's wrath would be even more fearsome. It might cut all trade with Australia; the dollar could fall to US25 cents, half its historic low.

Stokes wanted Australia to quell "Beijing's anger" as its priority. But was Beijing actually angry? Or was Stokes responding to party propaganda, a performative "anger" as carefully constructed as *The Red Detachment of Women*'s aiming of stage rifles into the audience?

LION DANCE

The British had a raging thirst for Chinese tea, silk and porcelain, and could not get enough to slake it. London sent a high-level envoy to China in 1792 with the mission of opening it to more trade. Lord Macartney was instructed to go to the very top. He must insist on an audience with the emperor himself. He travelled for a year with an elaborate entourage, including fifty armed redcoats, two hundred horses, three thousand porters and six hundred crates of gifts for the Son of Heaven.

What happened next is one of the most famous failures in the annals of diplomacy. Macartney was impatient to present the emperor with a jewel-encrusted gold box containing a letter from King George III, translated into Chinese, that wished the emperor would rule for "tens of thousands and tens of thousands thousand years", and also expressed the desire for more Chinese ports to open to British ships. But Macartney was kept waiting nearly a week at Emperor Qianlong's summer residence, while he negotiated with the imperial court over a key point of protocol – the kowtow. The emissaries of all nations were required to submit to the full ritual kowtow, kneeling before the emperor and touching their foreheads to the ground three times, then three times more, then three times again. It was an unmistakeable act of submission to establish the supremacy of China and the greatness of its ruler.

Macartney refused. He decided that this was too demeaning for a representative of Britain. He would kowtow to the emperor only if a Chinese official would reciprocate, kowtowing before a portrait Macartney had brought of the English king. Failing that, he told the Chinese officials, he would show the emperor the same deference he paid to his own king – going down on one knee and bowing his head once – and no more.

The Chinese court agreed. The English aristocrat was shown in for his imperial audience and presented the king's letter. The emperor sent Macartney home with a humiliating letter in response, rejecting every one of Britain's demands. He returned to London to become a laughing-stock in the British press. As Stephen Platt relates in his book *Imperial Twilight*, Emperor Qianlong had decreed to his court that "if they come in arrogance, they get nothing".

In the centuries since, it's commonly been asserted that Macartney failed because of his refusal to kowtow. This seems plausible. Except for the fact that the Dutch sent a similar mission to China soon afterwards, performed the full kowtow, and failed just as abjectly as the British. This suggests a different conclusion: the Chinese court just enjoyed the theatrical deference of other nations. Submitting made no difference to the emperor's policy. There were two levels to China's diplomacy: theatre, on the one hand; hard interests, on the other.

Over the last few decades, the Australian media have been conditioned to expect "anger" from the Chinese government. The media have put itself in a constant state of anticipation. Reporters and editors closely watch Australia's government for anything that might "make China angry". It has become the frame through which Australia interprets news about the bilateral relationship.

Editors at *The Daily Telegraph* and other News Corp outlets thought they'd spotted a forthcoming fit on 5 June 2020, running the headline: "Australian foreign takeover rule changes could anger China." And the ABC was sure it'd found an actual tantrum as well as a future one in December 2017, when it headlined a report: "China is furious and Australia should expect more backlash after questioning its influence." And here's the ABC again, in 2018 with the headline: "China furious, as government and Labor unite on barriers against foreign interference." *The Australian* decided that it'd identified another squall in September 2019: "China angry at Australia's warnings on Huawei." And *The Australian Financial Review* diagnosed another Beijing outburst in February 2020: "Chinese furious over Australia's travel ban 'overreaction'," blared its headline. And the *AFR* again, five months later: "China's fury over Australia's embrace of Hongkongers." Then there's *The Guardian* in May 2020: "Australia unnecessarily exposed itself to Beijing's fury, but relying on the US now is risky." And a number of the Murdoch tabloids ran a headline in August 2020 proclaiming: "China's growing fury with 'lying' Australia." And Channel 7 news ran with the headline from an AAP newswire report in the same month: "Chinese envoy reveals anger with Australia."

You can see the pattern. I'm guilty of falling into the same frame. The headline on a 2013 column of mine in *The Sydney Morning Herald* was "China vents its anger at Australia's stand on airspace rights", drawing on my use of the word "angry" in the story. This was before I came to understand the phenomenon I was witnessing.

According to a search of the Factiva database, Australian newspaper articles on Australia–China relations have featured the word "angry" on 1057 occasions between 2015 and 2020. That's an average of 211 times per year, or a report of China's "anger" at Australia every 1.7 days. These articles are usually interpretations by Australian journalists of remarks in the Chinese Communist Party's media outlets or from Chinese government spokespeople. But in the most direct instance, on 17 November 2020 a pair of officials from the Chinese embassy in Canberra handed a list of fourteen grievances about Australia to reporter Jonathan Kearsley of Nine News. They wanted their complaints addressed. As China's government was exerting economic coercion against Australia at the time, it seems the embassy wanted to leave nothing to interpretation. The Chinese diplomats asked the reporter not to use their names, but he was free to quote them and to report the list of demands. When Kearsley asked them how China viewed its relationship with Australia and Australia's conduct since the advent of COVID-19, one of the officials replied: "China is angry. If you make China the enemy, China will be the enemy." Did she seem angry to Kearsley? "It wasn't aggressive, they weren't berating me, there never was an angry point," reports Kearsley. The diplomat steadily looked him in the eye while she spoke.

There are three features of this standard framing of China as permanently "angry" at Australia that stand out. First, it is unique among Australia's international relationships. No other country's dealings with Australia are assessed consistently through the prism of anger, anticipated or actual. Australians are not told that they should live in fear of any other nation. Not bigger countries – the US or Indonesia – nor smaller – New Zealand or Papua New Guinea. Not democracies – France or India – nor autocracies – Vietnam or Russia. Australia has accepted the conditioning that it must live in fear of China's "anger", and no one else's.

Second, its truthfulness goes unchallenged. Is China actually angry? No one seems to bother asking the question. The major Australian media that report on the relationship are generally careful with their facts and accurate in their details, yet they never explain the essential assumption underlying the reports. They implicitly accept that when CCP mouthpieces use words with angry connotations, the party itself is angry, and that anger is then transposed onto the entirety of China, the nation. And CCP mouthpieces often claim to speak for all 1.4 billion residents of China.

When a Chinese foreign ministry spokesperson speaks sternly during a routine press briefing, Australian observers believe that she or he is actually angry. In my case, I was in an Australia–China dialogue where a succession of five senior Chinese representatives spoke harshly, with frowns and cross words, and I implicitly accepted that it was a display of anger. It was only in retrospect that I realised I should have given more weight to their demeanour during meals and casual conversation. They were generally relaxed and approachable, even friendly. If I'd contrasted the set-piece diatribes in the formal conference room with the affable, informal chats during coffee breaks, I'd have understood sooner that I was witnessing a performance.

"Performative outrage is a high art in China," observes the Australian Sinologist Geremie Barmé. "Within the Chinese system, developed under the Chinese Communist Party since the 1940s, it was carried out in rectification campaigns based on the Soviet show trials. They had criticism and self-criticism sessions for years. They had to learn Mao Zedong thought, they had to perform regret for the past, some had to be outraged for backward ideas, others had to perform fury, anger, repentance, renewal.

It began in a codified way then, and it's never stopped." Indeed, the Communist rectification campaigns live on today. The great reviver of Mao, Xi Jinping, has launched a series of rectification campaigns of his own, most recently in July 2020, to test the political loyalty of the police and domestic security apparatus.

So Barmé poses: "When a Chinese ambassador screams at a foreign diplomat, is it real anger or isn't it? I've been subjected to this sort of treatment frequently. Luckily, I spent my twenties with ex–Red Guards [the violent shock troops of the Cultural Revolution]." Barmé considers this lucky because it familiarised him with the thinking and methods to which he would later be subjected when living in China as an academic: "this rising, rhetorical, overblown behaviour, egged on by the Chinese Communist Party, and highly colourful language".

He cites the party's *Global Times* newspaper, usually the most stridently jingoistic among the official media. "These people are completely loony," says Barmé. "It's part of the competitive outrage in their system." Among classic insults from the *Global Times* was one from its editor, Hu Xijin, after the Morrison government proposed the COVID-19 inquiry. "Australia," he wrote, "is like chewing gum stuck to the bottom of China's shoe. Sometimes you just have to find a rock and rub it off."

Says Barmé: "Poor old Australia and NZ and Western countries are simply not built to respond to this highly theatrical, over-the-top stuff. It's very hard to read if you don't know the backstory. Do these people in the Chinese system know that they look like fools? It doesn't matter – they don't care. Because it's usually to play back to their superiors, performing for Beijing."

Malcolm Turnbull certainly thought they looked like fools. The former prime minister describes the response of the Chinese outrage machine to Morrison's proposal as "ludicrous". "Scott Morrison's proposal for an inquiry was unremarkable. It's like a train crash. If there's a train crash, there should be an inquiry, and there usually is. If there's a global pandemic, should there be an inquiry? Of course there should be an inquiry. Instead, their reaction was the story – it was crazy," he said in an interview. "The key point is that they try to present it as indignation, but their outrage is invariably confected and it's instrumental and it's controlled."

Kevin Rudd is, if anything, even more dismissive of China's so-called "anger". He says, "Anger is a useless term in international relations in general, certainly in seeking to understand the Australia–China relationship in particular. Chinese policymakers in Beijing are driven by a hard-line calculus of Chinese interests. Therefore, when Chinese interests conflict with Australian interests, China will be deploying every diplomatic and economic lever at its disposal in order to maximise its interests. Part of that repertoire will be varying versions of the idea that Australia has somehow 'hurt the feelings of 1.4 billion Chinese people'." This idea, says Rudd, is "nonsense". He argues that any such assertions of indignation or fury "are designed to apply leverage to Australian public opinion" and "should not be taken seriously".

> What we should take seriously, through a properly functioning diplomatic relationship – which we don't currently have – is a clear channel for looking way beyond the atmospherics to the essential conflicts of interests and values, and working out how to best and most effectively navigate them. Remember, the Chinese government is a Marxist-Leninist system. Leninists are not into hurt feelings; Leninists just act.

Every time an Australian reporter, editor, businessperson, analyst or politician represents a Chinese Communist Party statement or action as "angry" or "furious", they – or we, I should say – are presenting this propaganda as the party wishes it to be presented. We are unwittingly doing its work for it.

HOW MUCH CAN A COMMUNIST BEAR?

Xi Jinping is the world's most powerful person, ahead of the leaders of Russia and the United States, according to the most recent annual ranking by US business magazine *Forbes*. When Xi amended China's constitution in 2018 to remove the two-term limit on the presidency, the English-language media started referring to him as China's "president for life". He chairs so many of China's key institutions that Geremie Barmé has nicknamed him "chairman of everything". In China, an indicator of his power is that "Xi Jinping Thought" is enshrined in the national constitution. Only one other president has been named in the constitution while still alive, and that was Mao Zedong.

And in the world, China has risen to become one of the two most influential countries on earth. The US economy is still bigger in size based on market exchange rates, but China's in recent years has supplied more of the world's growth. The US still spends more on its military, but China has a bigger navy, measured by number of ships and submarines. The US is still ahead in the scientific frontiers of artificial intelligence and quantum computing, but China leads in 5G wireless and quantum communications, according to *The Wall Street Journal*. The US has many more allies than does China – sixty-four nations compared to just one or two – but China has signed sixty-six countries to its Belt and Road initiative. Total funding for the scheme has been estimated at anywhere between US$1 trillion and US$8 trillion.

Against the weight of this raw power, consider this fact: the Chinese authorities have banned Winnie the Pooh. The talking teddy bear may not be seen or mentioned on the internet in China. If anybody dare publish a picture of the children's character, created by A.A. Milne in 1924, it will be scrubbed from the web within hours or even minutes. Search his name on the Chinese web and it returns no results. The charming Disney movie based on Pooh Bear, *Christopher Robin*, was likewise banned.

Why? Because the round-bellied bear with the shy smile and benign expression is thought to resemble Xi Jinping. Playful comparisons and memes started popping up on the Chinese web, beginning with a 2013 photo of Xi walking next to Barack Obama. Some wag juxtaposed the picture with two characters from the Hundred Acre Wood: Winnie the Pooh, representing the plump Xi, walking along with Tigger, representing the tall, lean Obama. The joke soon became a way of mocking the Chinese president in a system that already censored any other hint of criticism of Xi. What was China's most censored image of 2015, according to the London-based Global Risk Insights? A photo of Xi standing in his presidential limousine, saluting at a military parade, juxtaposed with a picture of a toy Winnie the Pooh standing happily in a plastic toy car. That was it.

This raises an intriguing question. What sort of leader is so threatened by this sort of parody that the national internet must be purged of it? Nobody in the US was troubled by the portrayal of its then president as Tigger, the excitably foolish tiger. A similar meme representing Japan's former prime minister Shinzo

Abe as Eeyore, the sad, saggy donkey, caused not the least stir in Japan.

The British satirist Matt Forde said in 2020 that satire had lost its power. Forde, who supplied the voice for Donald Trump in a new series of the popular TV show *Rubbery Figures*, said: "Sadly, history shows that satire has no power whatsoever over politics. There's plenty of us taking the mickey out of governments all around the world, and I'm afraid it does not bring them down." The Chinese Communist Party, however, is not prepared to take the risk.

The extraordinary sensitivity of the Chinese regime to the gentlest mockery testifies not to great power, but to great anxiety – not to great strength, but to great fragility. The system that led to Xi's top spot in *Forbes'* most-powerful list is actually animated by fear. The party, anxious about its legitimacy and insecure about its fate, is frightened.

The English playwright Noël Coward once said, "I can take any amount of criticism, so long as it is unqualified praise." How much can Xi Jinping bear? None at all, in fact. Xi Jinping and the party – far from being "angry", as they're routinely portrayed in Australian media – are anxious. Deeply, existentially fearful.

Xi declared in 2013, his second year as general secretary of the CCP, that "control over the internet is a matter of life and death for the party". This control was considered more important than the internet's value as an information resource or a tool of commerce or a social avenue. Note that Xi spoke specifically about the party, not the nation. He would soon enough portray the internet as a threat to national security, but this reference to the party is a telltale sign that his core fear is about political survival and the power of the party.

He acted accordingly. Six months later, Xi created a new supervising body and appointed himself to be its head, as Willy Wo-Lap Lam has chronicled. In launching the Central Leading Group on Internet Security and Informatisation, Xi said: "No internet safety means no national security." In that same year, 2014, online opinion leaders were detained. They were not political agitators but high-profile people from a range of fields – an investor, a couple of online marketing gurus, an environmentalist, an entrepreneur. Their crimes? "Disturbing the public order" was one, "creating disturbances" was another, and one of the marketing geniuses was jailed for three years for defamation and "spreading rumours". Since then, the controls have only tightened and the punishments increased.

Of course, the Chinese market remains firmly closed to major foreign online sites, such as Google, Amazon, Twitter, Instagram and Facebook. This is in spite of the very best sycophancy from Mark Zuckerberg. The Facebook co-founder learnt Mandarin and delivered speeches in the Chinese tongue on visits to China. For a meeting with Xi Jinping, he dressed identically to the president. The US entrepreneur's signature style at home is a T-shirt. In Beijing, he adopted the president's trademark navy suit, white business shirt and red tie. Even more obsequiously, Zuckerberg told Xi that he was expecting a child and wanted to give him a Chinese name. Would Xi do him the honour of choosing a suitable name?

But Zuckerberg didn't stop there. He posted on Facebook a photo of himself jogging through Tiananmen Square, with a rapturous smile and the caption: "It's great to be back in Beijing!" He was so anxious to win over the Beijing authorities that he overlooked the fact that the great square was where they'd massacred students peacefully protesting in 1989, that the site he posted the picture to was censored in China, and that the smog he was running through was at such a dangerous level – over 300 on the air safety index – that physical exertion was not recommended. Implicitly, he would endorse anything he needed to – murderous repression, the censorship of his business, and environmental harm – in order to make money in the Chinese market. All expressed in a single photo.

Zuckerberg was prepared to go even further. When he gave the regime's chief censor a tour of Facebook's offices in California, copies of Xi Jinping's 2014 book, *The Governance of China*, were on conspicuous display. Zuckerberg explained that he'd bought them for his staff because "I want them to understand socialism with Chinese characteristics". He was explicitly promoting the propaganda of an authoritarian state. And boasting of it.

The technology tycoon had performed the full kowtow. He could not have gone any lower. His evident hope that this grovelling would work revealed a complete lack of understanding of socialism with Chinese characteristics. Zuckerberg had no comprehension of Xi's project for China, of the exceptional priority the party had given to excluding US corporations from its internet. Xi gave Zuckerberg a bonus tutorial. He refused permission for Facebook in China. And he declined to name Zuckerberg's first-born.

Xi later handed down the lesson of the age in the party's attitude to the private sector, and online entrepreneurs in particular. China's private sector had enjoyed relative freedom to manage itself, even as other areas of the economy have suffered a new repression under Xi. But in November 2020, the president imposed a landmark humiliation. His target was the wealthiest and most successful of China's modern tycoons, Jack Ma, with a fortune of US$65 billion, according to the *Forbes* "China Rich List" of the same month. His fame and fortune stem from co-founding China's major online marketplace, Alibaba.

Ma planned to list shares in a subsidiary, Ant Group. Don't be misled by its name. Ant is mammoth. It operates a mobile payments app called Alipay, which has loans to 20 million Chinese small businesses and to half a billion Chinese individuals. It's so successful that it's disrupted the banking system. It is used, one way or another, by 70 per cent of the population of China. For scale, in 2019 it handled payments of US$16 trillion, which is twenty-five times more than that well-known American success story PayPal.

"More important than its size is what Ant represents," said London's *Economist* magazine.

> It matters globally in a way that no other Chinese financial institution does. China's banks are huge but inefficient, burdened by state ownership. By contrast foreign financiers look at Ant with curiosity, envy and anxiety. Some hawks in the White House reportedly want to rein in the company or hobble its IPO [initial public offering]. Ant is the most integrated fintech platform in the world: think of it as a combination of Apple Pay for offline pay, PayPal for online pay, Venmo for transfers, Mastercard for credit cards, JPMorgan Chase for consumer financing and iShares for investing, with an insurance brokerage thrown in for good measure, all in one mobile app.

One example: if you apply for a loan through Alipay, the app will grant or refuse it within three minutes, using a system that can processes half a billion orders per second. "Ant is, in short," the *Economist* concluded, "the world's purest example of the tremendous potential of digital finance."

What a glorious triumph for an ascendant China, surely. The float of Ant shares was to be the biggest initial public offering in the history of world share markets. Investors paid US$37 billion to buy shares in a company described as the world's largest fintech or e-finance business, to be listed on the Hong Kong and Shanghai exchanges. Its total market value was to be over US$300 billion. That would make it more valuable than any bank in the world. The anticipation was tremendous, all the way up to the eve of the listing. Which was when China's regulators ordered it halted. It was a tectonic moment that sent "shockwaves" around the financial system of China, according to business news magazine *Caixin*. The big question was, of course, why was it blocked at the eleventh hour?

There seem to be at least two parts to the answer. The technical explanation is that Chinese authorities were not satisfied that Ant would comply with new regulations for such microcredit businesses, that it was playing fast and loose and posed a risk to the stability of the banking system. The political answer, however, is that Jack Ma had provoked Xi Jinping. Ten days before the IPO was due to launch, Ma gave a speech to a top-tier finance conference. *The Wall Street Journal* reported: "Mr Xi, who read government reports about the speech, and other senior leaders were furious, according to the officials familiar with the decision-making." Xi then "ordered Chinese regulators to investigate and all but shut down Ant's initial public offering, the officials said".

Ma was one of the least important people at the conference. The opening address was given by China's vice-president, Wang Qishan, described by Sinologist Bill Bishop as the "godfather of China's financial system". His speech was about the need to curb "wrong paths" that could destabilise the system. So when Ma spoke a couple of hours later, he did seem to be issuing a challenge to the government.

In his speech, China's most successful entrepreneur said: "China doesn't have a systemic financial risk and problem because China's finance doesn't have a system." Ma was scornful of the international rules to keep banks solvent, describing regulators as an "old people's club". He was critical of Beijing for sticking with a system he described as an outdated Western construct: "Don't just be guided by what others have done." To concentrate excessively on risk was to cheat China's younger generation of opportunity, according to Ma.

That was all it took. A few days later, the regulators called Ma in for "tea" – code for a reprimand – and the float was cancelled. Xi squashed Ant like a bug.

Jack Ma was not the first billionaire tycoon that Xi had disciplined. Before Ma became China's richest person, there was Wang Jianlin. He founded the real estate empire Dalian Wanda Group, China's biggest property developer. He had gone on an international buying splurge, including a Hollywood movie studio and the AMC cinema chain in the US, Hoyts cinemas in Australia and a $1.1 billion pair of Australian development projects, one at Sydney's Circular Quay and another on the Gold Coast. Until the authorities decided to rein him in.

Again, there was a technical reason. His companies were taking excessive risks, according to the authorities. And again, there was a political agenda. He was perceived as too big, too independent, too successful, putting too many assets overseas. The party decided it needed to assert its primacy over the private sector and the billionaire class. Banks were ordered to cut his firm's credit lines. Wanda Group was forced to sell foreign assets, including its two big Australian real estate developments. Wang's ostentatious only son was targeted too. Technically it was for excessive debt, but politically it seemed to be for excessive playboyism. A court order banned him from first-class air travel, luxury hotels, foreign holidays and playing golf, among other things.

But Xi meted out the harshest punishment to Wu Xiaohui of Anbang Insurance Group. Wu had transformed a small car insurance company into a swashbuckling investment firm that had a quarter-trillion American dollars' worth of assets and was China's third-biggest insurer. Wu's international spending spree included the trophy US$2 billion Waldorf Astoria hotel in New York. Wu's most important asset, however, was his wife. He was married to the granddaughter of the late Deng Xiaoping, China's paramount leader from 1978 to 1989 and author of China's modern economic success.

Wu's downfall was an unmistakeable assertion of Xi's power. In 2017 Wu disappeared without word, the usual precursor to arrest. He was later announced to be in detention on suspicion of economic crimes. His lawyers were not permitted access to him for a year. His company was taken over by regulators. Wu later appeared in a one-day trial accused of fraud and abuse of power. His assets worth US$1.65 billion were seized. But the show-stopper was his sentence of eighteen years in jail.

Dozens of other lesser businesspeople and tycoons have suffered similarly dramatic downfalls during Xi's reign. No one would suggest that they were all scrupulous characters with unimpeachable business dealings. And their persecution by the authorities was, no doubt, partly personal and specific. But it was also systemic and political. One measure: the number of billionaires in China's notional parliament, the National People's Congress. At the outset of Xi's term as general secretary, 209 of its approximately 3000 delegates were billionaires. By 2020, according to the Hurun report on China's wealthy, that number had dropped by two-thirds to seventy-four. The number of Chinese billionaires soars year by year, but their political participation, even in an ersatz kind of legislature, shrinks. Private-sector businesspeople were allowed membership of the party for the first time in 2002. It was considered a privilege.

The more the super-rich proliferate, and the more money they amass, the more Xi seeks to check them. "China's political class wants to avoid the 'Yeltsin problem' of permitting the rise of powerful oligarchs," said Scott Kennedy, an expert on Chinese business at the Center for Strategic and International Studies in Washington. Boris Yeltsin was Russia's first post-Soviet president. In moving from a rigid command economy to a market one, he privatised major state businesses and allowed a group of oligarchs to accumulate vast economic resources in the process. The oligarchs soon challenged state power.

Yeltsin's deputy for economic affairs, Anatoly Chubais, ran the transformation of Russia's economy. When I asked him in 1999, after he'd left office, about the problem of the oligarchs, Chubais said: "The existence of these guys is not the problem. There are two real problems. First is the problem of political strength of government. The solution is to strengthen the government, and in Russia that is a challenge for the next government and the next president. The other problem is not that there are too many oligarchs but too few. We need more billionaires." Chubais meant that the power of the oligarchs would be diluted if there were more.

Yeltsin's successor, Vladimir Putin, accepted the first part of Chubais' analysis, but rejected the second: he strengthened the government but ruthlessly curbed the power of the billionaires. Xi Jinping has also rejected Yeltsin's approach. He's not only embraced Putin's method, but has gone even further. For decades, China's big state-owned firms were required to support internal Communist Party committees so that the party could offer guidance to management and keep watch on its political loyalty. In 2016, Xi stepped that up. The state-owned enterprises should now be "integrating the Party's leadership into all aspects of corporate governance" and "clarifying" its legal status, he said in a speech. Hundreds did. They formally changed their corporate charters to specify a role for the party in running the firm. Four years later, the party made this practice compulsory.

But then Xi took this system to the next level – into private companies. In September 2020, the party's central office first published an "opinion" on "Strengthening the United Front Work of the Private Economy in the New Era". It meant that private businesses were about to be conscripted to serve the needs of the party. Private companies now needed to "help continuously strengthen the Party's leadership over the private economy, bring the majority of private economy practitioners closer to the Party, and gather the majestic forces that work together to build the Chinese Dream". Party members should "educate and guide private economy practitioners to weaponise their minds and guide their practice with Xi Jinping's Thoughts on Socialism with Chinese Characteristics for a New Era". And, among other purposes, this would "build a backbone team of private economy practitioners who are reliable and useful at critical moments".

Some specifics were spelled out a few days later in a speech by Ye Qing, the vice-chairman of the All-China Federation of Industry and Commerce and chair of Beijing Yeshi Enterprise Group Ltd. It turns out that private firms will now be expected to hand control of personnel to their in-house party cell. The party should be given power to hire and fire employees, and "advise" the company's management whom it's chosen. The internal party committee should also have the power to audit the company. And to investigate proposed projects or new business lines. Staff training should be led by the party organisation. Companies should be encouraged to participate in Belt and Road initiatives. And so on.

In other words, it's party takeover of all private firms from the inside. Privately owned companies account for 60 per cent of China's economy and 80 per cent of urban jobs. But the distinction between state-owned firms and private businesses is now blurring to the point of being indistinguishable. "China is trying to mobilise more resources around the national strategy amid the economic slowdown caused by the pandemic and the deterioration of diplomatic and trade relations with the US," said Yue Su of the Economist Intelligence Unit. "The authorities will give priority to companies that assist in realising policy goals when allocating financial and policy resources." The policy on private firms is not law. But if the increased control over the state-owned sector is any guide, ultimately it will be.

Xi's ever-tightening grip on the internet, on speech, on dissent, on public enterprises as well as private companies – on all aspects of China – is an outgrowth of the deep-seated fear at the centre of his rule. Since Xi took power, China has spent more on public security at home than on national defence. On top of China's pre-existing security structures, Xi added an overarching new Central National Security Commission in 2012. He appointed himself chairman. As Willy Wo-Lap Lam reported, the commission would "devote the maximum resources toward maintaining state security in the following areas: politics, territory, military, economy, culture, society, science and technology, information, ecology, resources-related security, and nuclear power". It's hard to imagine that Xi left much off the list.

Xi has described a new concept of "mega-security" which is "of utmost importance in consolidating the Party's ruling status". This is a telling choice of words. After more than sixty years of monopoly power without any evident internal challenge, the Chinese Communist Party still considers itself to be "consolidating" its ruling status under Xi. It is the most successful and durable one-party state in modern history, yet considers its reign tenuous.

"The authorities are very worried about stability despite the apparent achievements in economic development," said the economist and former Peking University professor Xia Yeliang. "There are parallels between the Central National Security Commission and the KGB," he said at the time of the commission's establishment.

"Well may Beijing be afraid," wrote Ross Terrill, the Australian-born Harvard Sinologist. "The Chinese party-state does not represent Chinese society, but takes its mandate from a Marxist-concocted 'history', the contemporary manifestation of 'heaven'", which is the mandate claimed by China's emperors. "This is the irreducible problem of legitimation of a government that has never been elected. It is a state that is oppressive, yet also afraid of its own people."

"WORLD IN GREAT DISORDER – EXCELLENT SITUATION"

Xi Jinping was not born repressive, paranoid and authoritarian. It didn't seem inevitable that he would take a harsh dictatorship and drive it towards even harsher totalitarianism. His personal story and his early political persona didn't suggest that sort of outcome. His father, his family and Xi himself suffered terribly during the Cultural Revolution, the ten-year eruption of mayhem and violence that Mao Zedong unleashed as a way of shocking society, purging his political enemies and regaining control of the party. As a teenager, Xi saw his father beaten relentlessly and imprisoned as a "party traitor", his mother tortured, the family home ransacked; the young Xi himself was humiliated publicly, locked up multiple times and at the age of fifteen sent to live in a cave in the provinces. One of Xi's sisters died at the same age amid the brutality, the exact cause unclear.

When Xi took power as general secretary of the Chinese Communist Party in 2012, there was a widespread expectation that his personal experience of Maoist repression would make him a liberal reformer. Even in his five years as China's vice-president, there was no outward sign that Xi would turn decisively to become the new Mao once he'd ascended to the top: returning China from group leadership to one-man rule;

abolishing term limits for himself; creating a cult of personality ~~cult~~ as no leader since Mao had done; launching wave after wave of crackdowns on lawyers, human rights advocates, religions, the private sector, journalists, feminists; crushing China's Uighur minority with industrial ruthlessness; breaking China's solemn commitment to preserve Hong Kong's liberties post-handover; asserting that domestic laws made in Beijing apply to all people in all countries; sweeping aside international law to occupy and militarise great expanses of ocean also claimed by China's neighbours; launching a new campaign of military intimidation and economic coercion against a score of nations all at once, ranging from immediate neighbours India and Japan to ones further afield such as Australia and Canada.

Indeed, the two Western leaders who spent the most time with Xi before his ascension – Joe Biden, as US vice-president, and Kevin Rudd, as Australian prime minister – didn't foresee how he would act once president. Xi visited both in their home countries and spent some days in intensive private discussions with each as part of his preparation to assume the presidency. And both Biden and Rudd came to the conclusion that he was "someone we can do business with". They were wrong. Like the CCP itself under Deng, Xi was biding his time, hiding his intentions. Until he assumed the leadership. Biden and Rudd have since offered much harsher opinions. In February 2020, Biden called him "a thug". The former Australian leader has said that the party under Xi is "the enemy of liberal democracy".

Xi was formed by trauma. Until the age of nine, he lived a privileged life in the comfortable home of one of China's most powerful and revered men. His father, Xi Zhongxun, was one of the storied leaders of the Communist Revolution. Xi senior was an early activist against the then Nationalist government in the 1920s, a guerrilla warrior in the uprising in the 1930s, a comrade in arms with Mao in the 1940s, and a shrewd commander in the final years of the Long March that brought the Chinese Communist Party to power in 1949. He saved Mao's life and helped deliver victory.

Mao rewarded Xi senior with key posts in the People's Republic, culminating in his appointment as secretary-general of the State Council, China's cabinet, and as vice-premier of the National People's Congress. He was also given living quarters in the leadership compound of Zhongnanhai, the former imperial garden, with its man-made lakes and pavilions and the Library of Chrysanthemum Fragrance that Mao turned into his personal abode.

This pedigree as son of one of the revolutionary leaders makes the junior Xi a "princeling" in the unofficial parlance, one of a few hundred such aristocrats of the revolution who might have been able to look forward to a life of comfort and ease, wealth and power. But for politics.

The Xi family's pampered existence came to a shattering end when Mao turned against Xi Zhongxun. The downfall began in 1962, four years before the Cultural Revolution began, when he supported the publication of a biography of a former friend and party martyr. His enemies claimed this was a covert act of subversion – the book, by praising another party martyr, could be read as an implicit criticism of Mao. Xi senior also was accused of sympathy for a former comrade in arms who'd been purged for daring to criticise the so-called Great Leap Forward and its ensuing famine, perhaps the deadliest event in history besides World War II.

In essence, Xi senior was on the losing side of factional intrigue. Suspicion descended. Mao never needed much of an excuse to feed his fears. Like many dictators, Mao was paranoid and ever seeking out traitors, real or imagined. Xi senior was banished to the provinces to work in a tractor factory. His son, Jinping, was set to a prestigious Beijing boarding school.

But when Mao launched the Cultural Revolution and chaos descended, the young Xi could not be protected any longer. Mobs of youthful Red Guards carried out Mao's instruction to purge China of class enemies and counter-revolutionaries by violently attacking anyone they deemed suspicious. Mao's political shock troops satisfied his paranoid craving to uncover any lurking plotters or potential enemies. Chaos, Mao decided, was his friend. It was amok authoritarianism. One of the Red Guards' slogans: "World in great disorder – excellent situation". As many as 1.5 million people died.

As a fallen official, Xi senior was designated part of a "black gang" with no way of sheltering his family as the fanatical Red Guards wreaked mayhem. His wife, Xi Jinping's mother, took all her children (including Jinping) to hide in the Central Party School, a Communist Party training academy for senior cadres. But there was nowhere safe.

Xi Jinping, aged thirteen, was paraded on stage at mass rallies, where crowds led by Red Guards demonstrated their Maoist fervour by denouncing him as a class enemy, a traitor, a rightist, a counter-revolutionary and all the rest, as he wore a conical hat, like a dunce's cap, a badge of shame. At the front of the chanting crowd was his mother. She denounced her son, along with the Red Guards, over and over with the rest of the mob.

The adult Xi Jinping once spoke of an encounter during the Cultural Revolution where some radicals detained him, still a teenager. "They asked me how bad I thought my crimes were. I said that they should make a guess, was it enough to deserve being shot? They said it would be enough to be shot 100 times over. I thought, what was the difference between being shot once and 100 times?" Yet it made an impression. "Afterwards, I recited the thoughts of Chairman Mao every day, late into the night." He was sent into the countryside and spent six years as a farm labourer.

Locals who helped the young Xi said he had difficulty adjusting. He first grasped that he was in a different world when he found a piece of stale bread in the bag he'd brought with him from Beijing. He fed it to a village dog. The locals looked on in puzzlement. Not because they wondered at his wastefulness, but because they had no idea what he was holding. "'What's that?' they asked me," Xi recalled decades later. They'd never seen bread, much less eaten any.

The cave he lived in, which he shared with five others, was infested with bugs. He was quickly covered in rashes in reaction to flea bites. He and the others commonly went months without seeing meat. When offered some, he would wolf it down raw, he has since recounted. The other workers initially rated him a feeble six out of ten for his physical ability, "not even as high as the women", he would later confess. "I was very lonely. I thought a lot about whether to live or die."

Xi was locked up "three or four times" when he was fifteen because of his father's crimes, according to *The Washington Post*. He had to attend daily "struggle sessions", where he was often forced to read out denunciations of his father. "Even if you don't understand, you are forced to understand," he later said. "It makes you mature earlier."

Within months he ran away to Beijing. This was common in Mao's China, when millions of privileged youth from the cities were sent "down into the countryside" to be "rustified" and discover the virtues of peasant life and hard work. The fugitive teenager was quickly caught and sent to dig ditches in a work camp as punishment.

He grew to accept his fate. The shy, soft-handed son of comfort developed. Within a year of arriving in the village of Liangjiahe, in rural Shaanxi province, he could walk ten miles carrying a large sack of wheat. He could carry a pole across his shoulders, balancing a bucket of water or manure on each end. There was no electricity, piped water, farm machinery or tools.

Meanwhile, his father was carrying wooden boards strung around his neck, painted with slogans to denounce his treachery. He was carted around on the back of a truck for ritual defilement by crowds, beaten and thrown into prison for almost the full decade of the Cultural Revolution, from 1966 to 1975.

The threshold moment for the future life of Xi Jinping was when he decided how he would respond to all of this pain. It was while his father was still imprisoned. Would he reject the party, reviling its potential for arbitrary viciousness? Or would he embrace its power as an escape from his suffering?

Xi Jinping decided he would join the Communist Party. First, he applied to join the Communist Youth League. His application was rejected but he kept trying. On the eighth attempt he was accepted, at the age of eighteen, in 1971. Next, he applied to join the party itself. Again, he had to show determination. He was accepted on his tenth application, in 1974. "My fundamental ideas", the contemporary Xi Jinping has said, "my whole life-path was decided there" in rural exile.

He saw his father only once, briefly, during the elder Xi's decade of confinement, and even that was only after a special intervention by Premier Zhou Enlai as a favour to Xi Jinping's mother. Battered and bewildered, the older man didn't recognise his sons at first.

Why did Xi Jinping decide to join an inhumane political party that could license such wanton mass brutality as a political tactic? Why did he choose to embrace a movement that had inflicted such deep trauma on his family and such suffering on himself?

In a word, survival. He seems to have calculated that his world was destined to be a savage struggle to stay alive, and that the best odds rested with the greatest power available: "He chose to survive by becoming 'redder than red'," according to a friend who knew Xi as a teenager, as quoted in a US government research report released by Wikileaks. The same friend said that Xi saw the party as a "system for survival". As a party elder told reporter Katsuji Nakazawa of Japan's *Nikkei* newspaper: "Xi Jinping believes political battles must be won at all costs. His father's life story taught him that lesson, and it has been etched into his mind."

In other words, it seems Xi was motivated by fear and desperation to escape oppression by joining the oppressors. Mao, "who caused his own father so much suffering, and who had such an impact on his own early life, may not be a person Xi harbours fond memories of", wrote the English Sinologist Kerry Brown of King's College, London. But Mao "the propagandist, the master of Chinese symbolic politics, the person in modern

China who could be said to have most truly understood where power was located, how to use it and how to keep it – his was an inheritance worth tapping into."

Xi didn't just join the party and attempt to master its power. He decided to employ Mao's methods to do so. "It does harken back to Mao, this personality cult, the concentration of power by casting aside the collective leadership," historian Warren Sun of Monash University explained. "Now his style is quite dictatorial, demanding loyalty ideologically. He's anti-Western, dismissive of universal values and he also rules by fear, in the form of the anti-corruption campaigns and cracking down on dissent and tightening the control on media, education, culture – all this does harken back to Mao's practice." Like Mao, Xi Jinping rules China "through a mixture of managed crisis and fear", according to Kerry Brown. "This, in essence, is his political program. And it is why Mao is still of immense importance for him."

If Xi Jinping decided that his father's response to factional intrigue was a negative model – something he would avoid at all costs – it seems he also decided that his father's ideology was another. Xi the elder was a leading moderate and political liberal within the party's ideological spectrum. The father was as tolerant as the son is repressive, as progressive as the son is regressive. If China operated a Westminster parliamentary system, Xi the elder would sit on the opposite side of the chamber to his son.

Before his exile, Xi senior wanted to allow China's ethnic minorities – the Tibetans and the Uighurs, for example – greater autonomy. He fought against the champions of repression who wanted to "tame" them through violent crackdown. He was friendly with the Dalai Lama before the Tibetan spiritual leader fled to India in 1959. The Dalai Lama gave him an Omega watch as a gift. The elder Xi treasured it, managed to hide it during his exile and imprisonment, and wore it for decades afterwards.

Xi the father was rehabilitated on Mao's death, and Deng Xiaoping brought him back into the party's upper echelons. In this capacity, Xi senior was a successful advocate of private capital and open trade. He persuaded Deng to open the special economic zones that brought tremendous investment and wealth to Guangdong, Shenzhen, Zhuhai and Shantou. These experiments were the models for China's wider economic opening and take-off, the foundation for China's modern power.

Xi senior tolerated political dissent. He famously rehabilitated young dissidents who had dared criticise the Cultural Revolution, tantamount to an attack on the late, great Mao himself. Xi the elder advocated for some freedom of expression. He even favoured a law to permit various opinions. The party had made errors in the past, he asserted, because free debate was not permitted. "That's exactly why we need a law to protect and accommodate different views, even 'wrong views'," the elder Xi said. Differing opinions should be allowed so long as they did not progress to substantive acts of subversion. He made the point that the special economic zones had been opposed as bourgeois. "There will be no reform, none whatsoever, if we rush to label any different views as anti-party or anti-socialism."

Xi senior even tried to prevent the crackdown on student protests that ended in the Tiananmen Square massacre. He advocated peaceful resolution though negotiation, not bloody resolution by the People's Liberation Army. When Deng moved to sack the liberal general secretary, Hu Yaobang, for being soft on the nationwide protest movement in 1987, Xi the elder went so far as to camp inside the Great Hall of the People for a week, a kind of political strike, to stop him. Xi publicly opposed the looming suppression. Deng prevailed, of course, and Xi senior fell from favour for a second and final time, although this time it was into retirement and not imprisonment.

Strikingly, Xi junior has embraced a diametrically opposite policy on every one of these issues. He has forcefully "tamed" the Uighurs and Tibetans, tightened party control over the private sector, crushed political dissent, and upheld the correctness of the Tiananmen massacre. If winning was all, Xi junior has been determined to be on the winning side.

He visited his father regularly in Xi senior's retirement. The president of the People's Republic has prominently displayed in his office a framed photo of himself, the filial son, pushing his dad's wheelchair, before his father's death in 2002. But in every political sense, he has repudiated his father in a quest to survive the party, master the party and drive the party. And he is driving it hard away from his father's ideological and policy preferences in every instance. Xi the younger is taking China on a fully reactionary course, inhabiting a political persona more recognisable as that of the son of Mao than the son of Xi Zhongxun.

The president of China has turned his years of hardship in rural exile into a narrative of the joyous discovery of peasant life and working-class solidarity: "After I got used to the local life, especially after I lost myself in the local people, I began to feel a happy fulfilment. We mustn't stand high above the masses or consider the masses as our fish and meat. The hard life of the grassroots can cultivate one's will. With that kind of experience, regardless of the difficulties I encounter in the future, I am fully charged with courage to take on any challenge." He has revived Mao's insistence that the party hew not to urban elitist thinking but to the "mass line", or what the masses are interpreted to think.

He has restored Mao to the centre of China's daily political propaganda diet. He has said that any repudiation of Mao, even his atrocities, would undercut the very existence of China's system of "socialism with Chinese characteristics". And he has adopted much of Mao's political style, including Mao's use of confusion and fear as a tactic to build power: "He's the first leader really to be born and grow up in the Mao era," explains Geremie Barmé. Xi was born in 1953. "The way he responds to threats and problems is according to the high socialism of the 1950s and '60s.

"Xi's formative years in the 1960s and '70s were an era of shrill propaganda, complaints against the West and a warlike atmosphere. He uses the word 'struggle' a lot, sometimes fifty or sixty times in a speech. He grew up with constant campaigns. Every six months to a year, there was a new campaign. He grew up with these on-edge, off-kilter social campaigns of disturbatory politics with constant tension, uncertainty and turmoil.

"In the early 1950s there was thought reform and landlords were killed, three million people killed, in 1956–57 there was the anti-rightist campaign, in 1958–62 you had the Great Leap Forward and maybe 30 million to 40 million people died, in 1962–63 there was moderate reform but that didn't last long and next you had the Cultural Revolution."

The US from 2016 to 2020 offers a clue to the atmosphere of Mao's reign, according to Barmé. "You now understand China better because you've had endless Donald Trump destabilisation by Twitter – Mao was constantly changing direction, issuing new directions. That's what China feels like now."

The depth of disturbance in Chinese society and economy today is not comparable with that of the Mao era. China is a substantive economy, no longer bare-bones and impoverished; its social systems are more stable. Xi has not sought to foment street violence or mob rule. On the contrary, the party has put a premium on stability post-Mao. And whereas Mao's political campaigns often ended in mass death, Xi's usually end in mass incarcerations, demotions and dismissals.

But Barmé's point is that Xi has created a much more unsettled political atmosphere than the one he inherited. It is more centred on one man than on a collective leadership, more prone to sudden changes of direction, more hysterically anti-West and nationalistic. Xi's anti-corruption campaigns, which are political purges with corruption as their putative target, are nonstop. By January 2020, more than three million party members had been caught up in investigations.

When I interviewed Barmé in mid-2020, Xi's regime was announcing the "rectification campaign" aimed at purging the domestic security apparatus, including the police, prosecution, courts, judges and the agents of the Ministry of State Security. The secretary-general of the political and legal commission, Chen Yixin, said that the campaign would "drive the blade in" and "thoroughly remove tumours". He said it was modelled on the "Yan'an rectification campaign" that Mao launched inside the party from 1942 to 1945 to cement his personal power while the party was still a guerrilla force based in mountainous Yan'an. Mao's supporters killed at least 10,000 people in the process. It's no coincidence that this new rectification campaign is set to run all the way into 2022. That's when the party holds its once-in-five-years congress. Among other agenda items, Xi will be expecting it to agree to his third five-year term as leader. He may have removed the limit on the number of terms a president can serve, but he still needs to serve them one at a time, and he still needs formal approval for each.

Xi is deliberately unsettling the system. Again like Mao, he is fomenting managed crises and fear to build power. Because he has seen the consequences of powerlessness in the Chinese Communist Party. Power is all. Survival itself is at stake – not only political survival, but the literal survival of himself, his family and his allies in a ruthless system. And he is determined to survive. As the Cultural Revolution slogan said: "World in great disorder – excellent situation."

WHAT DOES XI WANT?

What does China's supreme leader want? His primary objectives are survival for himself, his family and his allies, and to maintain his personal authority and the Chinese Communist Party's iron grip on power. All else exists to serve these core ambitions. All else is an extension of the overwhelming imperative of power. From that flows what else Xi wants – including his "China Dream" of the great rejuvenation of the Chinese nation. And his primary objectives also determine what he does not want. Only knowing that can we comprehend where Australia fits into his plan.

He has made cut-glass-clear what he does not want. In a secret directive that became famous as Document No. 9 after it was exposed by a Chinese journalist, Xi laid down what have become known as the "seven taboos" or "seven unmentionables" for today's China. It was written in the first six months of Xi's rule and issued by the General Office of the Central Committee of the Communist Party of China, which Xi, of course, leads. It demanded "intense struggle" against seven "false trends".

The first taboo is "Western constitutional democracy". It is denounced as a vessel for "capitalist class concepts". First among them is the separation of powers. This is the doctrine that puts checks on power, so that one branch of government can check another. Its purpose is to prevent the rise of a tyrant, to protect the rights of citizens. A practical example is that, in a liberal democracy, a citizen can challenge a government decision in court. But Xi's Document No. 9 encyclical specifically denounces "independent judiciaries". So too multi-party systems, general elections and "nationalised armies". What does this peculiar term mean? In normal countries, the army serves the state, regardless of which party happens to be in power. But in China it is fully owned and controlled by the party. As Mao said: "The principle is that the party commands the gun, and the gun must never be allowed to command the party." The army and the courts are not national institutions. They are partisan. They serve the party, and only the party.

Second, the concept of "universal values" is forbidden. The first of the universal values promulgated by the United Nations is a fundamental one: "All human beings are born free and equal in dignity and rights." Xi rejects this. He regards it as a challenge to the rule of the Chinese Communist Party. The party recognises collective rights – to development and security, for instance – while rejecting individual rights, such as the right to vote, to speak freely and to worship.

Third, civil society is taboo. That is, any community-based body, or non-government organisation – like a charity, environmental group, trade union, professional group or church – is forbidden. Document No. 9 says that "advocates of civil society want to squeeze the party out of leadership of the masses at the local level" and constitute a "serious form of political opposition". So organisations like Falun Gong, or Falun Dafa, are brutally repressed. Religions, always strictly controlled in modern China, increasingly are persecuted under Xi. The repression of China's Uighur Muslims, with a million or more detained indefinitely in mass camps from 2017 and denied the right to practise their beliefs, is a dramatic escalation.

Fourth, neoliberalism is a no-no. The doctrine of unrestrained market forces is the US-led Western world's attempt to "change China's basic economic system . . . under the guise of globalisation" and "weaken the government's control of the national economy". It should be noted that, since Document No. 9 was first drawn up, the United States under Donald Trump and then Joe Biden has ceased to advocate neoliberalism, which now stands friendless in the world.

Fifth, the West's idea of journalism is unmentionable. Why? Because it is "challenging China's principle that the media and publishing system should be subject to party discipline". Freedom of the press is a "pretext" for challenging the Marxist definition of news. The media are not "society's public instrument" but should be "infused with the spirit of the party".

Sixth, historical nihilism is banned. The document says that historical nihilism is "trying to undermine the history of the Chinese Communist Party and of New China". "In the guise of 'reassessing history'", says the encyclical, historical nihilism is "tantamount to denying the legitimacy of the Chinese Communist Party's long-term political dominance".

Finally, questioning reform and opening and the socialist nature of "socialism with Chinese characteristics" is forbidden. "The discussion of reform has been unceasing," says the paper. "Some views clearly deviate from socialism with Chinese characteristics." Decoded, this simply means that further major economic reform is off-limits and should not be discussed.

So Document No. 9 – or, more formally, the Communiqué on the Current State of the Ideological Sphere – has three striking characteristics. First, its unwavering theme is the imperative of party control above all else. Second, its psychological stance is defensive, even paranoid. Each of the central principles of Western civilisation is dismissed as "pretext" or a "guise" or a "political tool" for undermining the Chinese Communist Party. According to the document, the values and institutions of Western civilisation did not arise from Europe's historical experience over millennia – well before the West knew China existed – to be adopted and adapted by Europe's civilisational offspring to suit their own circumstances over the centuries. The communique casts Western civilisation as a conspiracy against China.

Third, it is a directive to all party cadres to snuff out the fundamental values and liberties at the heart of liberal democracy. It is hostile to the essence and the governing principles of societies such as Australia's. It defines the party's ideological sphere as directly opposed to the West's.

How do we know that Document No. 9 is authentic? One indication is that, while it was not publicised, it was posted on some Chinese government websites. Another is that the journalist who first published the document outside officialdom, Gao Yu, was arrested for publishing "state secrets", forced to make a televised "confession", and jailed, initially for seven years, later amended to house arrest with a reduced sentence of five years due to her poor health. Gao is seventy-five years old. Her treatment suggests that the party is not proud of its declaration of the seven perils. China puts great effort into projecting a positive image to the world. Its public pronouncements gush about peace, humanity and the boast that "China always attaches great importance to human rights", as it claimed in its declaration to the UN General Assembly in September 2019. A third indication is that its precepts have since been disseminated in compulsory study sessions, some of which have been documented on the internet. Corporate managers, university administrators and other officials have been instructed in the seven taboos. Finally, Document No. 9 has been enforced, the ultimate validation of its authenticity.

Democratic values and liberties are taboo, a threat to the survival of Xi and the party. These are exactly what Xi does not want. Then there is what he does want.

13

MAKE THE PAST
SERVE THE PRESENT

When President Xi Jinping visited Germany in 2014, his host, Chancellor Angela Merkel, gave him a gift, as protocol requires. She chose an old map, printed in Germany in 1750. Official photos show an animated Merkel enthusiastically presenting Xi with the framed map, but Xi standing back, stony-faced. He was unimpressed.

Why? As the BBC journalist Bill Hayton explains in his book *The Invention of China*, the map "included only the former provinces of the Ming Dynasty. It therefore excluded most of the other territories acquired by the Qing: Manchuria, Mongolia, Tibet and Xinjiang. To make things worse, Taiwan was outlined in a separate colour."

China's party-controlled media had a dilemma. They needed to report the official ceremony, but were not allowed to admit inconvenient historical fact. "They resolved it in the traditional manner of a one-party state: they faked the news," writes Hayton. The Chinese media reported the occasion but published the photo of the event with a different map. The version approved for Chinese audiences replaced Merkel's map with a much later one, from 1844, showing a much wider Chinese territory. Even an eminent Chinese professor fell for it. He went on to write about the deeper significance of Germany giving China such an expansive map of China's territory, even including some Russian land as a bonus for Beijing.

Funny, yes? But serious, too. Hayton explains that the tale "demonstrates the anxiety and paranoia that lurk just beneath the surface of contemporary China's politics. If Xi had given Merkel a map of eighteenth-century Prussia that excluded most of western Germany, the object would have been treated as an interesting curio."

> The People's Republic's sense of self, on the other hand, is far too fragile to admit that the shape of the country may have been different 300 years ago. No debate over the state's "core interest" of territorial integrity is permitted and the result is absurd denials of any historical evidence that underpins a different story of the past. The only acceptable version of history is the invented version that suits the needs of the Communist Party's current leadership.

Mao Zedong said it himself: "Make the past serve the present." Contemporary China does this relentlessly. Sometimes it's to erase history. The 1989 Tiananmen Square massacre, for example. It did not occur, according to the official version. This erasure has been so effective that very few of the younger generation growing up in mainland China today have heard of it. Some report their cognitive dissonance when they travel overseas to study and hear of it for the first time. Yet when China's defence minister, Lieutenant General Wei Fenghe, was asked about the massacre at a major international conference in Singapore in June 2019, he defended it unreservedly. The protests were "political turmoil that the central government needed to quell, which was the correct policy," said Wei. "Due to this, China has enjoyed stability." The party is pleased enough to endorse the massacre, yet guilty enough to censor it.

Sometimes it's to rewrite history. The COVID-19 pandemic, for instance, did not originate in Wuhan but was brought into China by US troops, according to the version that a spokesperson for China's foreign affairs ministry, Zhao Lijian, promoted by linking to a conspiracy-theory website. Party-owned media also propagated this version. When President Xi presented medals to China's pandemic heroes in September 2020, in a nationally televised ceremony, he spoke for more than an hour but did not mention the original hero, Dr Li Wenliang. Li was one of the handful of Wuhan doctors who sent out the first alerts, but he was shut down by the police and later died of the virus. Nor did Xi mention the weeks between Li's warnings of the outbreak and the government's acknowledgement of it. More than three weeks later. Instead, Xi said: "The CCP's strong leadership is the most reliable backbone when a storm hits. The pandemic once again proves the superiority of the socialist system with Chinese characteristics."

And sometimes it's to invent history. Bill Hayton catalogues quite a few such creations in *The Invention of China*. He describes what he calls the invention of sovereignty, of the Chinese nation, of the Chinese language, of a national territory, and a maritime claim. Much of what's presented as ancient, traditional and immutable in China today is actually recent, imported and defined by the political imperatives of the present.

For instance, the name "China" is not originally Chinese, but a European invention. In fact, the young political entity known as Australia, which only came into being at Federation 120 years ago, has had its official name for longer than the country we know as China has had its. The leading intellectual and politician Liang Qichao lamented in the late nineteenth century that "our greatest shame is that our country has no name".

It was only when the last emperor was overthrown, in the revolution of 1911–12, that the nationalist leader Sun Yat-sen declared the existence of an entity called the Republic of China, which the communists changed to the People's Republic of China. As the name of the country, "China" has stood for only 109 years. "Until the very end of the nineteenth century, rulers in Beijing would not even have recognised the name 'China'," Hayton writes. He describes how early European adventurers were puzzled when they reached a place they thought of as China – or Land of the Chins, probably from the name of the ancient Qin dynasty – only to discover the locals knew no such name. Before 1912, the territory we recognise today as China bore the name of each successive dynasty that ruled it. So, for instance, during the Ming dynasty people called themselves *Da Ming Ren*, or people of the Great Ming. Just as its name changed with each dynasty, so did the shape of its borders and lands. This is an uncomfortable reality for the party today, as it continues to make new claims in the name of historical "rights" to territories also claimed by its neighbours.

There are longstanding local names for China. *Zhonghua*, or central state or central kingdom or middle kingdom, has an ancient history but was not used as the name of the country in a fixed or exclusive way until the nineteenth century. It's now incorporated in the country's official name of *Zhonghua Renmin Gongheguo*, to equate to the People's Republic of China. The other more colloquial common name is *Zhongguo*. Either way, it wasn't called China.

Even the idea that the majority ethnic group in China, the Han, is the Chinese "race" is a relatively new construct. Hayton sets out how the nationalist revolutionaries in the late nineteenth century needed a tool to set the Qing rulers apart from the people. The Qing were Manchu invaders from the north who'd ruled "China" for nearly three centuries. The Confucian consensus of the time was that political legitimacy arose from engaging in the civilised culture, which meant that anyone from anywhere – even barbarians, even the Manchu – could participate in the nation if they adopted its culture. One of the nationalist revolutionaries challenged this cultural definition of the nation by replacing it with a racial one. Zhang Binglin, a classical scholar turned revolutionary, did it by, in Bill Hayton's words, "inventing" the Han race in 1899. This allowed the revolutionaries to delegitimise the Qing rulers.

"Change could only come from the Han, the sons and grandsons of the Yellow Emperor," writes Hayton. He points out that the Chinese Communist Party today uses its United Front Work Department to promote worship of the mythical Yellow Emperor among overseas Chinese communities, "an obvious example of a political strategy intended to change their identity and allegiances". This "traditional" annual ceremony was first conducted in Beijing in 2006. Indeed, there's a Yellow Emperor worship ceremony held every year in Sydney, supported by the United Front, to which Australian dignitaries are invited. Local politicians have attended, including Tony Abbott.

Explaining the invention of China is important because Beijing deploys its history as a powerful political phenomenon.

"The idea of China as this permanent and spiritual force in East Asia is probably the most important part of China's rise," Hayton told me in an interview. "We look at it and say, 'Wow, this great power that's always been there is coming back,' this idea that we're returning to a natural order where China takes the lead and we all bow our heads – the psychology of that is their most powerful tool."

And sometimes the past is conscripted to serve the present by being weaponised. Taiwan's status is one example. Taiwan is a self-governed democracy of 24 million people. Today, Beijing calls its claim to full sovereign ownership of the island a "red line", and commentators have described it as "the reddest of red lines" for mainland China. It "must and will be" reunited with the mainland, Xi has said. Peacefully, if possible, but Beijing always keeps alive the possibility of reunification by force.

For the first time in twenty years, in 2019 the PLA Air Force flew across the unofficial median line between the island and the mainland. It has since been intensifying its sorties into Taiwan's airspace. In the first ten months of 2020, Taiwan's air force scrambled to intercept Beijing's fighters and bombers 2972 times, at a cost of US$886 million to Taiwan's taxpayers, according to Taipei. The US is selling military hardware to Taiwan to help it protect itself, including more F-16 fighter jets.

China's Qing dynasty partially annexed Taiwan in 1684, and then signed it away to Japan in 1895 when it lost the First Sino-Japanese War. After the Nationalists removed the Qing and took power under Sun Yat-sen, they weren't interested in reclaiming Taiwan. And neither was the Chinese Communist Party. While the communists were still an insurgent movement, in 1928 at the Sixth Party Congress they recognised Taiwanese as a separate nationality. This consensus on Taiwan's status only changed in 1942 when China's Nationalist government made its first claim to Taiwan.

Despite the blowhard rhetoric and military intimidation from Xi's regime, its claim to Taiwan is not based on any ancient or continuous entitlement. Even the Communist Party initially didn't want it. Yet now Xi says that the "great rejuvenation of the Chinese nation" cannot be complete without it. He's declared a deadline: 2049.

In reality, it's not a pre-eminent matter of manifest destiny. It's a territorial dispute. There are few things so common in world affairs. There are some 150 current such disputes around the world, including territorial and border conflicts, on land and sea. Only about forty nations – fewer than a quarter of the world's total – are not engaged in some sort of territorial or border clash. What distinguishes countries is not whether they have such disputes, but how they handle them. Whether they respect international law, or whether they force their will onto others.

The party's rigid, shrill and intolerant insistence on a single version of history is not a sign of strength, but a symptom of fragility. Sun Yat-sen famously described China as a sheet of loose sand. He made the case for overthrowing the imperial system and building a new China as an aggressive Japan was inflicting stinging military losses on the country:

> Despite four hundred million people gathered in one China, we are, in fact, but a sheet of loose sand. We are the poorest and weakest state in the world, occupying the lowest position in international affairs; the rest of mankind is the carving knife and the serving dish, while we are the fish and

meat. Our position is now extremely perilous. If we do not earnestly promote nationalism and weld together our four hundred millions into a strong nation, we face a tragedy – the loss of our country and the destruction of our race.

China has transformed since. But the US Sinologists Orville Schell and John Delury wrote in 2013 that "the confidence levels of many Chinese, even after all the successes of their economic miracle, still lag behind their actual achievements in curing their historical sense of inferiority. Indeed, it may yet take another generation or so before confidence levels become better aligned with achievements." They observe that "despite China's enormous progress, a humiliation complex still remains, nationalism is still on the rise, and Chinese still so easily tend to feel victimised".

A country with a national inferiority complex, ruled by a fearful party and led by a paranoid leader, is a volatile place, not at ease with itself. Another example of the party's use of history to serve the political needs of the present is the mobilisation of China's "century of humiliation". Xi has engaged it as the engine of history to power China – and its supreme leader – into the very near future.

14

THE FALL AND RISE OF CHINA

Xi Jinping made his first public outing as the general secretary of the Chinese Communist Party to a monument not to China's glory, but to its humiliation. He took all the members of the Politburo Standing Committee, analogous to his inner cabinet, with him. He had been leader of the party for exactly two weeks. The venue was a very deliberate choice. It was 29 November 2012, and it was the starting point for the national narrative he is leading China through today.

He took the leadership group on a tour of an exhibition at the National Museum of China in Beijing. The exhibition was titled "Road to Renaissance", and was devoted to chronicling China's "century of humiliation". It begins with imperial China's defeat by Britain in the First Opium War in 1839–42, when the British took Hong Kong. It includes its defeat by Britain and France in the Second Opium War, less than twenty years later, when the invaders captured Beijing and burned the emperor's summer palace.

It also encompasses the Eight-Nation Alliance that brought the armed forces of Germany, Japan, Russia, Britain, France, the US, Italy and Austria-Hungary to Beijing in 1900 to crush a spontaneous popular uprising against foreign exploitation, the Boxer Rebellion. They stayed on to loot and pillage. And it includes multiple Japanese affronts, including Tokyo's Twenty-One Demands in 1915 and the Rape of Nanjing by Japanese troops in 1937 involving mass slaughter and systematic rape.

The humiliations continued until, as the exhibition's introductory placard puts it, "under the leadership of the Chinese Communist Party . . . all the ethnic groups joined forces to achieve national independence and liberation".

Xi stopped to speak, respectfully recorded by party-owned media: "In modern times, the Chinese nation was subjected to untold miseries and sacrifices rarely seen in the world's history." The speech became instantly famous for what he said next: his promise of the "China Dream", the hallmark of his presidency. But note that Xi began his promise of China's sweet future by plunging into its bitter past. The people were well primed already. The term "century of humiliation" was first used in 1915, the time of Japan's Twenty-One Demands. It's been a theme ever since, and understandably so.

China is not the only country to dwell on its defeats and losses. Australia has Anzac Day, for instance. US Confederate supporters commemorate their loss in the American Civil War; the state of Virginia had a public holiday to mark Lee–Jackson Day until 2020. South Korea holds a national ceremony on International Memorial Day for Comfort Women, remembering the women recruited into sexual slavery by the Japanese army.

China's situation stands out, nonetheless, for three reasons. First, for the remarkable pervasiveness of its "national humiliation discourse". Second, for its calculated distortions of history. Third, for its mobilisation for a partisan political agenda.

China has marked National Humiliation Day, now known formally as Defence Education Day, with remembrance events and public holidays since 1915. There are textbooks, novels, songs, museums, movies, parks and even an Atlas of Shame, officially known as the *Atlas of the Century of National Humiliation in Modern China*, devoted to the topic. William Callahan, a professor of international studies at the London School of Economics, has dubbed this national humiliation discourse "the master narrative of modern Chinese history".

To understand Chinese national security, he argues, it's necessary to grasp its national insecurity. Callahan explains: "Humiliation is not just about passive 'victimisation'. National humiliation discourse actually involves a very active notion of history and redemption: the ancient *Book of Rites* (*Liji*) tells us that 'A thing's humiliation can stimulate it; a country's humiliation can to rejuvenate it.'" National humiliation was the context for the founding moment of the People's Republic of China, when Mao Zedong announced that the Chinese people had finally stood up: "Ours will no longer be a nation subject to insult and humiliation. We have stood up." "In other words," concludes Callahan, "the narrative of national salvation depends upon national humiliation; the narrative of national security depends upon national insecurity".

The official narrative of China's humiliation is selective and distorted. The list of disasters, invasions and insults excludes China's most devastating upheaval of the nineteenth century: the Taiping Rebellion. This was one of the bloodiest civil wars in history. The total death toll is estimated at between 10 million and 70 million, comparable to World War I and dwarfing the American Civil War.

The Taiping Rebellion was a protracted armed effort from 1850 to 1864 to defeat the Qing dynasty by an uprising with religious, ethnic, class and ideological elements. Its leader was Hong Xiuquan, who titled himself the Taiping Heavenly King. Wherever he took territory, he imposed the rule of the Taiping Heavenly Kingdom. His army seized the city of Nanjing and he made it his capital. It wasn't just a struggle for the throne, though. Hong proposed a thoroughgoing upending of the social and economic order of China.

The rebellion was a religious movement because Hong declared himself the younger brother of Jesus and propagated his own version of Christianity and his own moral code. It was ethnic because he regarded the Manchu people, including the ruling Qing court, as monsters; his army killed all the civilian Manchus, as well as the armed ones, that they could find. It was a class war because the Taiping army was populated almost exclusively from the lower social classes, while the aristocracy sided with the emperor. And it was ideological because the Taiping Heavenly Kingdom had communist landowning policies and commonly killed wealthy landlords. The Qing, much weakened, prevailed. But at a terrible cost.

The Taiping Rebellion, in other words, was a sweeping and convulsive episode of shocking devastation. And it contributed to keeping China weak, poor and directionless, just as it was coming under severe pressure from the British and other colonial powers. In contrast, Japan responded to the Western imperialists with a remarkable modernisation, the Meiji Restoration, which gave Japan the power to preserve its sovereignty. China, however, was stunted as a result of the Taiping revolution.

But because it was a self-imposed humiliation, it's carefully excised from the official historiography of the "century of humiliation". The authorised causes of China's "untold misery" are foreign imperialism encouraged by domestic corruption. Civil war is self-harm and therefore not admissible.

While the "century of humiliation" has been a long-running theme, the party has emphasised it more in recent decades as it has eased its communist ideological fervour. The weakening of one unifying ideology requires the strengthening of another: nationalism. And national humiliation is an emotion that stokes nationalism. Xi Jinping is relying on nationalism to supply the motive force of history. His history, inseparable from China's – the "China Dream". In Xi's short speech at the National Museum, he defined the China Dream as the "great revival of the Chinese people". And he repeated the phrase. Seven times. As the *Book of Rites* says, "a country's humiliation can rejuvenate it".

"To understand how Chinese nationalism works," writes Callahan, "we need to reverse Paul Kennedy's famous thesis about 'the rise and fall of the great powers', to examine the 'fall and rise' of China", from humiliation to glory. "The discourse of national humiliation shows how China's insecurities are not just material, a matter of catching up to the West militarily and economically, but symbolic. Indeed, one of the goals of Chinese foreign policy has been to 'cleanse National Humiliation'."

Xi's employment of the "China Dream" is thoroughly unoriginal. Yet, for that very reason, it is electrifying. It rouses nerves deep inside the neural trunk routes of Chinese consciousness. Or, in another physiological metaphor, Orville Schell and John Delury invoke genetics: "Like a set of genes that is firmly implanted on a genome and is then faithfully transmitted from generation to generation thereafter, DNA coding for this dream to see China restored to greatness and a position of respect has been re-expressing itself over and over since Confucian scholars . . . first began fretting over the Qing Dynasty's early nineteenth century decline." As China suffered each new humiliation, "the scramble to find the keys to China's lost 'wealth and power' gained an almost unbearable urgency". Mao found the key to power, Deng found the key to wealth, and Xi promises to unite wealth and power in a heady, culminating key-turning that will unlock historic greatness. A nationalistic China Dream indeed.

*

What are the components of the cleansing "China Dream" that Xi has set out? Xi is specific about what his dream includes. Such as being a "moderately well-off society" by 2021. He doesn't apply an exact definition. The Chinese term is *xiaokang*, literally "small comforts". But if you apply the informal rule of thumb that defines a middle-income country as having US$10,000 in income per head annually, China already achieved this in 2019, putting it in the same income league as Malaysia and Russia. It's a serious accomplishment because it means that income per head had multiplied tenfold in just two decades. It won't be celebrated fully until 2021, however, because of the symbolism of the date – the centenary of the founding of the Chinese Communist Party.

Another achievement: in November 2020, authorities claimed victory over absolute poverty. Which they defined as achieving average incomes in all China's counties above the official income stipulation of about US$1.60 per person per day. Officials removed extreme poverty in the final nine counties, all in Guizhou Province, of China's total 1355 counties. Poverty was now zero per cent, and the satisfaction rate among locals was over

99 per cent, according to local officials – remarkably complete outcomes and, remarkably, just in time to meet the national deadline of 2020. China's authorities are known for their uncanny ability to meet their centrally imposed quotas and targets. No less a figure than China's premier, Li Keqiang, observed years ago that China's GDP statistics were "man-made". Manufactured, in other words. Regardless of such sleights of hand, the transformation of income and living standards in China has been palpable and undeniable.

Xi dreams of a fully rich China by 2049, the centenary of Mao Zedong's founding of modern China. The country will be "closer to centre-stage" of world affairs, in Xi's vision. This refers to China's ancient name for itself – the two characters that are sometimes translated as "Middle Kingdom" can also be rendered "Central Kingdom".

A fond fantasy? Not at all. China's economy was the biggest in the world for at least half a millennium, until as recently as 1820. It is not inevitable that it will vault over the United States to recover that title, but it is likely, and likely by about the time today's newborns are ready to start high school. It's a distinction without much of a difference. China will have about the same economic heft as the US, maybe a bit more, maybe a bit less. But whichever it is, it is already well advanced towards superpower status, its economy as big as the European Union and Japan put together. Economic bulk is the base feedstock of national power. Pre-pandemic, China's economy was adding so much new activity that it was "growing" another Australia every two years.

Imperial China, a world leader in technology, also pioneered the capable, modern nation-state. It took Europe almost two millennia to catch up. China is again thrusting to the forefront of technological know-how and again pioneering a more effective nation-state. For instance, in less than half the time Australia has spent debating inconclusively whether to build a single fast rail line to connect its major cities, China built a network of over 20,000 kilometres of fast rail.

Its return to imperial-era greatness has many modern touches. To keep the kids connected to the spirit of nation-building, China's gaming behemoth, Tencent, launched a new game. Patriotically titled *Homeland Dream*, it went live just in time for the celebrations of the seventieth anniversary of the founding of the People's Republic in 2019. As described by *The Financial Times*, the game "allows players to build virtual cities filled with Communist slogans and landmarks". It went instantly to the top of the list of most popular games. "For China's biggest video game company, a patriotic business strategy appears to be paying off." Unpatriotic ones are less likely to succeed. Every new game needs the approval of the state. And for lovers of liberty who fret over China's tech-enhanced surveillance and control – the US-based independent watchdog organisation Freedom House has dubbed the game "techno-dystopian expansionism" – China has become hyper-capable in a troubling way.

The spirit of the once-mighty empire that built the Great Wall and the Great Canal is taking concrete form once more with Beijing's imperial-scale ambition for its vast intercontinental Belt and Road scheme for connecting the world through Chinese money and power. The Central Kingdom has every prospect of being much "closer to centre-stage", just as Xi wishes.

And by the same date of 2049, he sees Beijing "recovering" the self-governing democratic island of Taiwan for the party, a prospect that troubles most of Taiwan's 24 million people. It's no coincidence that Hong Kong's special autonomy under the

"One Country, Two Systems" formula is due to expire on the same date. But Xi was unable to wait and asserted full control over Hong Kong's internal affairs in 2020. This provoked a storm of outrage, erased Hong Kong's remaining liberties and broke China's solemn pledge to the world. Xi calculated that the world would do nothing to stop him. He was right.

That's what Xi wants. A country as rich as the richest on earth, with all its territories united under the centralised rule of the CCP, in a magnificent restoration of China's sovereign splendour before it was torn apart by British, European and Japanese forces after 1842. Xi's dream is to end the ignominy of the "century of humiliation" in glory.

Xi intends to be nothing less than a threshold figure in world history. The Soviet Communist Party collapsed because "in the end nobody was a real man", Xi said in his first months in power. Implicitly, he was asserting that only a "real man" could hold China together. He was that man. The iron fist had announced itself. There would be no ideological wavering or political timidity from China's future "president for life".

The leader went further. Not content to assert unassailable power at home, he overturned the famous maxim that had guided China's overarching strategy for almost a quarter-century. Paramount leader Deng Xiaoping in 1990 urged restraint on a China that was beginning to pulse with the possibilities of its own rising power. Deng urged his compatriots to "hide your brightness, bide your time". Xi declared that China was now "striving to achieve." This is a crystallising statement of China's transformation. It was a status quo power. It's now an ambitious one. Barack Obama accused China under Xi of using "sheer size and muscle to force countries into subordinate positions".

Like the narrative of national humiliation, the "China Dream" is monolithic and centrally planned. China has a new master narrative, courtesy of a new master with a new narrative. And Xi Jinping has extended his dream beyond China to embrace the world. China seeks to build "a community of common destiny" for all people of the world. And his main mechanism for achieving it, the Belt and Road initiative, is well under way.

15

DRAGON IN YOUR LIVING ROOM

For a country that has defined itself as fiercely anti-imperialist, the People's Republic of China today is employing tactics that the imperialist powers of two centuries ago would have recognised instantly. Like Japan after its Meiji Restoration, China is mimicking some of the behaviours of the colonial powers but dreadfully, unfashionably late. It started with Mao's forced integration of the peoples on its periphery, continuing a project of Imperial China's Qing dynasty. "Shouting anti-imperialism, China hid its own imperial acts," Harvard Sinologist Ross Terrill said. "China managed to have its steady integration of Manchuria, Tibet, Xinjiang, and Inner Mongolia judged unobjectionable by much of the international community." Xi has extended the project, notably with his mass incarceration and re-education of the Uighur Muslims and other Turkic minority peoples in Xinjiang. Mao would have envied the Xi regime's use of high-tech digital surveillance to bring social control to totalitarian fulfilment.

Xi has now flung wide the imperial project. His signature formulation of his plan for the world is to create a "community of common destiny", also translated as a "community of shared destiny". It's a warm and inclusive rhetorical construct. When Xi propounded the idea of a "community of common destiny" in a speech, it was translated into English and posted on the homepage of the Chinese embassy's website in Canberra. Asked which countries were envisaged as being part of this community, an embassy official replied: "All countries."

"At its heart, the concept of a 'community of shared destiny' is essentially about ensuring peace and stability in China's external strategic environment through the development of good relations with neighbouring countries," explained the ANU's Richard Rigby and Brendan Taylor in 2014. "Ironically, it is difficult to recall a period, in recent history at least, where there has been such a substantial gap between Beijing's public rhetoric and what it has been doing in practice, with the result that it has alienated, alarmed and infuriated many of its neighbours." Beijing's relentless creation of a "community of shared destiny" in its near neighbourhood is a forerunner, a case study and an object lesson in the reality of what Xi's regime has in mind. It is where a nation has its greatest power, where it is least constrained, that its truest self is on display.

Consider the "shared destiny" that Xi's regime is shaping along its maritime frontier. It has been negotiating a set of basic rules for countries' conduct in the South China Sea with its ten neighbours in ASEAN, the Association of Southeast Asian Nations, since 2006. While all sides have agreed that they will commit to a code of conduct, for a decade and a half Beijing has shown no serious intent to finalise one. China's foreign affairs minister, Wang Yi, has said, "China believes that there should be no rush." He wasn't kidding. That was in 2013.

"Fundamentally, the situation is simple: ASEAN countries want to curb China's behaviour, but China does not want its actions to be constrained," wrote Viet Hoang, an expert on the law of the sea and a lecturer at the Ho Chi Minh City University of Law, in *The Diplomat*. "ASEAN has little or nothing that it can do to force China to agree on an effective and substantial [code of conduct], so the negotiations have continued to deadlock on key issues." In 2002 the eleven nations agreed to a holding position in the interim, pledging to exercise self-restraint, to settle disagreements through dialogue, and to observe the UN Convention on the Law of the Sea (UNCLOS).

Of course, in the intervening two decades China has trampled on this agreement spectacularly, shocking the world with its assertions of raw power over its neighbours. It has ignored their competing claims, brushed aside a ruling from The Hague that it has "no legal basis" for its claims on areas of the South China Sea also claimed by the Philippines, and constructed substantial military bases on minor reefs and outcrops also claimed by four other nations. The biggest military bases it has built in the sea are 1000 kilometres from its own coastline. The Filipino foreign secretary, Teodoro Locsin, has likened China's behaviour to having "a dragon in your living room".

The ASEAN states are not blameless. Some have built their own facilities on contested maritime features over the decades. But the scale of China's creations dwarfs all others combined, and their military capabilities set them apart.

The stakes are high. The South China Sea is the world's most valuable commercial artery. On a strategic level, it's about control of the world's busiest shipping route. It is an international sea route and a lifeline for most of the region's countries. About half of the world's commercial shipping passes through the area, including 60 per cent of Australia's exports. China is laying claim to 90 per cent of the South China Sea, marked out by a so-called "nine-dash line" drawn on the map, which has been compared to a vast tongue lolling south into the sea and slurping up against the sides of Vietnam, the Philippines, Malaysia and Brunei. On a resources level, it's about some of the world's wealthiest fisheries and most prospective seabed oil and gas deposits. On a military level, it's about China's avid desire to push the US navy away from its coast and establish itself as the regional hegemon. And on the level of global governance, it's about whether a country can break the rules and get its way through using force. So far, China is winning on every level.

Xi ignored Barack Obama's urging to stop using sheer muscle to claim the maritime territories. His regime built artificial islands atop the reefs and rocks and then, when they were built, at a 2015 press conference Xi promised Obama that China had no plan to militarise the islands: "Relevant construction activities that China is undertaking in the Nansha [Spratly] islands do not target or impact any country and China does not intend to pursue militarisation." Xi proceeded to break this promise. The Spratlys now have concrete runways kilometres long; hardened bunkers for fighter and heavy bomber aircraft able to operate in a radius of more than 5000 kilometres; complexes of radar, anti-ship and anti-aircraft cruise missile systems; barracks buildings and other facilities. Beijing has denied that this comprises militarisation, calling these "defensive" measures against an unnamed enemy. Long-range, nuclear-capable Chinese bombers have conducted demonstration touchdowns on its newly built runways in the Paracel Islands, also a contested area of the South China Sea now militarised by China.

Three years after Xi's "no militarisation" remarks with Obama, the head of the US Indo-Pacific Command, Admiral Philip Davidson, told the US Congress that "China is now capable of controlling the South China Sea in all scenarios short of war with the United States". Obama's senior Asia adviser at the time of the Xi encounter, Danny Russel, when asked whether in retrospect the US might have handled China's ambitions better, told me: "There was no clear path to blocking Chinese expansion in the Spratlys and Paracels short of the use of force. And China was prepared to overtly lie about its plans for the South China Sea."

The US, like Australia, takes no position on any of the territorial claims. But it does urge all the claimants to avoid destabilisation and to observe international law, specifically UNCLOS. The US is in a feeble moral position here, having not ratified the convention itself – the US Senate has rebuffed it repeatedly. But successive US administrations have committed to abide by it, nonetheless. Australia is a signatory to the convention. Its deepest interest is mere stability, allowing the international waters to remain exactly that, a shared resource for the world and not claimed as one country's territory.

China's strategy for conquest of the South China Sea has been described as "salami slicing", a series of small increments that together achieve an eventual transformation. China's strategists prefer to call it a "cabbage leaf" strategy. Meaning? China puts down one "cabbage leaf", or layer of territorial assertion, over another. First are its fishing boats, then the official vessels of its fisheries administration, then its maritime surveillance vessels, then its coastguard and then, finally, its navy. Layer on layer – the least objectionable first, the most intimidating last – is its way of patiently building a thickening circle of claim by force.

It uses a "swarming" technique, deploying scores and even hundreds of Chinese vessels of various types to block, intimidate and surround those from other countries. A pair of Filipino fishing boats was swarmed by ninety Chinese civilian, coastguard and naval vessels, for instance. Another swarm of 200 Chinese ships, comprising fishing boats and coastguard ships, blocked Filipino fishing access to a tiny island claimed by both. In 2016 Japan protested against a swarm of 230 Chinese fishing and government ships crowding the contested Senkaku Islands, called Diaoyu by China, in the East China Sea.

One curious fact about China's many swarming fishing vessels is that they appear to do little fishing. In fact, they try not to "appear" at all, in any formal, traceable sense. Most are more than the 450 tonnes above which vessels are required to carry automatic identification system transceivers. These broadcast crucial safety data, such as position and heading and so on. "But fewer than 5 percent of them actually broadcast AIS signals at any given time," observes Gregory Poling, the director of the Asia Maritime Transparency Initiative at the Center for Strategic and International Studies. "This suggests a fleet intent on hiding its numbers and actions. These large, modern vessels represent a stunning level of sunk capital costs but do not engage in much commercial activity. Frequent satellite imagery shows that the vessels spend nearly all of their time anchored, often in large clusters."

This is an example of "grey zone" warfare. Below the threshold of traditional armed conflict, yet an intimidation exercise for a state-directed strategic purpose. Notionally a civilian economic activity, but one escorted by government vessels. Unarmed, but with the navy in support, commonly out of view beyond the horizon. It is designed to win without fighting.

In a sign of things to come, China also has tested a swarm of fifty-six small robotic or drone ships in the South China Sea. The test models were unarmed, but the same manufacturer has produced armed versions.

The major proponent of the "cabbage strategy" is Major General Zhang Zhaozhong, a military theorist with the PLA National Defence University. In 2013 he explained how ordinary fishing boats were being used as the advance force in an integrated national intrusion onto a reef also claimed by the Philippines. The Scarborough Shoal is a small ring of reefs 230 kilometres from the Philippines' closest uncontested land and 580 kilometres from China's. In a famous standoff that lasted over a year, China blocked Filipino fishing boats from access while protecting Chinese fishing boats. As Major General Zhang told *China Daily Mail*:

We have begun to take measures to seal and control the areas around the Huangyan Island [Scarborough Shoal], seal and control continuously up till now. In the over one-year period since then, there have been [Chinese] fishermen in the inside. Our fishermen are often there because there is lot of fish there. Fishermen go there in large ships and then sail small boats in the lagoon to fish. They can have shelter in the lagoon when there is a typhoon.

The [Chinese] fishermen conduct normal production there. In the area around the island, [Chinese government] fishing administration ships and marine surveillance ships are conducting normal patrols while in the outer ring there are [Chinese] navy warships. The island is thus wrapped layer by layer like a cabbage. As a result, a cabbage strategy has taken shape.

If the Philippines wants to go in, in the outermost area, it has first to ask whether our navy will allow it. Then it has to ask whether our fishery administration ships and marine surveillance ships will allow it. Therefore, our fishermen can carry out their production safely while our country's marine rights and interests as well as sovereignty are safeguarded. Is that not satisfactory? We can adopt this method elsewhere. We have not resorted to war and we have not forced the others to do anything, have we? . . . For many things, we have to grab the right timing to do them.

Zhang said that much more work was needed to "coordinate various efforts" and consolidate China's grip on the Spratly Islands and the Paracel Islands. "We should not rely only on military effort. In the military perspective, fighting is the last resort while before it there must be production on a large scale and with high enthusiasm and large-scale production on the sea", including fishing and tourism.

Today, China presses ever outward against its neighbours. It has been harassing with increasing intensity the fishing boats, survey vessels and oil rigs of its neighbours deep within their own exclusive economic zones, which extend 200 kilometres from shore under UNCLOS. In 2020 Chinese coastguard ships rammed Vietnamese fishing boats, sinking one and disabling another. China's coastguard also harassed a Malaysian oil drilling rig and its resupply vessels just 80 kilometres from Malaysia's coastline, leading to a standoff with the Malaysian navy.

And at the southern extremity of the South China Sea, China has resumed pushing into Indonesia's EEZ. After three years without any clashes, in early 2020 China sent sixty-three fishing vessels, with an escort of two coastguard ships, to the Natuna Sea. Jakarta's reaction was spirited. President Joko Widodo sent a diplomatic protest, dispatched the navy and

some F-16 fighter jets, made a public statement of "no compromise", called on Indonesia's fishing fleet to send hundreds
of vessels to the area, and then visited the island in the middle
of the contested zone, Natuna Island, home to about 170,000
Indonesian citizens. All within a few days. The Chinese armada
disappeared, but a large Chinese coastguard ship reappeared
in September. A spokesperson for Beijing's foreign ministry
replied to a fresh Indonesian protest with the bland statement
that China was operating "normal patrol duties in waters under
Chinese jurisdiction".

For context, Natuna Island is closer to the coast of Australia
than it is to China's southernmost uncontested territory, Hainan
Island. Indonesia's foreign affairs minister, Retno Marsudi, told
reporters: "Indonesia will never acknowledge the Nine-Dash
Lines claimed by China. This is clearly our sovereign right . . .
the lines we drew for Indonesia's EEZ are in line with the
UNCLOS. All we want is for China as a party to UNCLOS is
to abide by what's in there."

For all Xi's happy talk, this is the actual "shared destiny" his
regime is creating. At international gatherings he gushes about
"win-win" partnerships, but at sea his fleets operate under the
doctrine of "zero-sum", where the more he wins, the more you
lose. It is the assertion of China's interests above all else. Above
those of its neighbours, above its own international commit-
ments. China's Southeast Asian neighbours are much smaller
and less capable powers, so Xi treats them with contempt. When
the cameras are rolling, he is the magnanimous statesman.
When the seas are rolling, he is an unabashed buccaneer. It's his
destiny, and he's not sharing. As for the "community", welcome
aboard. You can join the crew, or you can walk the plank.

He offers a "shared destiny", but its authorship is exclusive to Beijing. There is no suggestion that Bangkok, Seoul, Manila, Hanoi, Jakarta, Ulaanbaatar, Canberra, Suva or Delhi is to be given a say in the form of this destiny. Yet all are conscripted into it by its designers in Beijing.

If imitation is the sincerest form of flattery, as Oscar Wilde maintained, Japan's fascist leaders of the 1930s and '40s would have been flattered. Xi's "community of shared destiny" has overtones of General Hideki Tojo's "Greater East Asia Co-Prosperity Sphere". Both sound benign and inviting, yet both are contrivances to conceal ambition and extend control.

Japan's former prime minister Shinzo Abe was not gulled by the offer of "shared destiny". After all, his grandfather, Nobusuke Kishi, was a minister in Tojo's war cabinet. He knew all about imperial projects: Kishi had been the ruler of Japanese-occupied China. His nickname was the "Monster of Manchuria". So his grandson immediately rejected Xi's "common destiny".

Abe accused China of being a destabilising force in Asia. He said that relations between Japan and China today were in a "similar situation" to those between Britain and Germany before 1914. Britain and Germany had very close ties, yet went to war against each other nonetheless, he said. Beijing scolded him for this.

Of course, the defining difference between the imperial projects of Japan and China is that Japan's was carried out at the point of the bayonet. Xi's is a more sophisticated twenty-first-century version. It has the coercive elements of military force, grey-zone intimidation and economic techniques such as trade sanctions.

But it also has the lure of temptation: the offer of untold billions of dollars in infrastructure. This is Xi Jinping's Belt and

Road initiative. And the billions are literally untold, or at least uncounted. Beijing has not put a figure on it, and the plan seems open-ended and ever-changing. It's had three names since Xi launched it in 2013. It began as One Belt, One Road, then Belt and Road, now the Belt and Road Initiative (BRI).

According to China's authorities, 138 countries had signed a memorandum of understanding to join Beijing's plan by late 2020, although there are not active investments in all. That's most of the countries on the planet. And Xi has called for more to join. Australia is invited too. Victoria's government controversially said yes, only to have the federal government say no. It cancelled the deals in 2021. Beijing threatened to respond "firmly and forcefully". Of course, China would do the same in the same circumstances – its national government doesn't allow its provinces to enter deals with foreign powers. Beijing is not interested in reciprocity, however, only dominance.

Xi poetically proposed Belt and Road as a twenty-first-century version of the ancient Silk Road. The Silk Road was actually many, the storied routes trod by traders from Europe selling horses, honey and slaves to the East in exchange for silk, spices and gunpowder. The Silk Road operated from the time China's Han dynasty decided it would trade with the West, 130 years before the birth of Christ, until the Ottoman empire closed it 1500 years later. In between, Marco Polo travelled the Silk Road and brought back to European readers their first glimpse of the wonders and riches of Asia in his *Marvels of the World*. It was indeed a marvellous time for China, then the world's dominant economy. It had built "a centralised, merit-based bureaucracy that was able to register its population, levy uniform taxes, control the military and regulate society some eighteen hundred years

before a similar state was to emerge in Europe", Francis Fukuyama notes. Imperial China built the Great Wall and the Great
Canal, projects on a scale dazzling to Europeans. So for China to
launch a modernised Silk Road redolent of its glories of yester-
year was a clever domestic political stroke by a leader promising
the great rejuvenation of the Chinese nation: the "China Dream".

The BRI is also designed to restructure the world's power
relationships. It's an expression of China's ambitions in global
foreign policy and economic policy, by building interconnect-
ing networks of rules, scientific research, roads, railways, ports,
power grids, communications and other systems spanning most
of the planet with Beijing at its centre. The "belt" part refers to
land routes connecting Europe to Central Asia and then across
to China's Pacific coast. The "road" is about sea lanes stretching
south from China's coast through Southeast Asia and the Pacific,
then across the Indian Ocean to Africa.

It was clever as political economics. At a time when then US
president Donald Trump was calling for an end to globalisation,
Xi was opening new channels of economic activity for China
and its many partners. While the United States is trying to work
out how to extract its remaining troops from the never-ending
war in Afghanistan, Chinese engineers are laying thousands of
kilometres of fibre-optic cable through that country. Yes, the Silk
Road encompasses Afghanistan, too.

It's also a clever strategic initiative. China uses infrastructure
as the friendly forerunner of political power. A Chinese military
theorist and a former general in the People's Liberation Army
Air Force, Qiao Liang, described Belt and Road as "truly the
strategy of the shrewd". He explained, "If you tell people, 'I come
with political and ideological intentions,' who will accept you?"

But if one offers to build scores of highways, fast rail networks, ports and power plants, who can resist?

The offer of infrastructure is a well-tested Trojan Horse for Chinese power. It was tested on the people of Tibet and Xinjiang. The Chinese Communist Party built a road into Tibet and the Tibetans were excited – it was their first highway: "We were promised peace and prosperity with the highway, and our parents and grandparents joined in building the road," as the president of Tibet's government in exile, Lobsang Sangay, tells the story. "In fact, they were paid silver coins to help them build the road. So there was a popular song during those days, it goes like this: Chinese are like our parents; when they come, they shower you with silver coins," the Harvard-educated lawyer recounted at the National Press Club in Canberra in 2017. The Chinese soldiers were patient with the local kids and bore their taunts with smiles, he said. "Then they built the road. Once the road reached Lhasa – the capital city of Tibet – first trucks came, then guns came, then tanks came. Soon, Tibet was occupied. So it started with the road."

The CCP built roads into Xinjiang, the Muslim-majority lands just to the north of Tibet, too. "When the Chinese people first went to Xinjiang, we all thought, what nice people," says the voice of the ethnic Uighur people's independence movement in the region, Rebiya Kadeer. "We treated them nicely, we expected some investment and development. Initially they said, 'We will help you with development, but you will rule over the land,'" says Kadeer, once one of the richest women in China and a member of China's National People's Congress. "Only 3 per cent of the people in Xinjiang were Chinese," Mandarin-speaking ethnic Han Chinese, distinct from the Turkic-speaking Uighur who make up the biggest ethnic group in what is now a province of China. The Beijing government operates a transmigration policy in Tibet and Xinjiang, relocating Han people from the south to change the ethnic and political composition. Han Chinese now make up about 40 per cent of the population in Xinjiang. "They increased and increased and now they are killing us," says Kadeer, who now lives as an exile in the US. The CCP has built a network of re-education camps for the Uighurs. Kadeer calls them concentration camps, where more than a million Uighurs, typically Muslims, are detained indefinitely without due process, stripped of their culture and religion, forced to learn Chinese and sometimes subjected to forced sterilisation.

The cases of Tibet and Xinjiang are ones where China has a historical claim, dating back over centuries, for asserting sovereign ownership. Both involve lands adjoining China's heartland. They are cases of China consolidating power on its periphery. They are not stories of the CCP conquering foreign nation-states. But they are, nonetheless, instructive tales of how Beijing has used attractive infrastructure as the undeclared vanguard of an uglier political dominance.

Although Beijing does not publish official figures, an association of major international banks, the Institute for International Finance (IIF), has estimated that Chinese lenders supplied US$690 billion to finance overseas projects, which is a pretty good proxy for Belt and Road lending, in the six years from the policy's inception to September 2019. The money went to seventy-two countries. That's already more than five times the US$130 billion cost of the US post-war Marshall Plan that helped rebuild Europe, adjusted to current dollars. By another count, it's much bigger. A total of US$2.1 trillion had been

invested in 1574 Belt and Road projects with Chinese involvement, according to the US financial data supplier Refinitiv.
Not all the money was necessarily from China. In other words,
it includes some investment from other sources. If the Belt and
Road vision is fully built as originally described by Xi, the total
cost would be as much as US$8 trillion, estimates China's State
Council, or cabinet.

The BRI is already the biggest international infrastructure
project since the Roman Empire. Indeed, the home of Rome
itself, Italy, has signed up to participate. It is important to note
that it's not a charitable or philanthropic enterprise. Whereas
Australia's foreign aid is mostly through grants, not loans, China
generally only extends loans. Although Beijing is generous with
the scale of the loans and doesn't require high governance standards, it's not so generous with the terms. The interest payable
varies depending on a range of factors, and some Chinese loans
to African states are interest-free, but for most borrowers it's at or
above market rates.

In addition to nation-states, there are hundreds of lesser
entities that have joined the BRI. It's not clear why Victoria, a
developed economy with a stronger credit rating than China itself,
needed to borrow money from Beijing. It can raise debt at lower
interest rates on its own terms. Without needing to cede any
power to an autocratic foreign country in the process.

The list of recipients of China's money includes some rich
countries, like Italy and Austria, but it's mainly a who's who of
the desperate and the destitute. China's easy money is appealing
not only for poor countries, but also for awkward projects. Most
of the beneficiaries – also known as the debtors – are developing countries. Of a group of countries identified by the IIF as

the seventy-two "core" Belt and Road borrowers, forty-four have no credit rating or a junk rating. These are the desperados who cannot borrow on the world market and who rely on foreign aid and concessional lending from official international institutions, like the World Bank. As for awkward projects, the IIF found that 80 per cent of Belt and Road money has gone to "sectors with high carbon footprints". Many, presumably, would have had trouble getting loans from more conventional sources for high-carbon projects.

Some of the poorest countries have really loaded up on Belt and Road debt. Kyrgyzstan and Timor-Leste have borrowed the equivalent of 30 per cent of their GDP. For scale, that would be the equivalent of Australia borrowing over half a trillion dollars, as much as the annual federal budget. All from one country. And five Belt and Road countries have been named by the International Monetary Fund as being at "high" risk of not being able to service their China debts – Djibouti, Ethiopia, Laos, the Maldives and Tajikistan. This is what China's critics have called debt-trap diplomacy. Lend more than these poor countries can handle, and they're in a debt trap. This gives the lender great power as the indebted country's leaders plead for better terms or for debt forgiveness.

Beijing's strategic use of its Belt and Road billions is an economic "cabbage leaf strategy", analogous to its military-strategic "cabbage leaf strategy" in the South China Sea, according to Richard Javad Heydarian of National Chengchi University in Taiwan. "From Malaysia to Maldives, China has sought to dominate critical infrastructure across sea lines of communications, gradually building a global network of access and dependencies, often at the expense of smaller nations' sovereignty."

Indeed, the two sets of cabbage leaves can be visualised as piling one on top of the other, gradually thickening the layers of Chinese power and presence, militarised and monetised, gradually solidifying into an overarching claim on the sovereignty of the countries in its realm. If Japan's plan to impose its Asian sphere of influence was conducted at the point of a bayonet, China's could be described as being conducted by swarming boats and swarming billions in a campaign of overbearing influence.

Beijing has shown willingness in some cases to renegotiate the terms of its Belt and Road loans. Indeed, in 2019, one-sixth of all its outstanding foreign loans were under renegotiation, according to research house T.S. Lombard. Sometimes it swaps debt for equity, as in the famous case of Sri Lanka's Hambantota port, where a Chinese firm took a 99-year lease on the port in return for forgiving the outstanding debt of US$1.1 billion.

Sometimes it agrees to renegotiate to meet the demands of a strident new government. As it did when Malaysia's Mahathir Mohamad won the election in 2018 and simply refused to honour the deal his predecessor had made with China to build and finance the East Coast Rail Link. The rail line is to run across the Malay Peninsula, to connect the Strait of Malacca on the west coast to the South China Sea on the east. Mahathir said the terms were unfair and "very damaging to our economy". China eventually agreed to cut the cost by about a third to US$10.3 billion.

Indonesia has asked Beijing for money for projects under the Belt and Road rubric. In March 2019 it pitched twenty-eight separate projects, seeking US$91.1 billion in Chinese money. Beijing and its big policy banks agreed to most of the projects within six months, according to Jakarta. Landmark Chinese-financed projects were already underway, including the US$7.8 billion high-speed rail line from Jakarta to Band-ung. But Indonesia insists these existing projects are not actually part of the Belt and Road, and only the new ones will be. It's a semantic point. Indonesia has taken major loans from China, and is seeking more to fund its development.

But hold on. This is the same country chasing China's vessels out of its territorial waters. In a case like Indonesia's, how does its maritime rejection of China on the one hand reconcile with its development dependency on the other?

Beijing made an attempt to reconcile the two in January 2020, when its foreign ministry spokesman hinted darkly that Indonesia's uncooperative behaviour over the South China Sea might endan-ger its Belt and Road projects. So Beijing seems to think it can use its loans to Jakarta as a pressure point to paralyse Indonesia's defence of its maritime territories. And Indonesia has extraordi-nary maritime territories. It's the biggest archipelagic state in the world, with some 17,000 islands strung along a 5000-kilometre stretch of the equator. If China were allowed to operate with impunity in Indonesian waters, it would be a geopolitical coup.

But Indonesia isn't the only one caught in this apparent dilemma – so is China. If Jakarta calls Beijing's bluff, Xi's Belt and Road strategy to advance his South China Sea policy would be damaged. The BRI and the South China Sea may be two halves of Xi's overarching plan to assert China's power, but in such an example they come into conflict with each other.

And if Xi thinks that an Indonesian president has scope to kowtow in the face of Chinese border aggression, he understands neither Indonesia nor democracies. Jakarta's elites are very com-fortable with the Chinese Indonesian minority, but China and the Chinese are deeply unpopular with the great bulk of Indonesians.

And long have been. Which is why, whenever there's a breakdown in civil order, Indonesian mobs immediately burn and loot Chinese businesses and neighbourhoods. Jakarta's Chinatown still hasn't fully recovered from the last outbreak of such violence. To kneel before Beijing's demands would bring down a firestorm of fury on the head of an Indonesian president. It's not tenable.

China has already thoroughly alienated Vietnam through its aggressive seagoing ventures, and it now risks relations with Indonesia as well. "Alienating yet another powerful ASEAN member state could prove to be a foolish mistake for Beijing," said RAND analyst Derek Grossman. The two strategies for building China's power – one through oceanic intimidation and the other through massive investment – seem to be operating in an ad hoc and uncoordinated way. In truth, the BRI itself is not a detailed blueprint but a high-level concept – flexible, open-ended, ever-changing and only loosely coordinated. One academic, Lee Jones of Queen Mary University of London, went so far as to describe it as "a mess, not a master plan", and it certainly has messy elements in its sprawling, multi-continental ambition. But it is still early days; Xi plans to be in power till at least 2035.

While the transport projects have been its most publicised features, Belt and Road encompasses much more. Indeed, in Xi's original exposition of the plan's "five links", he didn't list the infrastructure first but "policy coordination", government-to-government links and dealings to establish agreed protocols and rules. In other words, harmonisation with China's systems and standards to more smoothly interconnect.

Only after that did Xi rank the other four: "infrastructure connectivity, unimpeded trade, financial integration and people-to-people communication". It includes a fibre-optic "digital silk road", an "academic silk road" connecting scores of universities across dozens of countries, and an "investment silk road" flowing with tens of billions of dollars' worth of corporate investment already and strewn with Chinese economic cooperation zones. And embedded within it is the "string of pearls", a poetic name for a military project.

The "string of pearls" is an international chain of ports that China is building or leasing to allow China control of the Indian Ocean. The ports in Myanmar, Bangladesh, Sri Lanka, the Maldives and Pakistan reach along the vital maritime trade corridor connecting China to its oil supply in the Middle East. Beijing emphasises that all its port arrangements are strictly commercial. Analysts in India, the United States and elsewhere point out that the ports are dual-use, able to accommodate Chinese warships as well as merchant ships. An anxious India is seeking to counter with its own "chain of flowers". India fears that China's command of the shipping routes of the Indian Ocean could jeopardise its own access to oil and other essential imports, especially in a blockade, war or other crisis.

One particular inclusion in China's Belt and Road deals is GPS. The US is not the only country with a satellite-based global positioning system. China is urgently building its own, as Russia has. The reason? So that Beijing can operate a global navigation system independently of the US. Recall that GPS isn't just a handy way to get you around town. It is the essential navigational tool for systems ranging from air travel to missile guidance. Like the internet, America's GPS started as a government tool and was only later extended to allow civilian access. The US can change or shut down its GPS if it so chooses. China, like Russia, does not want to allow America that level of power. By building its own, China will be able to operate even in a crisis where Washington might choose to disrupt Chinese access. Beijing launched the thirtieth and final satellite for its system in June 2020. The Belt and Road fits into the plan because Beijing is asking participatory nations to accept China's Beidou GPS stations to improve its global reach. Already, most countries, including Thailand and Pakistan, are using its system for at least some purposes, according to Beidou. The US, Russian and Chinese systems are operated by their militaries. The European Union is in the process of completing its Galileo system as a civilian-operated one.

Again, China's techniques for dominance have modern features, but the face itself is familiar. It's the face of an emperor seeking to extend his realm. The original Belt and Road was built 2000 years ago; the Roman Empire was its forerunner. As their empire grew, the Romans built a network of paved roads 80,000 kilometres long to move their armies at speed in straight lines. Today the roads would be called a "dual use technology". They were built chiefly for the army to extend Rome's power, but they also served as the most important trade routes and cultural vectors of their time, generating wealth and spreading Christianity. The roads allowed Rome to bind a polyglot of peoples, races, languages and kingdoms. They put Rome at the centre. It was a truism that "all roads lead to Rome".

The Romans were audacious in the scope of their roads and pioneering in their engineering, with mountains tunnelled, swamps drained, valleys levelled, and soaring aqueducts built. They endure today. Not only in the physical fragments that remain but in the power of their patterning of human organisation. A 2018 study by four Danish researchers sought to test how much the patterns of settlement and economic activity had shifted over the last two millennia in Europe, North Africa and Britain where the Romans had built. They reported "a clear tendency for persistence in road density within the areas covered by the empire by 117 CE" or AD. "Areas that featured relatively high road density in antiquity on average also feature relatively high road density today," wrote Carl-Johan Dalgaard and his group. The Roman routes created a public good so powerful that it still generates an economic return today, holding cities and patterns of movement in thrall to toga-clad engineers who were measuring road gradients when Christianity was new. Infrastructure can be a tool with great power and durability. Beijing seeks to be the next Rome.

And conquest by debt-trap diplomacy is instantly recognisable as a well-worn instrument of colonialism. In the nineteenth and early twentieth centuries, the newly independent countries of Latin America and the Caribbean borrowed heavily from financiers in Europe and the US to fund their development. When they ran into repayment problems, they discovered that one form of oppression can be readily replaced by another. Their unhappy creditors called upon the coercive power of the governments standing behind them. The European powers backed their banks' claims with diplomatic pressure and sometimes armed force. The British invasion of Egypt in 1882 is one example. The Venezuelan crisis of 1902 is the most famous. To recover debts, Britain, Germany and Italy sent their navies to blockade Venezuela's ports and destroy its coastal defences. It worked, and Venezuela agreed to a settlement.

Modern finance has had plenty of quasi-imperial debt-trap episodes too. Indonesians who were old enough to understand the news in 1998 will never forget the picture of their strongman ruler, Suharto, sitting at a desk while meekly signing away fiscal control of his country as the IMF's French head, Michel Camdessus, stood above him sternly with his arms folded.

Another familiar mechanism for imperial control is the 99-year lease. In 1898 the collapsing Qing dynasty, the "sick man of Asia", appeased Britain by agreeing to London's demand for a 99-year lease on the New Territories, including the jewel, Hong Kong. The British representative in the negotiations, Claude MacDonald, settled on a 99-year lease because he thought it was "as good as forever". Germany and France took other pieces of China under 99-year leases at the same time. Beijing mimics this mechanism today with its 99-year leases on Sri Lanka's Hambantota Port and the Port of Darwin.

State-approved narcotic trafficking is another time-tested technique for eroding the sovereignty of target powers. China's Opium War with Britain in 1839 illustrates the point. China's governments had been struggling to stop the inflow of opium for a century. Addiction among its southern population was a serious and growing social problem for the Qing dynasty. Although the Portuguese had been the main suppliers, the trafficking burgeoned when Britain's East India Company entered the business. The East India Company, a privately capitalised firm but operating with the full mandate and protection of the British government, shipped increasing quantities of opium from India to China for profit. Fabulous profit. American traders also joined in, exporting Turkish and Indian opium to China. An estimated 12 million Chinese had become addicted to the drug by the time of the First Opium War. The emperor called it "the flowing poison".

When the Qing cracked down on the trade in 1839 in the southern Chinese city of Canton (or Guangzhou), they seized

British inventory of 1300 tons of opium. It was such a vast amount that it took "500 men twenty-three days to mix it with salt and lime in pits, 'where it boiled like soup', after which it was sluiced off into the sea", writes Lucy Inglis in her history of opium, *Milk of Paradise*. The British traffickers, now led by the merchant William Jardine, demanded that London go to war with China to protect the opium trade and entrench the British trading base.

Britain's modern warships easily outgunned China's junks and killed 18,000 Chinese troops, with the loss of fewer than seventy British sailors. The Qing emperor was helpless to prevent the British taking control of five ports plus Hong Kong. The young Queen Victoria wrote to her uncle, the King of Belgium, that "Albert is so much amused at my having got the Island of Hong Kong". China's "century of humiliation" had begun.

By the time Barack Obama was US president, it was the illicit flow of opioids from China to the US that was reaching crisis proportions. One opioid was a particularly poisonous Chinese export to America: fentanyl. This synthetic narcotic is about 100 times more potent than morphine and thirty times stronger than heroin. The legal form was an advance in blocking pain experienced by patients suffering from cancer and other diseases, but the illicit trafficking of the drug was an advance in the scale of addiction and death suffered in the US. A mere 2 to 3 micrograms can kill. Not milligrams, which are thousandths of a gram, but micrograms, which are millionths.

Because of its potency, fentanyl needs to be dispensed with the greatest care. Drug dealers are not known for their concern for customer wellbeing. They mix fentanyl with other drugs, including methamphetamine, heroin and cocaine. This increases its potency, and it's cheaper than heroin. And because of fentanyl's intensity, it's easy to mail commercial volumes in small packages. Which is generally how it reaches the US. Its American street name is "China girl" or "China white".

America's Big Pharma had already primed the US population for this problem. The legal pharmaceutical industry recklessly marketed and pushed pharmaceutical painkillers in the US so that Americans had become accustomed to overusing well before the fentanyl flood. But then the flood: "In 2013, its illegal supply from China initiated the third phase of the US opioid epidemic – and the deadliest," writes Vanda Felbab-Brown of the Brookings Institution. Other major sources are Mexico and Canada. It's a lucrative trade. One kilogram can be bought in China for US$3000 to US$5000 and resold in the US for US$1.5 million, according to the American Drug Enforcement Administration.

Obama sought Xi's help in 2013. After a couple of years, Beijing made some token efforts to oblige. In each year from 2013 to 2016, the number of US overdose deaths involving fentanyl rose by an average of 113 per cent, according to the US Centers for Disease Control and Prevention. Donald Trump took up the cause when he became president and the US again won some superficial concessions from Beijing. By 2017 there were 70,230 drug overdose deaths overall in America. Of those, 28,400 involved fentanyl.

In the same year, websites in China were openly advertising and selling fentanyl. It was readily available, both wholesale and through retail. Nearly one hundred Chinese companies were selling the drug on a single website, Weiku.com, based in the eastern city of Hangzhou, for instance. Compared to Beijing's energetic commitment to political censorship of the web, its interest in shutting down the fentanyl trade was evidently a very low priority.

It was only when Trump put fentanyl on the table in late 2018 as part of his "trade war" with China that Xi committed to properly trying to control the trafficking industry. The first serious Chinese crackdown began in 2019. In return, Xi asked Trump to remove punitive tariffs that the US president had imposed on hundreds of billions of dollars' worth of China's exports to America. Trump refused but did agree to a ceasefire in the trade war. Trump hailed the agreement as a possible "game-changer" in America's opioid crisis.

Beijing hadn't been sponsoring the trafficking of illicit fentanyl to the US. But it hadn't really been trying to stop it either. Xi's regime was prepared to allow it to flourish largely unchecked for years in spite of sustained American requests. Yet China has cracked down on illicit trade when it's so chosen. Felbab-Brown of Brookings gives two examples. One is its cooperation with Australia in suppressing the trafficking of meth from China to Australia under the joint Taskforce Blaze in 2015. "The buildup of Australia's cooperation with China, featuring the strongest and longest police-to-police relationship with China of any Western liberal democracy, succeeded in significantly suppressing the production in China of meth heading to Australia," she writes in her report *Fetanyl and Geopolitics*. "It also dramatically reduced the trafficking of meth from China to Australia."

Xi was prepared to cooperate because he wanted to suppress the drug in China itself, because it suited his image to be tough on drugs, because he wanted to cultivate Australia in pursuit of an extradition treaty with Canberra, and because it helped him centralise power, according to Felbab-Brown. The success in stemming the flow of meth from China to Australia was soon offset, however, by a rising inflow from Myanmar to Australia.

Felbab-Brown's second example: China's energy in cracking down on the trade in illicit wildlife products, such as ivory. And since Xi's deal with Trump on fentanyl, many of the websites and easy supplies in China have vanished. There is evidence of real progress for the first time.

So why the reluctance to stop the flow of fentanyl to the US for the first five years? Considering the three cases, Felbab-Brown observes: "The following pattern emerges: The government of China at first tends to deny the existence of a problem. Under international or strong domestic pressure, it eventually moves to tighten regulation. But its enforcement tends to be limited and subverted by powerful vested interests of industry representatives, officials of line ministries charged with regulating or promoting the industry, and government officials. Geostrategic interests also trump other considerations." In other words, it takes a lot of political will to break the nexus of profiteers and corrupt officials. Unless it's overcome by geostrategy. In the case of fentanyl, it appears that Xi lacked the will to act, or it suited his geostrategy, or both. Whichever it may have been, the conclusion is the same: Xi was content to allow an accelerating medical, social and political problem unfold in the US while Chinese businesses and officials were making money from it. Until Trump applied the force majeure of trade sanctions. The Opioid War of 2013–18 seems to have ended in a negotiated truce, temporarily at least.

*

The idea of Xi's "community of common destiny" derives from an ancient Chinese concept, All-Under-Heaven or *tianxia*. On the basis of this concept, Chinese emperors claimed the Mandate of Heaven to unite all under their rule on earth. Xi's "community of common destiny", says the Australian Sinologist Geremie Barmé, "provides substance and diplomatic architecture to the revived concept of all-under-heaven or *tianxia*, one which assumes a belief that China can be a moral, political and economic great power".

And it's using implements that imperial powers have wielded for centuries to establish empires. Xi now pursues a modernised suite of neo-imperial policies to impose China's agenda. After the forced integration of the peoples on the periphery of the Chinese heartland, Xi's project is extending far beyond. With the promise of a benign shared destiny, yet the reality of "grey zone" coercion in the South China Sea. With the tantalising offer of a China-funded Belt and Road of shared prosperity worldwide, while inviting countries into debt dependency in the process. Extending the imperial interest through 99-year leases and opiate flows, the very techniques used against China by earlier empires. It's a twenty-first-century construct but with readily identifiable imperial impulses. An empire with Chinese characteristics.

Orville Schell and John Delury in their 2013 work, *Wealth and Power: China's Long March to the Twenty-First Century*, wrote presciently of the temptation beckoning to an increasingly powerful Beijing. There was "always the danger of a new sentiment – one not unknown among those once acquainted with oppression – arising: the temptation to do unto others what has been done unto them".

16

PARADOX OF PARANOIA:
ELEVEN TYPES OF PAIN

It's a paradox. While China's conduct outwardly seems offensive, from within it is designed to be defensive. "The Chinese Communist Party's priority is to pre-empt all perceived threats to state security," says Samantha Hoffman of the Australian Strategic Policy Institute, an expert on China's use of technology for social control, "which means the Party must not only protect its existing power, but also continuously expand its power outward in what feels like an attack to China's targets."

Anne-Marie Brady explains why this came about. From the very beginning of the People's Republic in 1949, "influenced by China's recent history and guided by Marxist-Leninism, the Chinese Communist Party stressed the importance of resolving the foreign presence in China, eradicating the harmful, taking what was useful and bringing it under Chinese control". The system for doing this, its "*waishi*" system for managing the foreign world, "is a defensive tactic to control the threat of the impact of foreign society on the government's political power", says Brady. The system is "part of a cultural crisis, a conflicting inferiority/superiority crisis that Chinese society has faced since its earliest contacts with the technologically superior Western world in the nineteenth century". To the outsider, it appears that today's

China is so mighty that it must have outgrown such timorousness. Yet the psychology and the policies of an impoverished and uncertain new republic of seventy years ago remain operative today.

While the party's aggression is based on its insecurities, that's little consolation because its intrusions are aggressive nonetheless. Further, it means that its quest for perfect protection is both paranoid and never-ending. You cannot reassure a paranoid person that he or she is secure; nor can you reassure a paranoid political party-state that it is safe. Its systems and policies are structured to expand endlessly. Under this mindset, the greater China's reach, the greater its ability to protect itself. So it must not stop reaching.

Xi has told his party that it must brace for a long ideological struggle. Early in his tenure as president he gave an internal party speech, not released until six years later, in which he portrayed China as the challenger striving to defeat a stronger, more established West: "We must profoundly understand the self-regulating ability of capitalist society, fully appraise the objective reality of the long-term advantage of Western developed countries in the economic, scientific and military spheres and conscientiously prepare for all aspects of long-term cooperation and struggle between the two social systems." He warned his party that strengthening and advancing China would not be "a walk in the park". It was likely to continue long beyond the lifetime of anyone alive today.

The gilded lure of a Chinese-funded "community of common destiny" isn't Beijing's only mechanism for making the foreign serve China. Economic coercion is an important tool of Chinese statecraft. When the Reserve Bank's Philip Lowe cited the "political difference" between Australia and China, he was too diplomatic to speak plainly about the central one: China is an authoritarian country. Australia is a democracy. And this introduces a peculiar risk. The Chinese authorities don't think of international business or finance in the same way that people elsewhere do. For decades, whenever an Australian business manager celebrated a breakthrough into the Chinese market, a CCP official would quietly note it as a possible future pressure point. Whenever an Australian government minister proudly announced a new trade opening into China, Beijing silently counted it as a new source of leverage against the Australian government. Beijing's motto could be summarised as: "Your deal, our leverage." It's an alien concept for most people in democratic systems, where trading is conducted for mutual advantage. That's naive in the worldview of the CCP. The trade will be allowed to proceed to mutual advantage unless and until Beijing needs to take control for sole advantage. Then it's zero-sum.

When First Vice-Premier Zhu Rongji proposed that we "all get rich together", he didn't disclose the second half of the formula. Getting rich with China means getting ready to be pressured by China. In China, business does not exist in a universe separate to politics. Business, like everything else, is subordinate to politics. Xi has given this new stridency with the requirement that all listed companies in China, including foreign ones, set up internal CCP committees. The party's intrusion into private firms "is not a discrete effort to infiltrate the private sector per se, but rather is a manifestation of the CCP's desire to have insight and input into all economic, civil, and political activity within the country", says Jude Blanchette, China adviser with the US-based geopolitical advisory business Crumpton Group.

A pair of China experts tried to warn Australian business-people and government officials about the CCP's intentions in 2017. Australia's economic relationship with China has flourished, "but this flourishing relationship also gives ... China the increased ability to threaten and use economic coercion in its relations with Australia", wrote Linda Jakobson and Bates Gill in their book *China Matters: Getting It Right for Australia*. "Australian political leaders and the broader public need to be aware of the pronounced intertwining of security and economic interests with China [and] the ways in which Chinese can exercise economic hard power." Their warnings and those from others were ignored as Australia's corporate profits and export dependency on China continued to grow. Sydney University's James Reilly said in 2013: "Never in world history has one government had so much control over so much wealth. It is no surprise, therefore, that Beijing is deploying its vast economic wealth to advance foreign policy goals. China is using economic statecraft more frequently, more assertively, and in more diverse fashion than ever before." As Reilly wrote those words, Xi was only just unveiling the Belt and Road initiative. Australian companies, industries and governments behaved as if they had some secret magic protection against the risks of their overexposure to China's market.

In fact, nothing could be as ordinary as Beijing using economic coercion against its trading partners. In the past dozen years, Beijing has imposed economic punishment on at least eleven countries, for a wide range of perceived offences. This does not include China's trade war with the United States in 2019, where the US was the aggressor and China the respondent. In each of the eleven punishments, Beijing imposed an economic penalty for a non-economic action. They varied in the particular but were consistent in the pattern. The Chinese government went after countries large and small, on several continents, over a range of grievances. The countries punished were, in chronological order, France, Japan, Norway, the Philippines, Britain, Taiwan, Mongolia, South Korea, Palau, Canada and Australia. Typically, the Chinese government found a pretext rather than announcing a reason. Ambiguity is important to Beijing, as we'll see. It generally chose very specific interests to hit, rather than imposing economy-wide sanctions. And while it has not met with 100 per cent success, and its tactics have sometimes backfired badly, it has had substantial impact. If China's government were aiming to train the world to fear its wrath, it would seem, by and large, to be succeeding.

A brisk walk through these cases starts with the 2008 decision by French President Nicolas Sarkozy to meet the Dalai Lama, considered a spiritual leader by many Tibetans and a reviled "splittist" pursuing Tibetan independence by the CCP. In response, Beijing suspended a multi-billion-dollar order for 150 Airbus planes and cancelled two big-spending trade missions to France. The link was clear, but never stated openly. China's then premier, Wen Jiabao, leading a major Chinese trade delegation around Europe, winked: "I looked at a map of Europe on the plane. My trip goes around France ... We all know why." Paris recanted within weeks. The flow of deals resumed. Sarkozy's meeting with the Dalai Lama was the last by a French president. Asked in 2018 whether he would meet the spiritual leader of the Tibetan people, President Emmanuel Macron said: "Is it good for my people if I have a sort of counter-measures coming from China" as a result of such a meeting? "For sure, no."

The next case grew out of a Chinese territorial dispute with Japan. In maritime jostling in 2010, a Chinese fishing trawler near the Tokyo-controlled Senkaku/Diaoyu Islands collided with two Japanese coastguard vessels. The Japanese detained the Chinese skipper. Beijing retaliated, while never drawing the connection explicitly. It said that it was cutting exports of rare earths, a group of seventeen metals of strategic importance, to countries including Japan. It so happened that Japan was more acutely affected than others. Rare earths are essential to a wide array of computer and electronic products, from mobile phones to guided missiles. Beijing controlled about 95 per cent of global exports of refined rare earths at the time. While China's government said that it was restricting output for environmental reasons, the World Trade Organization rejected this explanation and ruled against it. Japan decided it needed to protect future access to these strategic metals by sponsoring more developments outside China. This included critical Japanese support for an Australian company, Lynas Corporation, which is today the most important source of refined rare earths outside China. In this way, the episode rebounded on Beijing because Japan took insurance against future coercion. China's grip on the global supply slipped to 85 per cent. But it also worked for China: Japan has not detained any more of its ships' crews. In 2019, Beijing's official media again threatened to use its rare earths dominance for coercive purposes – this time against the United States as part of the trade war between the two great economies. Alarmed at the risk, Washington began coordinating with Canberra over ways to bring more Australian rare earths onto the market to dilute Chinese dominance, much as Japan did after the maritime incident.

The month after the clash with Japan, China acted against Norway, case study number three. The Norwegian Nobel Committee awarded the Peace Prize to Chinese writer and democracy advocate Liu Xiaobo. China froze diplomatic contacts, suspended free trade negotiations and cut imports of Norwegian salmon, supposedly because of "food safety" concerns. The sanctions remained in place for more than three years, until Norway buckled. Its prime minister declined to meet the Dalai Lama, and the foreign minister pledged not to support "any behaviour that harms China's core and important interests".

In the fourth case, that of the Philippines, Manila was punished for standing up to China over a territorial dispute in the South China Sea in 2012. Beijing cut imports of its bananas, supposedly over pests in the fruit. And while bananas may sound a trivial target, they're a serious export for the Philippines and the losses were in the billions of dollars. When President Rodrigo Duterte buckled, visiting Beijing in 2016 and announcing the Philippines' "separation" from its long-time ally, the United States, the banana trade rebounded and Xi Jinping announced US$24 billion in new investments.

In the case of Britain, high-level contact was frozen after then Prime Minister David Cameron met the Dalai Lama in 2012. It resumed after Cameron emphasised in the House of Commons that Britain was firmly opposed to Tibetan independence. He told Chinese investors: "We want to be the destination for Chinese investment. Tell the other Chinese investors – come to London; spend your money." Beijing responded by announcing £14 billion in investment in 2014.

When Taiwan's voters ignored Beijing's preference in 2016 and elected as president the candidate for the Democratic

Progressive Party, Tsai Ing-wen, in a landslide, China cut its flow of tourists to the island. The number of mainland visitors fell by more than one million a year, a quarter of the total. Beijing imposed a political freeze and other measures, including intensified military exercises. It sent an aircraft carrier to circle the island, just 180 kilometres from the Chinese mainland. And Beijing continued building up its massive missile forces just across the strait.

Beijing regards Taiwan as a rebel province that must be united with the mainland at any cost. Tsai's DPP favoured eventual independence from Beijing; her main rival, the Kuomintang party, favoured unification. Tsai has not resiled from her party's position. In 2019, she was an outspoken supporter of the Hong Kong protest movement. Beijing, which had until then only restricted tour groups, said in July 2019 that it would also curb individual Chinese travelling to Taiwan. Tsai was due to face an election in just six months' time. Xi interfered through a major disinformation campaign. Taiwan depends on mainland China to buy 40 per cent of its exports, almost exactly the same as Australia's China export dependency pre-pandemic of 38.8 per cent. But Xi's bullying, coercion and interference failed. The people of Taiwan re-elected Tsai resoundingly. Voter turnout jumped to 75 per cent, its highest in a dozen years. And Tsai's share of the vote increased slightly, from 56 per cent to 57. "Democratic Taiwan and our democratically elected government will not concede to threats and intimidation," Tsai told a cheering crowd after the election. "The results of this election have made that answer crystal clear."

Case seven. Mongolia allowed the Dalai Lama to visit in 2016, his third time in a decade. It was one of his predecessors who brought Tibetan Buddhism to Mongolia in the sixteenth century. But neighbouring Beijing buys 90 per cent of the tiny democracy's exports. It punished Mongolia by imposing tariffs on its mining exports and freezing negotiations over loans. The government in Ulaanbaatar quickly expressed regret and promised not to repeat the offence. China relaxed its sanctions. In this case, China did not try to conceal the cause and openly cited the Dalai Lama's visit. "We hope that Mongolia has taken this lesson to heart," said its foreign ministry.

In 2017 it was South Korea's turn. When it sought to protect itself from North Korean missile attacks by installing a US-made and -operated missile defence system called THAAD, Terminal High Altitude Area Defense, China cut its group tours. Tourism numbers fell by 60 per cent. The cost to South Korea's tourism industry was US$6.8 billion, according to its parliamentary budget office. Beijing also shut down much of the "K-pop" industry's burgeoning sales to China – music, TV and film. The sanctions affected 57 per cent of all South Korean firms, according to a local trade association's survey. The sanctions played directly into South Korea's presidential elections: the opposition candidate, Moon Jae-in, took advantage of the situation by promising to cancel THAAD's deployment if elected. Moon won the 2017 election and remains president. He was going to win in any case – the election was brought forward because the incumbent party was in deep disgrace after its leader, Park Geun-hye, was impeached over a corruption scandal, removed from office and later jailed for over thirty years. But China counted it as a success for its policy of coercion. Once elected, President Moon retained the elements of the THAAD system already in place but froze any further deployments. He gave Beijing a three-part undertaking: South Korea would not build up THAAD any further; the existing THAAD batteries would not be integrated into a regional US missile defence system; and Seoul would not enter a trilateral alliance with the US and Japan. South Korea remains a US treaty ally and hosts 28,000 US troops on its soil. But the trade embargo successfully conditioned South Korea into fearing future disagreements with China. Whenever there is any possible clash with Beijing looming on any issue, the South Korean media fret about a possible "second THAAD". China insisted throughout that its punishment of Seoul was, in fact, the "voice of the people", a spontaneous Chinese people's consumer movement that had nothing to do with the government.

It was also the year to punish Palau, case nine. Palau is a country so remote and so small that many have never heard of it. This South Pacific micro-state has a population of 20,000. It is a sovereign state in a close relationship – "Compact of Free Association" – with the United States, which provides its defence and funding for other services. The other key fact about Palau is that it is one of the very few countries to recognise Taiwan, not Beijing, as the sole legitimate government of China.

In 2008, there were just 638 Chinese visitors to Palau. China's tourism industry pumped this up to 91,000 by 2015. At its peak, the flow of tourists from China was the biggest part of Palau's biggest industry. China supplied 54 per cent of an industry that was generating 42 per cent of the island state's GDP. And then, two years later, Beijing told its tourism operators to shut off group tours to Palau under pain of fines. No explanation was given. The number of Chinese visitors fell to 58,000 in 2017, an abrupt decline of more than a third, and it kept falling. The reason behind Beijing's embargo on Palau was clear: to force it to dump Taiwan and switch diplomatic recognition to China instead.

China's campaign to persuade nations to switch recognition from Taiwan to Beijing has intensified. Since Tsai first won Taiwan's presidency, seven countries have changed allegiance to Beijing. That includes two South Pacific nations, Solomon Islands and Kiribati. Only fifteen capitals worldwide remain allied to Taiwan. Despite the shattering effect on the Palau economy, its then president, Tommy Remengesau Jr, stood firm in the face of what the locals call "the China ban", refusing to switch recognition to Beijing, and seeking economic help from the United States, Japan and South Korea. Remengesau said that "friendship is earned, not forced".

Besides, he said, Palau had too many tourists. When the Chinese tourism flood peaked, it put strains on Palau's electricity and water supplies. Chinese buyers brought suitcases of cash to buy property. Rents and land prices soared. The island environment suffered. So in 2015 Remengesau cut the number of charter flights from China. "We definitely got out in time, this pain we're going through, it would have been so much worse," said one tourism operator, Leilani Reklai, also president of Palau's tourism association.

In the face of "the China ban", Remengesau stayed calm and turned to the US. When then US defence secretary Mark Esper visited in 2020, the Palau president proposed that Washington build military facilities in Palau. And a US coastguard presence to protect Palau's fisheries. "There are so many things that the US can show leadership, as you can see China seems to be the main nation showing initiative and aggressively coming to the Pacific and establishing their mark," said Remengesau.

He reached his term limit as president and his brother-in-law, Surangel Whipps Jr, won the election to replace him in 2021. Whipps isn't expected to change policy and, with Palau closed off to protect itself against COVID-19, tourism was a hypothetical question going into 2021.

Canada was next, number ten. Its crime was to act on an American request to arrest in December 2018 a Chinese business executive accused of committing bank fraud in the United States. Meng Wanzhou worked as chief financial officer for Huawei. A US request to extradite her to America for trial is before the Canadian courts. Beijing demanded her immediate release and threatened unspecified "serious consequences". Nine days after the Canadians arrested Meng, the Chinese authorities detained two Canadians, former diplomat Michael Kovrig and business consultant Michael Spavor. They remain under arrest accused of spying in general, without specific charge. Prime Minister Justin Trudeau described the arrests as arbitrary, the men "detained for political reasons". He added: "China is making stronger moves than it has before to try to get its own way on the world stage and Western countries and democracies around the world are pointing out [that] this is not something we need to continue to allow." But more than two years later, it was still being allowed.

Beijing inflicted the further punishment of cutting imports of Canadian canola, potentially a US$2 billion loss, and beef and pork, a possible further loss of half a billion US dollars a year. The Chinese government says the food bans are due to food safety issues. Beijing cut off political contact. The Canadian opposition leader accused Trudeau of weakness in the face of Chinese bullying and urged him to impose retaliatory trade sanctions on China. It was a contested issue heading into Canada's October 2019 election. Trudeau won re-election but lost his majority. In late 2020 his government was still treading very softly with Beijing – Ottawa dithered over banning Huawei and resisted opposition pressure to take other measures. Trudeau backed away from a proposal for a free trade agreement with Beijing, yet offered a sector-by-sector deal instead. This was even as China's trade sanctions remained in place, and with two Canadian citizens held hostage in China's jails. Canada's parliament grew so frustrated with Trudeau that the opposition parties united to outvote his government to demand tougher action. The House passed a motion 179 votes to 146 calling on the government to decide within thirty days whether to allow Huawei to supply Canada's 5G wireless networks; Trudeau refused to respond to the deadline and was dithering over a decision in early 2021. The House further demanded that the government "develop a robust plan, as Australia has done, to combat China's growing foreign operations here in Canada and its increasing intimidation of Canadians living in Canada". The opposition leader, Erin O'Toole, said that "the democratic world must acknowledge that the approach to China over the last two decades has not worked. In fact, the situation has gotten worse." He railed against CCP agents interfering in Canada and threatening Chinese Canadians, against Confucius Institutes pushing party propaganda, and the bullying of university professors into self-censoring on human rights issues. The Conservative leader said that "Canada should work very closely with our Five Eyes allies ... so that it's difficult for China to use its immense economic size to intimidate smaller economies like Canada", a reference to the intelligence-sharing alliance between Australia, Canada, New Zealand, the UK and the US.

Finally, Australia. In February 2019, it became clear that China's authorities had ordered extra checks on Australian thermal coal imports. The news agency Reuters reported that Australia's product was to be subject to extra "environmental" inspections and clearing time would be extended. Normal processing time of between five and twenty days was to be extended to at least forty days. While China was seeking to reduce its overall imports of coal, imports from Indonesia, Russia and elsewhere were not affected. The Australian dollar lost 1 per cent of its value on the news. Australia's thermal coal exports to China in 2018 earned $4.9 billion in export income, not the biggest item but among the top half-dozen. The Morrison government said it would seek clarification from Beijing. By July more than $1 billion worth of Australian thermal coal, used for generating electricity, was piled up on China's docks awaiting customs clearance, according to industry newsletter *Platts*. "People who are buying Australian coal have switched," Rory Simington, principal analyst at global energy consultancy Wood Mackenzie, told *The Guardian*. "If you have a vessel that is sitting outside a port for three months waiting for clearance you're going to buy Indonesian or Russian coal which isn't going to be delayed." By August the Morrison government was still "seeking clarification" from Beijing. Six months after the Reuters report, trade minister Simon Birmingham said, "We do want to get to the bottom" of the situation and that he was seeking "further dialogue".

Why the go-slow? And why the mystery? The former secretary of the Department of Foreign Affairs and Trade, Peter Varghese, now chancellor of the University of Queensland, said at the time: "Personally, I think they probably are trying to [send a] signal to Australia." It was a clear signal of displeasure. Beijing made clear privately to Australian officials that it was unhappy at Australia's ban on Huawei and ZTE building the 5G wifi network, as well as the new laws to curb foreign interference. "Taking countries in and out of the deep freeze is a well-tested Chinese strategy," said Varghese. Confirming that this is exactly what Beijing had done, the director of Australian studies at East China Normal University, Chen Hong, said in September 2019 that Australia's relations with China had entered a "freeze". The freeze extended to high-level diplomatic visits. By the end of 2019, it was clear that Australian coal exporters were unharmed by Beijing's ban. The short-term holdup was costly, but the coal companies quickly rerouted shipments to other countries. The verdict from one senior executive: "It was real, but it ended up being a drop in the ocean." The ban on political contacts remained.

So why didn't Beijing just openly say why it was imposing sanctions? Why not let countries know explicitly that they are being punished, as the United States does when it imposes trade sanctions on other countries? The US announces its displeasure, gives its reasons and imposes punishment accordingly. Sometimes, especially in the Trump presidency, the official justification is disingenuous. But the transgressor state knows exactly who is hurting it and they have a pretty clear idea why.

The CCP operates differently. "You are never going to get clarification from the Chinese system of whether they are signalling something or whether it's a more routine trade matter," Varghese explains. "It's part of their strategy. They leave it to you to guess. They let you go through the process of thinking, 'What could we have possibly done to upset the Chinese?' They leave us to use our imaginations to think of what we might have done." This is the same principle – of self-criticism – that the party used to pressure suspects during the Cultural Revolution. "Vague warnings frighten more people than precise warnings do," said the US Sinologist Perry Link, and "vague charges allow for arbitrary targeting". Peter Varghese expands: "Then they wait while you take it to the next step. You identify it yourself. Once you've come to your list of possibilities of what they might be upset about, you try to fix it. There's an element of tactics to it. The whole pattern of Chinese exercise of influence and control is to bring pre-emptive concessions to China so that they don't have invade or do anything so unsubtle."

It is, in other words, a process of conditioning. Beijing uses uncertainty over the reason for punishment to train countries into anticipating its wishes and fearing its wrath. Better than telling other countries how to serve China, Beijing trains them into doing it themselves. Unbidden.

Beijing's policy of aggressive ambiguity serves three other purposes. It allows China to pose outwardly as a benign power offering only "win-win" outcomes. It protects China from any country that might want to take formal recourse by taking a case to the World Trade Organization. And it gives uncertain or fearful governments the option of pretending nothing political is going wrong, of playing along with the Chinese fiction to avoid open confrontation. Australia fell into this category, preferring not to talk about the problem all through 2019.

There are six important features of the policy. First, this is not a policy that Xi Jinping started. The People's Republic of China has used it for decades. But it has been extended to more countries, more aggressively, under Xi. Second, it's being used as an all-purpose punishment. In this sample of eleven cases, it was used to influence other countries' election outcomes, defence options, territorial claims, peace awards, telecommunications decisions, laws against foreign interference, arrests of Chinese citizens wanted abroad, diplomatic recognition of Taiwan and hosting of the Dalai Lama. Third, pain was applied across a wide variety of economic fields. Beijing has applied it to trade in goods from aircraft to bananas, services like tourism and music, infrastructure such as telecommunications, and investment, too. This means that any company or any industry anywhere can be punished for the decisions of a country's national government, or even for the choices of its voters. It is a form of collective punishment. Fourth, China generally deploys economic pain quite carefully to avoid hurting itself where possible. It targeted Norwegian salmon, for instance, rather than its oil drilling firms, on which China relies. It chose to hit Australian thermal coal, a commodity in plentiful supply from many suppliers, including domestic Chinese ones, rather than its iron ore, on which China heavily relies. Fifth, a country cannot assume it will be protected by its size or geography. Beijing has struck major powers as well as minnows, in Europe, Asia, the Pacific, North America, Oceania. Only one country has been conspicuously spared: the United States. While France and Britain were punished for hosting the Dalai Lama, the US hosted him without consequence. Beijing presumably did not want to provoke Washington because of America's size, its readiness to retaliate, and the fact that China's grand, systemic challenge to US power is a much greater priority than the urge to deter Dalai Lama visits or other lesser matters. Finally, and most importantly, China's coercion doesn't always work. Sometimes it simply meets resistance. The coal ban certainly didn't change Australian policy. Canada has not yielded to China's tactics – not yet, at least. Even tiny Palau is standing its ground, putting bigger powers like Britain and France to shame. Sometimes China's bullying backfires. The attempt to pressure Japan only made Japan more resilient.

In the eleven case studies, five countries yielded to Beijing's coercion: France, Norway, Britain, Mongolia and South Korea. Of those, three related to Dalai Lama visits, one to human rights and the fifth to defence policy. In the three cases where nations stood firm – Japan, Taiwan and Palau – China's coercion backfired against Beijing. In the case of the Philippines, it yielded to China when Duterte took office. But in its earlier resistance, the Philippines won a ruling in The Hague against Beijing's claims in the South China Sea. This was damaging to China's credibility and the legitimacy of its actions. It was now unmistakeably marked as an outlaw under the UN Convention on the Law of the Sea and a global rule-breaker. It's probably best scored as a draw or a lose-lose, as both the Philippines and China suffered some serious harm. The Canadian case was unresolved by early 2021. Finally, Beijing's attempt to punish Australia's coal trade was a failure – Canberra neither revoked its Huawei ban nor its foreign interference laws, and the damage to coal revenues was insignificant. But it might be too early to judge that a victory for Australian pluckiness. It might have had the effect of helping persuade Xi to change China's tactics of coercion and strike Australia harder at the next opportunity. To impose pain on Australia even when it hurts China. To set ambiguity aside and make Australia an example to the world.

17

CYCLOPS

Like Odysseus forcing his weeping ship's crew to leave the Land of the Lotus-eaters, dragging them out of the narcotic haze that had made them forget themselves, the Australian government met resistance when it decided to prioritise national sovereignty over profits from China. For Australia's elites, endlessly rising corporate profits and the heady privilege of a seat at the top table of imperial power proved every bit as addictive as the opiatic blue lotus did to Odysseus's crew in the tale told nearly three millennia ago.

The closest thing Australia had to that hero of ancient Greece was Malcolm Turnbull, the prime minister who led Australia's awakening to the danger of creeping CCP dominance. He had the support of his Coalition crew, but also the Labor leadership and most of the Australian people, judging by the Lowy Institute's polling. But just as some of Odysseus's crew cried and resisted, so did some of crew Australia. Notably some of its business and political elites.

The Chinese Communist Party's most important remaining Australian advocate was Paul Keating. The former Labor leader gave a spirited pro-China speech at the end of 2019. Then fell silent on the topic. Keating was the archetypal crazy-brave political warrior of his time, a fearless reformer who never took a backward step. He'd long advocated for an enlarged Chinese "strategic space" in the Asia-Pacific and urged the US to "share" its own. Of course, the strategic space that China took initially was not America's but that claimed by its immediate neighbours – the Philippines, Vietnam, Malaysia, Brunei, Indonesia, then in a wider arc Beijing advanced its claims against Japan and India. Keating was genuinely persuaded of the need to give Beijing its due as a great rising power. The former prime minister also had tasted the lotus. He had served on the international advisory board of the China Development Bank, a state-owned institution. And he'd been a much-honoured guest of Beijing for many years. Yet Beijing's behaviour finally became so ugly, so aggressive that even the fearless Keating would no longer defend it publicly. He is no longer on the board of the Chinese state bank. As tensions worsened in 2020 and into 2021, he kept his own counsel throughout. Stubborn, but not stupid.

But some leading entrepreneurs, businesspeople and state premiers struggled with the unfolding reality. Even after Australia's moment of truth arrived: when China's ambassador to Australia, Cheng Jingye, said in an interview with the *AFR*'s Andrew Tillett that China would impose trade sanctions to punish Australia for proposing an international inquiry into the global pandemic. From that moment on 26 April 2020, Australia was presented with an explicit choice between sovereignty and money. It's business as usual for Beijing to preach mutual respect and non-interference while intimidating countries to get its way. "The economic coercion looks pretty standard, comparable to what China has done in South East Asia and Europe," observed an expert on the subject, Zack Cooper of the American Enterprise Institute in Washington. What was

new, however, was that until that day in April 2020, Beijing bul-
lied Australian officials and ministers behind closed doors. Now
it was casting aside any pretence that it was following its self-
described "win-win" diplomacy. It was a zero-sum confrontation,
stark and public.

Turnbull had banned Huawei and created the foreign interference laws. Now the Morrison government had proposed an
independent, international inquiry into the cause and spread of
COVID-19. This was "dangerous", according to Cheng Jingye.
A pandemic that, at that point, had infected more than 3 million people, killed nearly a quarter of a million and plunged the
world into economic depression was tolerable, apparently. But an
inquiry? That's dangerous.

The Morrison government was much criticised for its handling of the inquiry idea. And it was, indeed, a ham-fisted
piece of diplomacy. Whereas Turnbull's government had quietly
briefed Beijing and Washington and others before announcing
Australia's Huawei ban, Morrison laid no such groundwork with
Beijing over the COVID-19 inquiry. His foreign affairs minister,
Marise Payne, simply went on ABC TV one day and announced
the proposal. The other intelligent groundwork would have been
for Canberra to make the proposal jointly with some other capitals. Instead, Payne walked onto the world stage alone. Yet while
the execution was inept, the policy itself was entirely reasonable.
Indeed, it was necessary that the world learn honestly the lessons
of the outbreak. An arms-length international inquiry would be
the best mechanism to investigate. But of course Xi's autocratic
regime cannot tolerate any independent scrutiny. Which is why
China's media are strictly censored and the internet controlled as
a matter of "life and death for the Party", as Xi has said.

So Cheng delivered the ultimatum: if you want to go ahead and make policies according to your national interests, and not ours, we will cut your income. Specifically, Cheng threatened boycotts of four Australian industries' sales to China: those of the wine, beef, tourism and education sectors. Sovereignty or money. Independence or income. Simple. What was Australia's choice?

It was the moment when Australia discovered the price it would pay for rejecting the lotus and asserting independence. It had escaped the seductive lure of the opiate but now faced the coercive danger of brute force. Or, to revert to the farmyard metaphor, the carrot had lost the power of its allure, and now the stick made its appearance.

Much as Odysseus's crew escaped from the Lotus-eaters only to sail directly, unwittingly, to the island of the Cyclops. The Cyclops was a man-mountain, living alone in his cave with his flocks of sheep and goats, a single eye in the centre of his forehead, a "giant, lawless brute", in Homer's telling, "a savage deaf to justice, blind to law". On first facing the Cyclops in his cave, the courage of Odysseus and his men is shaken. "The hearts inside us shook, terrified by his rumbling voice and monstrous hulk." The Cyclops lifted an enormous boulder and jammed it across the cave's entrance. "No twenty-two wagons, rugged and four-wheeled, could budge the boulder off the ground." The men were trapped in the Cyclops' cave. The giant proceeded to eat a couple of them.

The iron ore billionaire Andrew "Twiggy" Forrest, founder of Fortescue Metals, didn't like the turn of events. Faced with the choice of independence or income, he wanted Australia to take the money. The founder of the Russian Communist Party,

Vladimir Lenin, is credited with the saying that "the capitalists will sell us the rope with which to hang them". Updating this for contemporary Australia, the CCP might say that "the capitalists will sell us the iron ore with which we shackle them". Two days after Cheng delivered Beijing's ultimatum, Forrest became the personification of the capitalists Lenin had in mind – the capitalists Beijing hopes will prevail in Australia's debate. Forrest has the right to free speech, still upheld in Australia though long denied in the People's Republic of China. And he's entitled to his views. He's also entitled to considerable respect. He is one of Australia's most successful entrepreneurs and perhaps its most impressive philanthropist.

But on the China question, Forrest chose to campaign for a foreign authoritarian political movement. He made the case for Australia to surrender. Any inquiry into the outbreak and spread of COVID-19 should be shelved until after the US presidential election in November, he said. Why? His stated logic was that "there's a bloke in the White House who really wants to stay there and he's pushing blame as fast as he possibly can and from anywhere else but himself. I don't think this should be politically orientated." This was a clever way to discredit Morrison and the whole idea of an inquiry. This was, in fact, one of Beijing's talking points: Australia "dancing to the tune" of the US. In truth, the proposal came from Canberra, indeed from Morrison himself.

In a modified form, an international inquiry was eventually co-sponsored by China itself in a resolution adopted unanimously by all 194 member governments of the World Health Assembly, the decision-making body of the World Health Organization. The assembly decided to "initiate, at the earliest appropriate moment, and in consultation with member states, a stepwise process of impartial, independent and comprehensive evaluation, including using existing mechanisms, as appropriate, to review experience gained and lessons learnt from the WHO-coordinated international health response to COVID-19, including the effectiveness of the mechanisms at WHO's disposal". China was prepared to accept this resolution because the WHO, not Beijing, was the focus of the inquiry. And the timing, designated as "the earliest appropriate moment", was eminently postponable. Still, it demonstrated that the idea of an inquiry, even a limited one, to learn the lessons of the outbreak was not just reasonable but universally supported. It also reinforced the clumsiness of the Morrison–Payne initiative. With some deft private handling, they could have achieved the same outcome through early negotiation, without making Australia the sole target for Beijing's aggressive paranoia.

Forrest's intervention suited Beijing for another reason. He was saying that Australia's motive was political, while China's was not. This is, of course, ridiculous. The ultimate aim of every policy of the party is the further entrenchment of the party. Says who? The party itself, at its Nineteenth National Congress in 2017: "Party, government, military, civilian, and academic; east, west, north, south, the party leads everything."

But Forrest went a step further. He ambushed Australia's health minister, Greg Hunt, at a press conference in Melbourne by bringing a Chinese official, unannounced, to speak alongside him, forcing Hunt to share the podium or abandon the press conference. Forrest had every right to be there. The press conference was to announce that Forrest had used his connections in China to procure 10 million virus test kits for use in Australia for the COVID-19 pandemic. He put up the $320 million to buy them, although the Australian taxpayer is to reimburse him. Hunt had no idea that Forrest planned to bring along China's consul-general to Victoria, Zhou Long, to make a presentation of his own. The health minister stayed calm in the face of this poor etiquette, but, once again, it raised the question of Forrest's interests.

It's not just Forrest, whose Fortescue Metals Group counts China as its biggest customer, who can't tear himself away from the lotus. Another China-dependent West Australian billionaire, Kerry Stokes, chairman of Seven West Media, took a similar position that week after Beijing's ultimatum, calling for Australia to back down. So, too, did the national president of the Australia China Business Council, David Olsson, whose day job is as a lawyer advising Australian companies on entering the Chinese market. These businesspeople are deploring the confrontation as a "blame game" or "tit for tat". Which is a way of giving Beijing equal moral standing with Australia on this. You decide where the moral balance lies: one allowed a global pandemic to ravage the earth; the other wants an independent international inquiry into the pandemic. Is this a "blame game"? One threatens the other with illegal economic coercion; the other stands its ground while its prime minister declines to criticise Beijing and says China's position is "a matter for China". Is this "tit for tat"? All of which was exactly as prophesied one week earlier: "An Australian prime minister who ends up in conflict with China cannot expect any support or solidarity from the Australian business community," wrote Malcolm Turnbull in his memoir, *A Bigger Picture*. "Overwhelmingly, they're totally invested in the economic benefits of the relationship."

Forrest's public stance seemed to change over the months. He fell silent after his intervention received sharp and wide criticism.

And in February 2021 the global anti-slavery campaign funded by his Minderoo charitable foundation, Walk Free, denounced Beijing's treatment of China's Uighur Muslim minority, specifically its "forced labour and human rights abuses". But not all Australian business leaders are reflexively myopic. Innes Willox, the chief executive of the Australian Industry Group – which represents some 60,000 businesses employing about a million people – wrote in early 2021 that as the diplomatic relationship with China had worsened, "industry did its best, often in its naive way, to carry the relationship". But it was now up to the federal government to do what it could to manage the relationship while industry was powerless to intervene. "A high-level business delegation to Beijing or Shanghai would say what to pacify the Chinese leadership?" posed Willox. "What would we give up to meet China's so-called fourteen grievances? Our press freedom? Our ability to drive our economic destiny? Our democracy?" Companies, he said, should "look to other markets and opportunities. ASEAN, India, the Middle East, Latin America, the Pacific, a refocused Britain and Europe. And in time, we all hope, China once again." But, in the meantime, business had to bear the hard reality of China's coercion, and be prepared to endure it for years: "We will miss their students, tourists and the market they provide. We won't miss the abuse, our lobsters being left to die at their airports, our coal being left at ports for months at a time, their petty bureaucracy, their authoritarianism and their determination to punish."

Fiona Simson, the president of the overarching agricultural lobby group, the National Farmers' Federation, calmly committed full support to the government. The Australian government. "Australia has ideals that the government is responsible for upholding and I don't think any Australian would want them to back down on that," she said, as Beijing announced new bans on yet more of her members' exports to China in late 2020. She cited democracy, liberty and a rules-based international trading order. And she said that producers had to take the initiative to diversify: "It is a very important market for us but we need to make sure we continue to look at other markets as well and how we can diversify our offering." The farming sector produced a total output valued at $61 billion in 2019–20, and planned to reach a target of $100 billion by 2030. That target, she said, was still achievable. "For us to get to $100 billion, it is not all riding on China." As she spoke, Beijing had put in place new tariffs, bans or other restrictions on barley, beef, wine, seafood, cotton and timber, and had just added lamb. Australian officials were briefing the wheat industry to expect their product to be added to the hitlist.

Here's a puzzle: why would China, a country with a long-standing fear for its food security, block food imports from a major supplier? Even more jarring is the fact that even as Xi's regime was cutting food supplies from Australia, Xi himself announced a nationwide campaign to clamp down on food waste in China. On 11 August 2020, Xi declared that China's food waste was "shocking and distressing". He had implemented a ban on lavish official banquets in 2013 because of public anger at officials' indulgence at taxpayers' expense. But now he was taking the movement to the general population. It was quickly named the "clean plate" campaign. "Relevant departments are implementing the spirit of Jinping's important instructions, formulating and implementing more powerful measures, and pushing the whole society to advance the work of preventing

food waste," according to the party's Xinhua news wire. "Cultivate thrifty habits and foster a social environment where waste
is shameful and thriftiness is applaudable," urged the president
whom party media have christened "Papa Xi". Schools, restaurants, companies and institutions joined the effort. Sometimes
with great zeal. One school got publicity for refusing scholarships to gluttonous students. The campaign resonated widely in a
country with a history of food shortages and, at its worst, Mao's
man-made famine of the Great Leap Forward. Mao had urged
his people to limit themselves to two meals a day, and to make
one of them liquid or "soft".

In the month before Xi's announcement, average food prices
across China had risen by 13 per cent, chiefly because of a surg-
ing pork price. And the authorities warned that food supplies
could be threatened by the widespread flooding in China in
2020, as well as the "geopolitical risk" created by the COVID-
19 pandemic. "In an ideal environment, international relations
would be very good and China could freely import food from
other places," said a Beijing-based political economist, Hu
Xingdou. "But practically speaking, China may have some big
problems."

So why impose bans on food from Australia at the same
time? The fact that Xi is prepared to limit food imports from
Australia even as he asks his people to exercise food frugality is
an indicator of his determination to punish Australia. He will
inflict political and economic harm on Australia even at the
expense of his own people. There was much commentary in Australia anticipating that China would only limit imports in areas
where it would harm Australia but not China. So Australian coal
would be cut because China has easy alternatives for coal, but

iron ore would not because of a lack of alternatives in a tight global market. Yet the food import bans reveal a different reality. Xi is prepared to offend a major, longstanding food supplier and crimp supplies at home in order to assert his political dominance over Australia. This suggests a high degree of punitive political intent. The old-fashioned Australian colloquialism for such behaviour is "bastardry". This is a very one-eyed and determined Cyclops bearing down.

Fortunately, self-interested businesspeople do not get to decide national policy. There is more at stake than money. Australia has three big interests to protect in dealing with China. First and foremost is its sovereignty. If Australia buckles, "Beijing will see that it can use economic threats to change behaviour and continue to use them, if anything it may accelerate its willingness to use them against Australia," suggests Zack Cooper. Capitulation is Australia's path to vassaldom. The demands would never end. Second is social harmony. Australia has a Chinese Australian community of 1.3 million people, overwhelmingly a national asset, not a liability. It must be protected from CCP demands and nurtured as a source of Australian strength. "If we begin distrusting our own citizens," says Jason Yat-sen Li, chairman of investment group Vantage Asia and president of Chinese Australian Forum, "that will do more damage to Australian democracy than the Chinese Communist Party ever could." Third is the economy. The economy is best protected by not surrendering national sovereignty. That's a false trade-off. Once sovereignty is lost, Australia's control of its economic and commercial decision-making is soon lost too. In fact, sovereignty and the economy are complementary. Australia can only protect its economic interests by keeping a robust national independence.

This is also the best way of defending social harmony. The more control Australia cedes to Beijing, the more mischief it will wreak in demanding the loyalties of Chinese Australians. The three core interests – sovereignty, social harmony and the economy – are interlocked, and sovereignty is the greatest, the key to holding all three together for Australia's benefit.

It's Australia's great fortune that not only the government understands this, but the Opposition does too. Labor under Albanese has stood firm with the Coalition in this confrontation with Beijing. So the demand for an inquiry into the pandemic was not merely a government position. It was a national one. This bipartisanship is a critical source of national strength. So long as it continues, the Australian capitalists will not be allowed to sell out the national interest in pursuit of private interests.

There's a qualification to the quote attributed to Lenin about capitalists selling communists the rope. According to the *Oxford Dictionary of Political Quotations*, it's apocryphal. Lenin actually wrote that the capitalists would so help the communists that "they will work on the preparation of their own suicide". He couldn't have made it plainer.

18

NEW GOLD MOUNTAIN

Chinese immigrants invented a new name for Australia in the 1850s: New Gold Mountain. Hundreds of thousands of people from across the world surged to this exotic "new" land with the tantalising promise of instant riches. The gold rush had begun. California was the original Gold Mountain of the Chinese imagination; its gold rush started in 1848. When Australia's authorities decided in 1851 to stop suppressing news of gold finds, the excitement spread from the old Gold Mountain to Australia. New Gold Mountain gleamed and glinted with allure. The British government colonised the continent for one nation; the gold rush populated it with people from many. The first fleets created a penal colony; the gold rush flotillas created a boom. Convicts, soldiers and settlers set up an Anglo-Celtic settlement; the gold rush influx broadened it into a multicultural one. Chancers, dreamers and risk-takers of all trades and professions came from Europe, North America and China, tripling the population in twenty years and bringing the broad range of skills needed to build a modern industrialising country.

To the world today, Australia remains a land of promise. To China today, Australia remains a New Gold Mountain. The Chinese Communist Party sees Australia as a tremendous resource to supply the strategic needs for its rise to historic greatness.

At the same time, it sees Australia as a real threat to its strategic ambitions for hegemony. To secure its supplies and neutralise the threat, the party for many years worked by stealth, cautiously, to win influence over Australia's decision-making system. When it was caught and exposed in 2017, the CCP changed its tactics but not its strategy. Unhappy to be unmasked, it was, nonetheless, unembarrassed and undeterred. Beijing from 2020 began an open campaign to break Australia's sovereign will. When asked what he thought China's ultimate aim was in its policy towards Australia, Prime Minister Scott Morrison gave an extraordinary answer: "I think it would be dangerous for me to speculate publicly, and I don't think it would be helpful," he told me in September 2020.

It is a remarkable situation: Australia's leader will not speak openly about the intentions of its biggest trading partner, a country that has acquired Australian assets worth $218 billion, including those bought by Hong Kong investors, according to the Foreign Investment Review Board, and the greatest power in Asia. Why won't he? Presumably because he thinks China's policy towards Australia is so unpalatable that even speaking it could be disruptive to relations, dispiriting to Australians or provocative to Beijing. Or all three.

Former prime ministers, however, are not so constrained: "China's policy towards Australia since 2017 has been hostile," Kevin Rudd said in an interview in late 2020. "That is evidenced across all the instruments of Chinese policy – foreign policy, security policy, economic policy – and reflected in the fact that there have been no ministerial visits in either direction for some period of time. In half a century of bilateral relations, this is unprecedented," said Rudd, a recognised authority on China and the only Australian known to have a personal relationship with Xi Jinping.

What is China's policy end-point? China would like to silence Australia on human rights protests against Chinese domestic practices. China would want Australia to disengage, in foreign policy and naval policy terms, from the South China Sea. China would like Australia to separate itself from trilateral military collaboration with the US and Japan. China would like Australia to be a reliable trading partner with an open investment environment, and a safe destination for Chinese tourists and students. China would prefer a close collaborative relationship with Australia in the G20 on global financial and climate management.

Rudd continued: "Of course, many of these Chinese aspirations are incompatible with Australian national interests and values."

Duncan Lewis is well qualified to answer about China's intentions. "They are trying to place themselves in a position of advantage," he said in an interview shortly after retiring from ASIO in 2019. "Espionage and foreign interference is insidious. Its effects might not present for decades and by that time it's too late. You wake up one day and find decisions made in our country that are not in the interests of our country. Not only in politics but also in the community or in business. It takes over, basically, pulling the strings from offshore." Note that, although Lewis was a long-time soldier, traditional military invasion does not feature in his answer. This is conquest and control by the modern way of intelligent statecraft, without open kinetic war.

Another expert comes to the same conclusion from a very different lifetime of experience. Anson Chan, the former chief secretary of Hong Kong, occupied a position of trust unique in history. She was the last head of the Hong Kong civil service under the British, and the first under the Chinese. She served four years under each, evidence that both powers trusted her impartiality and professionalism. The career civil servant, nicknamed the "Iron Lady of Hong Kong", is now eighty. During a visit to Melbourne in 2016, pre-Dastyari and Australia's awakening, she told me:

> I don't think Australians understand the sort of country they're dealing with. Look at the way they are infiltrating, even in Australia. Australia is a very open society, so it wouldn't occur to most people the designs of the one-party state. And it wouldn't have occurred to the people of Hong Kong until we experienced it first-hand. No one should be under any illusions about the objective of the Communist Party leadership – it's long-term, systematic infiltration of social organisations, media and government. By the time China's infiltration of Australia is readily apparent, it will be too late.

Chan stepped out of retirement to support the campaign to keep Hong Kong's autonomy, as promised by Beijing under the Basic Law. As a result, once trusted by Beijing to administer Hong Kong, she is now denounced in party media as "an important pawn for anti-China forces in the West to meddle in Hong Kong affairs".

The Chinese embassy in Canberra took some of the guesswork out of the equation in November 2020 when two officials gave reporter Jonathan Kearsley the now infamous list of Beijing's fourteen demands. Kearsley had been seeking an interview with the ambassador or deputy for eighteen months; he was now called to the meeting on forty-eight hours' notice. They gave him a single sheet of paper with the typewritten list, without title or preamble. While it does read as list of "grievances", as Kearsley described it, China's foreign affairs ministry a day later said that Australia should "correct its errors". At the same time, Beijing was announcing new trade boycotts on billions of dollars' worth of Australian exports. Taking everything together, it was not a passive list of fourteen grievances, but an active set of demands.

One of the embassy staff framed the document's demands by telling Kearsley: "China is angry. If you make China the enemy, China will be the enemy." Below are the fourteen demands in full. Each is followed by a brief decoding by me:

1. foreign investment decisions, with acquisitions blocked on opaque national security grounds, in contravention of ChAFTA [China–Australia Free Trade Agreement]/since 2018, more than ten Chinese investment proposals have been blocked by Australia citing ambiguous and unfounded "national security concerns" and putting restrictions in areas like infrastructure, agriculture and animal husbandry

Decoded: Australia may not make its own decisions on which foreign investment to allow or refuse, but must accept Beijing's choices.

2. the decision banning Huawei Technologies and ZTE from the 5G network, over unfounded national security concerns, doing the bidding of the US by lobbying other countries

Decoded: Australia may not decide which telecommunications suppliers are allowed to operate its 5G network, but must accept Beijing's choices.

3. foreign interference legislation, viewed as targeting China and in the absence of any evidence

Decoded: Australia must accept any interference Beijing chooses to impose.

4. politicisation and stigmatisation of the normal exchanges and cooperation between China and Australia and creating barriers and imposing restrictions, including the revoke [sic] of visas for Chinese scholars

Decoded: Australia must cooperate with the party on the party's terms. Beijing will decide who gets Australian visas.

5. call for an international independent inquiry into the COVID-19 virus, acted as a political manipulation echoing the US attack on China

Decoded: You may not uncover what we cover up. The deaths of your citizens, and the costs to your economy, are none of your business unless we choose to make it so, on our terms.

6. the incessant wanton interference in China's Xinjiang, Hong Kong and Taiwan affairs; spearheading the crusade against China in certain multilateral forums

Decoded: We aren't proud of what we are doing within our borders, or of what we would like to do in Taiwan, so don't draw attention to it.

7. the first non-littoral country to make a statement on the South China Sea to the United Nations

Decoded: There is no such thing as territorial rights for anyone but China, no such thing as the international law of the sea, and no global commons of free navigation and overflight, so be silent.

8. siding with the US's anti-China campaign and spreading disinformation imported from the US around China's efforts of containing COVID-19

Decoded: We don't expect you to join our disinformation campaign to rewrite the history of the pandemic, but we don't want you to give credibility to America's version.

9. the latest legislation to scrutinise agreements with a foreign government targeting towards China and aiming to torpedo the Victorian participation in B&R [Belt and Road]

Decoded: We have entrenched programs to subvert Australia's sovereignty by exploiting the unwary or the unscrupulous – you have no right to interfere in our interference.

10. provided funding to anti-China think-tank for spreading untrue reports, peddling lies around Xinjiang and so-called

China infiltration aimed at manipulating public opinion against China

Decoded: We have thousands of government-affiliated think-tanks – how dare you have one?

11. the early dawn search and reckless seizure of Chinese journalists' homes and properties without any charges and giving explanations

Decoded: We repeat, you have no right to interfere with our interference in your country.

12. thinly veiled allegations against China on cyber-attacks without any evidence

Decoded: You still can't prove that it's us!

13. outrageous condemnation of the governing party of China by MPs and racist attacks against Chinese or Asian people

Decoded: We tried to buy off your MPs but it seems sterner measures are required to shut down their criticisms of the CCP. Let's start by calling them racists.

14. an unfriendly or antagonistic report on China by media, poisoning the atmosphere of bilateral relations

Decoded: Step aside and let us teach you about freedom of the press.

*

If we step back from the particulars and look at them as a collection, these fourteen points provide us with a key, a Rosetta Stone, for reading the psychology of Xi Jinping's regime. By specifying Beijing's sensitivities, they reveal the party's hopes and fears more honestly than its rhetoric does. The fourteen demands break into three sections. The first four all relate to Beijing's efforts to get its hands on Australia, overtly or covertly, to increase its degree of influence or control. China's government wants to buy or bully or break Australian sovereignty, and the list reveals the frustration that its officials feel at Australia's attempts to protect itself. The first four points constitute a demand to be given more power over Australia. The next four expose the party's sensitivity to Australian criticism for its activities outside Australia. Just as it cannot abide the least criticism at home, it cannot tolerate criticism abroad. It is fearful for its legitimacy and power at home, and insecure and self-conscious about its image abroad. The two come together when foreign governments make principled complaints about its flaws and failures. They can feed dissent at home and cost China prestige abroad. This second set of four points represents a demand that Australia exercise self-censorship over the party's actions in China and in the world at large. The remaining six points reveal the brittleness of Beijing's self-image and self-confidence. Each of the points is an objection to some sort of slight, or perceived slight, on its prestige or respectability within Australia. Together, they form a demand that Australia show more deference to Beijing.

The fourteen points violate the essential concepts of national sovereignty, international law and basic respect. It was accompanied by the threat that China would become "the enemy", delivered by a pair of diplomats who insisted that their names not be disclosed. Aware of the dishonour of their mission, they handed over the fourteen points anonymously, not to an official but to a reporter, without giving the document a title or any formal standing, so that they could later disown the whole exercise if necessary. In sum, it was a grubby, nasty attempt at thuggery against their host country.

Beijing's fourteen points of intimidation also exposed the dishonesty in the speech by China's deputy ambassador, Wang Xining just three months earlier. "China does not interfere in Australia's internal affairs. Nor do we have any intention to change Australia's political and social culture," he told the audience at the National Press Club. To meet the regime's demands, Australia would have to hand Beijing control of its foreign investment regime, telecommunications laws, anti-interference laws and visa policy; muzzle its free press, censor its members of parliament, suppress free speech, and surrender its voice to speak on world affairs; abandon its international treaties guaranteeing freedom of navigation and overflight, and stand silent when China commits human rights outrages or makes demands on the sovereign rights of other countries. The punchline to Wang's joke: "China respects Australia's sovereignty."

When the fourteen demands were delivered, the then director of China strategy at the Brookings Institution in Washington, Rush Doshi, pointed out that they were a blueprint for the sort of world that China wants to create: "The deployment of coercive economic leverage to shape [Australia's] internal behaviour is a kind of illiberal order-building. This list is a partial guide to the norms of that illiberal order." Doshi was later appointed to serve in Joe Biden's White House as China director on the National Security Council.

Xi wants Australia to be its Judas goat – a liberal democracy that surrenders its liberties in fear of China, paving the way for other free countries to yield their sovereignty and betray their people's freedoms, so that Xi Jinping can feel more secure in his Paranoid Republic of Coercion.

Obversely, the Chinese government's fourteen demands can be seen as Australia's roadmap to resistance. If these are the policies and principles that Xi finds most obstructive to his plans to assert dominance, then perhaps Australia should pursue them avidly as a central part of its project to maintain sovereignty.

19

NOT WITH A BANG

"What constitutes a weapon ... no longer has to go 'bang'," remarked the chief of the defence staff of the British Army, Sir Nick Carter, in 2018. "Our state-based competitors have become masters at exploiting the seams between peace and war ... I fear our 70-year long holiday from history may well be over." He was quite right. He was also about a generation too late. Because while a complacent Western alliance was enjoying its "holiday from history", more ambitious nations were designing and executing the next form of war – one that intelligently avoids the alarming old-fashioned "bang". Why alert the enemy while they are so busy feeling smug? As the twentieth century drew to a close, the West was relaxing after its defeat of the Soviet Union, and the big worry was whether computers would fail when the date ticked over to the Y2K.

It was just then, in 1999, that two colonels in the Chinese army imagined how those computers, with the newfangled internet, could open the way to a new type of war: "We can say with certainty that [information technology] is the most important revolution in the history of technology. Its revolutionary significance is not merely in that it is a brand-new technology itself, but more in that it is a kind of bonding agent which can lightly penetrate the layers of barriers between technologies and link various technologies which appear to be totally unrelated." This thought led them to an idea that seems to prefigure using 5G wifi technology as a weapon of war: "The new concept of weapons will cause ordinary people and military men alike to be greatly astonished at the fact that commonplace things that are close to them can also become weapons with which to engage in war. We believe that some morning people will awake to discover with surprise that quite a few gentle and kind things have begun to have offensive and lethal characteristics."

The 5G network will reach inside everyone's homes, as well as offices and hospitals and factories and universities and water systems and electricity networks, connecting everything in a system that dispenses with the previous design of core and periphery. To penetrate any part of the network is to penetrate every part. As Malcolm Turnbull liked to say in internal government discussions, "the core is no more". So a malicious intruder could, for example, burn your house down by accessing your toaster through its network connection, or kill you by running your driverless car off the road, or messing with your 5G-enabled pacemaker. These examples of "gentle and kind things" taking on lethal powers have been used commonly to illustrate one of the risks of the so-called "internet of things". And a malevolent hacker could do such things from anywhere, near or far, undetected, and "lightly penetrate the layers of barriers between technologies and link various technologies which appear to be totally unrelated".

In the year that internet access in Australia hit 22 per cent, US researchers connected a Coca-Cola vending machine to an internet cable and conceived the term "internet of things", and colonels Qiao Liang and Wang Xiangsui published their landmark book that later carried the English title *Unrestricted Warfare*. Qiao and Wang argued that while the Americans were limited by an infatuation with the latest expensive high-tech military hardware, the revolution in military affairs was not to be found in traditional weaponry but in a new concept of what a weapon might be: "As we see it, a single man-made stock-market crash, a single computer virus invasion, or a single rumor or scandal that results in a fluctuation in the enemy country's exchange rates or exposes the leaders of an enemy country on the Internet, all can be included in the ranks of new-concept weapons." Even if there is no bloodshed, it is still war: "Even if some day all the weapons have been made completely humane," they wrote, "there is no way to change the essence of war, which is one of compulsion, and therefore it cannot alter its cruel out-come, either." *Unrestricted Warfare* was published by the PLA Literature and Arts Publishing House, which indicates that this new conceptualisation of war enjoyed the support of at least some elements of the Chinese military leadership. The book has since been published in multiple editions in English. Its title is taken from a remark by one of the authors that "the first rule of unrestricted warfare is that there are no rules, with nothing forbidden".

Thirteen years later, the then top military officer in the United States, the chairman of the US Joint Chiefs of Staff, Martin Dempsey, described the military application of the internet as an "inflection point" in the history of war. It was so profound that it "eclipses the introduction of nuclear weapons, the introduction of the air domain and the airplane, and the transition from battleship to aircraft carrier". By the time of Dempsey's pronouncement in 2012, Qiao and Wang's work had been turned from concept to daily reality. The Second Bureau of the People's Liberation Army General Staff's Third Department, also known as PLA Unit 61398, was conducting all the activities that Qiao and Wang had prefigured: malicious hacking, malware, cyber-attacks and disinformation campaigns.

Around the time of Dempsey's observation, I found myself on the deck of the USS *Blue Ridge*. The *Blue Ridge* is the flagship of the US Seventh Fleet, the force that was created in Brisbane in 1943 as the US led the Allies' historic fightback against a rampant Japan. Today the Seventh Fleet is based in Japan and responsible for patrolling oceans covering almost half of the earth's surface. It's been the physical manifestation of Pax Americana in the Asia-Pacific for three-quarters of a century. It is the biggest of the forward-deployed American naval fleets, with some seventy to eighty ships and submarines, 140 aircraft and 40,000 sailors and marines. The USS *Blue Ridge* is also the "smartest" of the fleet's vessels, the brain and central nervous system of this warfighting constellation. Sophisticated command, control, communications, computers, and intelligence systems are jammed below its decks. I asked its commander how vulnerable the *Blue Ridge* was to cyber hacking. He gestured expansively with his arm, encompassing its bridge, radars and high-tech communications gear. "One successful hack and all of this is a floating pile of junk," came his reply.

Unrestricted Warfare has become a handbook for US–China hawks who believe it is a guide to Beijing's plan for asymmetric war against Washington. Later English editions carried a subtitle: *China's Master Plan to Destroy America*. American analysts have seen in the book an echo of the cunning of the ancient Chinese strategist Sun Tzu: "If one party is at war with another, and the other party does not realise it is at war, the party who knows it's at war almost always has the advantage and usually wins."

The Chinese are not alone in conceiving of asymmetric war against the United States. If your adversary has the biggest collection of military firepower on earth, a smart warrior doesn't come up with ways to confront it, drawing its fire for certain defeat. A smart warrior thinks of ways to circumvent it. Osama bin Laden didn't attack the Pentagon with guns in 2001, but with flying lessons for his men and the hijackings of civilian airliners. The 9/11 attacks provoked America into turning its own might against its own interests. Twenty years later the US is still counting the costs in blood and treasure of its poorly executed invasion of Afghanistan and its ill-conceived invasion of Iraq. Bin Laden could not have dreamed of inflicting the harm that only the US was capable of inflicting on itself.

The Russians didn't risk US intervention in their invasion of Ukraine by flying Sukhoi bombing runs against Kiev and marching infantry columns across the border. They used cyber-war to shut down parts of the Ukrainian electricity grid. On 23 December 2015, the computer systems that control Ukraine's electricity system were taken over by unseen agents. The power plant operators sat helplessly as "ghostly hands moved cursors across their computer screens, opening circuit breakers at fifty substations and shutting off electricity to about 700,000 people", reported *The Wall Street Journal*. Putin sent so-called "green men" in unmarked fatigues, former Russian soldiers or Russian soldiers on leave, to invade. Invasion? asks Putin. What invasion? In fact, Russia was the first state in history to use a cyber-attack to "soften up" an enemy in preparation for a conventional military strike. That was in the prelude to its invasion of Georgia in 2008. Four years before Martin Dempsey's remarks.

But by far Putin's greatest victory with cyberwar was his calculated interference in the 2016 US presidential election. Russia sowed confusion, mistrust and division that roils the US leadership and political system to this day. It destabilised its principal adversary more effectively than any military strike could have; where a physical attack would have unified the United States against a foreign enemy, cyberwar has turned it against itself. Notably, the Russians don't use the term "cyberwar". They call it "hybrid war", the merging of conventional and unconventional methods to subdue an enemy.

China is building aircraft carriers, but it isn't relying on them in any clash with the US. Because its inferior force would lose. Not just today. It would take China many years to match the United States in carrier-based warfare. Beijing, thinking asymmetrically, fast-tracked the development of long-range hypersonic missiles, the DF-20 and DF-21, the so-called "carrier killer" missiles. Armed with these, China doesn't need its own fleet of aircraft carriers to force America's carrier battle groups far from the Chinese coastline. US carriers would need to stand offshore at least 1000 nautical miles from China, according to US analysts, in the event of a crisis, to stay beyond China's range. That's new. The missiles do the job much more cheaply and effectively than Chinese carriers could. The US so far has no effective countermeasure. The latest version of these hypersonic missiles would force back the Seventh Fleet some 1500 nautical miles.

And, of course, China has put great effort into its offensive cyber capacity. A senior US official used a telling metaphor in 2019. The National Security Agency's cybersecurity adviser and a former White House cybersecurity coordinator, Rob Joyce, told reporters: "I kind of look at Russia as the hurricane. It comes in fast and hard." China, on the other hand, "is climate change: long, slow, pervasive". Russia strikes for particular disruptive advantage. China wants to take overall advantage of the entire system. And it's winning.

China spends much less on its military. While the United States spent US$731 billion in 2019, China – number two in the world – spent US$261 billion, according to the Stockholm International Peace Research Institute. It was the second time in nine years that US spending had risen. China's has risen annually for twenty-four years now, according to the institute, holding steady at 1.9 per cent of GDP, the same as Australia's ratio, compared to America's 3.4 per cent. The two great powers have different missions, with the United States the only truly global military power, while China's emphasis is the Indo-Pacific region. For now, Beijing isn't seeking to outmatch Washington globally, but to outsmart it in its priority region.

According to war games conducted by the US RAND Corporation, the US would lose a war where it fights China and Russia. "In our games, when we fight Russia and China," RAND analyst David Ochmanek said in March 2019, "blue gets its ass handed to it." "In other words, in RAND's wargames," summarised a reporter for the US site *Breaking Defence*, Sydney Freedberg, "the US forces – colored blue on wargame maps – suffer heavy losses in one scenario after another and still can't stop Russia or China – red – from achieving their objectives, like overrunning US allies." In the simulations, the United States is capable of defending its own territory but not others' against a Russian and Chinese attack. RAND is not a fringe group of publicity-seekers, but a think-tank often commissioned by the Pentagon for research projects.

Even without help from Moscow, China can now match America in the Asia-Pacific theatre. Michèle Flournoy was the chief Pentagon strategy expert in the Obama administration, with the title of US Undersecretary of Defense for Policy. In 2020 she described how far China had advanced its ability to suppress American power: "Ranging from persistent precision strikes on US logistics, forces, and bases to electronic, kinetic, and cyber attacks on digital connections and systems inside US battle management networks, these capabilities are designed to prevent the US from projecting military power into East Asia in order to defend its interests or allies," Flournoy wrote in the journal *Foreign Affairs*.

> As a result, in the event that conflict starts, the United States can no longer expect to quickly achieve air, space, or maritime superiority; the US military would need to fight to gain advantage, and then to keep it, in the face of continuous efforts to disrupt and degrade its battle management networks.
>
> The Chinese military has also made rapid advances in cyber- and artificial intelligence – thanks to China's massive theft of Western technology, state support for its leading technology companies, and doctrine of "civil-military fusion", which requires that any commercial or academic technological advancement with military implications be shared with the PLA ... China's theory of victory increasingly relies on "system destruction warfare" – crippling an adversary at the outset of conflict, by deploying

sophisticated electronic warfare, counterspace, and cyber-capabilities to disrupt what are known as C4ISR networks (command, control, communications, computers, intelligence, surveillance, and reconnaissance), and thereby thwarting its power projection and undermining its resolve. Among other things, this means that the United States can no longer assume that its satellites – essential for navigation, communications, early warning, targeting, and much more – would escape attack during a conflict.

The two stand-out features of China's military strategy are, first, its ability to connect capabilities, and second, its emphasis on asymmetry in defeating an enemy. Knowing the history of the CCP as a covert, guerilla revolutionary force, which successfully permeates all elements of society at home, and abroad where it can, these strategic strengths are no surprise. In the introduction to *Unrestricted Warfare*, its American publisher William Birnes describes its strategy as one of "waging a war on an adversary with methods so covert at first and seemingly so benign that the party being attacked does not realise it's being attacked". This is merely a military analogue to Beijing's political strategy.

The essential lessons for Australia today? First, this is not an argument to break the US alliance. Australia needs every asset it possesses. It has only one alliance with a great power. It would be reckless to throw this away. The alliance is a force multiplier for Australia. If Canberra were to junk it, Australia would have to spend at least twice as much, 4 per cent of GDP, to re-create the essential benefits that it now enjoys from the alliance, according to Peter Jennings of the Australian Strategic Policy Institute and former chief strategist for the defence department. Neither

Beijing nor anyone else is offering to replace the benefits of the US alliance for Australia. But it is an argument that Australia cannot rely on the United States for its security. Through long custom and wishful thinking, Australia clings to the vision of the US as its mighty and ever-dependable saviour. But today, Australia has to accept that this is an imaginary America.

One big change has been in the United States itself. Any pretence of an American security guarantee has been stripped of credibility by its erratic former president. It's not just the fact that Donald Trump routinely treated America's friends poorly that makes the United States a less reliable ally. That was a passing phase, as any presidency is. It's the fact that American alliances have become politicised. This takes them into a new realm. The standing and even the existence of US alliances became an issue in US politics at the 2016 presidential elections for the first time since World War II. The Democratic candidate staunchly defended the status quo; the Republican candidate promised a new policy of conditional support for America's alliances. Once elected, Donald Trump followed through on this. His rough handling of US allies won solid support among Republican voters, but not Democratic ones, illustrating that this has become a polarising political issue. This is not reversed simply because there is a new US president. Biden inherits this recent suspicion of the US. As the Harvard political scientist Joseph Nye has written: "Biden will still face a deeper trust problem. Many allies are asking what is happening to American democracy. How can a country that produced as strange a political leader as Trump in 2016 be trusted not to produce another in 2024 or 2028? Is American democracy in decline, making the country untrustworthy?"

Another feature of Trump was his reluctance to use military force. He campaigned to end America's agonisingly long wars in Afghanistan and Iraq and bring an exhausted military home. His defence secretary, James Mattis, resigned when Trump sought to continue this policy in Syria, prematurely in Mattis's judgment. Trump pulled US troops out of north-western Syria ten months later regardless, stepping aside so that Turkey could attack. Trump did order the flinging of some fistfuls of missiles at a Syrian air base early in his presidency. This was sporadic and ineffectual and no measure of his preparedness to use force to defend allies. In campaigning for re-election in 2020, one of his favourite refrains was "We are bringing all the troops home".

But Trump was not the first. Barack Obama was fond of saying that "I am the president who ends wars". They are part of a continuum, a Democrat then a Republican reflecting the American people's deep disillusionment with war. Joe Biden won the presidency promising to "end the forever wars in Afghanistan and the Middle East", knowing that he had the support of three-quarters of the American people to do so. Hollywood has always made it look easy. The reality is always shocking, bitter failure, dead Americans, no solutions.

The Biden administration promises to be far more supportive of American allies: "Allies are going to have pride of place in the hierarchy of priorities in a Biden administration foreign policy," Jake Sullivan said, before Biden nominated him as his national security adviser. "And yes, the rise of China is at or near the top of the list of big global challenges that we all have to be working effectively together on." Two weeks after winning the election, Biden himself said: "America is strongest when it works with its allies. That's how we truly keep America safe without engaging in needless military conflicts, and our adversaries in check and terrorists at bay." The obvious question here: which wars might be needless, and which necessary?

America is minded to confront China; it is not in a mood to enter a new war. Most Americans – 59 per cent – consider China a military threat, according to a YouGov poll in 2020. But most don't support the statement that the US should get involved in a war to defend democratic states against China in either of the two cases specifically polled – India and Taiwan, according to a 2020 YouGov poll commissioned by the Charles Koch Institute. Only 12 per cent think America should help militarily to defend India against China, and 30 per cent to defend Taiwan militarily against an invasion from the Chinese mainland. If the chances of an American intervention to protect Australia in a crisis previously resembled those of a game of two-up, they are now more like those of the roulette wheel. Would you accept those odds on the preservation of your country?

The other big change is the rise in Chinese capability and ambition. In its chosen theatre of the Asia-Pacific, China is now a peer competitor of the United States. This is new. Even if it were to directly engage China in war, there is no longer any certainty that the US would prevail.

The choice for Australia is not the one we're always being told we have to make – between America and China. It's the choice between the status quo, a wilful complacency, on the one hand. And, on the other, taking action to preserve our liberties from Chinese intrusion and American unreliability.

20

INTELLIGENCE TEST

Test your knowledge. Here's what you probably know. That the United States has the CIA to do its dirty work abroad, and the FBI does counterespionage and security at home, while the NSA does electronic spying. The whole world knows that James Bond worked for MI6. And Her Majesty has a domestic secret service, MI5, as well. Everyone knows the name of the Soviet Union's notorious secret police and foreign espionage service, the KGB, the training ground for Russian president Vladimir Putin. It lives on not only in Putin's mindset and methods but in its successor agency, the FSB. Most people have heard of the ruthlessly efficient Israeli Mossad. Australia's intelligence organisations have a much lower global profile. Most Australians have heard of the domestic spy agency, ASIO, and perhaps a few will know of the overseas one, ASIS. And some will know that Australia conducts signals intercepts and cyberwar through the ASD.

But can you name any of China's intelligence services? Or just one? Unless you're one of the handful of people who work in this area, it's likely you can't. Which is remarkable, considering that it has been more than fifteen years since Chinese diplomat Chen Yonglin defected to Australia and warned of the CCP's concerted attempts "to infiltrate Australia in a systematic way". Why have we remained so ignorant for so long? It's a testament to the party's carefulness and censorship, and it's an indictment of Australia's wilful refusal to take China seriously as anything other than a merchant. But we shouldn't feel too bad. Even former US secretary of state Mike Pompeo muddled his description of a Chinese intelligence outfit in a 2020 speech, confusing one agency with the United Front Work Department, the party organ charged with mobilising China's worldwide diaspora to advance the CCP's agenda in their host countries. Pompeo was a previous director of the CIA. It was "a telling error", in the words of Sinologist Anne-Marie Brady.

For the last few years ASIO has told us that spying and hacking in Australia is so rife that it's "overwhelming" the agency's resources, and we know that this hostile activity is mainly from China. The federal government even introduced new laws in 2018 to try to limit Chinese spying and interference. But we can't name the agencies doing it. Is it because they are so small and insignificant? Today, China has more people engaged in its spying effort than any other country, according to the 2019 book *Chinese Communist Espionage: An Intelligence Primer* by Americans Peter Mattis and Matthew Brazil. That makes sense; it has more people than any other country. So how can we be so blind to such a big enterprise? Brady suggests a couple of reasons in a 2020 essay in *Australian Foreign Affairs*. One is what she calls "decades of post–Cold War complacency, arrogance about the superiority of liberal democracies over communist systems". Another is a post-9/11 preoccupation with terrorism among Western intelligence systems, including Australia's. A third is public sector cutbacks. But there are other reasons, too. Penetrating the veil of the Chinese language is hard. The West has lacked the interest to make the effort. Another reason: popular culture hasn't created, or been allowed to create, a Chinese James Bond. Yet. The hero of the hyper-nationalist *Wolf Warrior* movies is in the army, not the intelligence services.

Finally, a deep-seated reason is that we haven't wanted to know. In an interview, Brady recalled when Chen Yonglin defected and issued his warning. "When Chen said there were all these Chinese spies in Australia, everyone in Australia said, 'Yeah, right,'" Brady told me. "It turns out he was right." But even now, as Australia has started to wake to the risks, "Australia doesn't yet have the critical mass in the police and other agencies to deal with the problem", she said. Australia has long been enjoying the economic benefits of a relationship it didn't want to scrutinise too carefully. Brady's essay will make uncomfortable reading for some politicians, academics, businesspeople and officials who've been warmly hosted by Chinese organisations they've not understood or failed to probe.

In her essay "Party Faithful", Brady offers a basic rundown of China's main intelligence agencies. Here's what you likely don't know. First is the Ministry of State Security, the MSS, which translates into Chinese as *Guoanbu*. It's modelled along the lines of the KGB. Brady describes it as a "full-spectrum intelligence agency", spying inside China and globally. Its public face is a think-tank, the China Institutes of Contemporary International Relations. Some Western academics and other foreign visitors to China will recognise its name – it has served as a valued host for trips to the country for many years. One of the jobs of the MSS is to spy on foreigners in China. It also directs a network of spies in countries around the world.

It's thought that it was MSS operatives who kidnapped people from Australia to take them to China in secret and illegal "rendition operations" over the last decade or more. China's agents have been conducting these kidnappings for years in many countries. At first, Australian officials refused to believe that it was happening in Australia. These operations seem to have been targeting ethnic Chinese, often Australian citizens. Now, Australian officials privately recognise that it was going on under their noses. "Among US allies, Australia seems to have borne the brunt of China's efforts," wrote the US investigative journalist Zach Dorfman in a 2018 report for *Foreign Policy*, titled "The Disappeared". "The number of suspected kidnappings in that country is approaching double digits and includes multiple cases where individuals were beaten or drugged and then dragged onto a boat destined for China, according to former senior US intelligence officials. In other instances, Chinese operatives detained individuals in Australia and used threats to coerce them into leaving the country voluntarily, says one former Australian intelligence official. That official places the number of people coerced into returning to China at 'significantly' higher than ten."

The defector Chen Yonglin said in 2005 that he had heard discussions in the Sydney consulate about two kidnappings conducted in Australia and one in New Zealand, and he named two of the victims. Some such renditions are of people wanted in China for corruption, often an explanation for political purges. Beijing says it has repatriated some 3000 people from a range of countries since 2014 under its Skynet and Fox Hunt campaigns. Other victims in Australia are people who have been critical of the party. Beijing would call them criminals or troublemakers. Australia would call them citizens. Families and friends have generally been reluctant to report such cases to Australian authorities for fear of even more drastic consequences.

The MSS has a division explicitly tasked with monitoring Chinese students and Chinese academics abroad. It's called the External Security and Anti-Reconnaissance Division. It also has an Imaging Intelligence Division to do hacking, and an Enterprises Division to manage the ministry's many front companies.

Next is the Ministry of Public Security, whose Chinese acronym is *Gonganbu*. It monitors dissent in China – including in Hong Kong, as Beijing imposes its new "national security" law. The MPS also operates the hundreds of millions of surveillance cameras throughout China. Ever checked into a Chinese hotel and wondered why your passport and visa status are being checked so carefully? It's because the MPS collects the information to monitor your location and that of all foreigners in China.

Politicians in Australia and elsewhere will recognise the name of the Chinese Communist Party's International Liaison Department. Because it has hosted just about any politician who has visited China. Brady writes that the ILD is "tasked with gathering intelligence on foreign politicians and political parties, and developing asset relations with them".

The military is another essential player. The People's Liberation Army has two key sections dedicated to intelligence. First, its overseas spy agency, the Joint Staff Department Intelligence Bureau. Its job is to support decisions on warfare. The JSD Intelligence Bureau also sends its people abroad as undercover operatives in companies, universities and other outfits. It has its own front organisation for welcoming foreign military officials, the China Institute for International Strategic Studies. It also operates the PLA Institute of International Relations. The second key PLA agency, the Strategic Support Force, carries out global cyberwar. It also operates political interference abroad, siphons off military and commercial secrets, and conducts psychological and political war overseas. Apparently, it's quite good at it. *The Washington Post* summarised the consensus of US agencies last year as "China's eating our lunch in cyberspace".

Within the PLA there is also a paramilitary force, the People's Armed Police, or PAP, mostly responsible for controlling social unrest and protests. Estimated to have over 1.1 million personnel, it is separate to the regular police force. If you've ever visited Tiananmen Square, you'll have seen PAP officers on duty, looking out for any hint of protest or disturbance. They're equipped with, among other things, fire-smothering blankets and extinguishers for Tibetan monks attempting self-immolation. An alleged PAP force of some 4000 troopers is now based in Hong Kong in case of any escalation of protests, though Beijing denies this. The PLA and the PAP both report to the party's Central Military Commission, which today is chaired by Xi Jinping.

The PAP sometimes operates abroad in civilian garb, posing as tourists, undeclared to host governments. Remember the controversy over the Olympic torch relay as it ran through the world's cities before the 2008 Beijing Olympic Games? It was big news when the torchbearers, including in London and Paris, were heckled and jostled by protesters, mostly against China's repression in Tibet. Just weeks before the torch relay, Tibetans had demonstrated against China's occupation by rallying on the streets of Lhasa. They'd been put down forcibly. It was an emotionally charged time.

The Olympic torch was to be carried through the streets of Canberra. Pro-Tibet activists planned to demonstrate. The Australian Federal Police prepared by putting steel barricades along the torch route and deploying large numbers of police. But the Chinese authorities took measures of their own. The theme for the Beijing Olympics was "one world, one dream" and no protesters, whether in Tibet or Canberra, were going to be allowed to disturb the dream. As Reuters reported on the Canberra relay: "More than 10,000 Chinese Australians staged the biggest pro-Beijing rally of the protest-marred Olympic torch relay on Thursday, bringing a sea of red Chinese flags and drowning out Tibetan demonstrators." The torchbearers were unhindered, and police arrested two pro-Tibet activists. "Chinese six-deep lined the 16-km relay route, and hundreds of cars drove around Canberra carrying Chinese flags," Reuters continued. The Chinese Students and Scholars Association, which had marshalled the crowd, estimated it at over 20,000. Chinese government officials declared the day a great success and a rousing display of spontaneous Chinese patriotism.

It was not spontaneous, however. The CCP had mobilised the turnout to suppress any potential protests in Canberra. The Chinese Embassy had helped get sixty busloads from Melbourne alone, according to a statement by the head of the Chinese Students and Scholars Association, Zhang Rongan, a statement he later withdrew. US magazine *The Atlantic* wrote that a "feature of the torch relay that clearly foreshadowed the years to come was China's opaque deployment of its own security forces abroad. Tall, well-trained men in blue-and-white tracksuits appeared alongside torchbearers in many of the cities along the route, without public explanation by Olympic organisers. When questioned, Chinese officials insisted that the men were volunteers." In fact, they were a contingent of PAP officers deployed as a "Sacred Torch Guard Team" to supervise the relay and direct the pro-China protesters. *Time* magazine's Beijing correspondent reported in 2008: "The group formed last August and trained by running six miles daily. While their chief mission is to protect the flame, they've also cracked down on protesters. Sebastian Coe, a two-time medalist and chairman of the London Games in 2012, called them 'thugs' and said they tried to push him" during the London leg of the relay. "A torchbearer in Paris, environmental journalist Yolaine De La Bigne, told the Associated Press that the team snatched away the Tibetan flag headband she was wearing."

The "patriotic" Chinese crowd in Canberra got a little carried away in their enthusiasm. *The Sydney Morning Herald* reported:

> Alistair Paterson, 52, from Lake George outside Canberra, said he was standing with his seven-year-old daughter on Limestone Avenue with an older couple, their teenage son and two other young women when they were attacked by a group of about 50 people draped in Chinese flags. Mr Paterson said he was holding a "Free Tibet" banner and the older couple also had a pro-Tibet placard, which angered the group as it ran along the crowd side of the barrier.
>
> I got a flying kick in the leg, another bloke was hit in the head with a stick with a Chinese flag attached to it and our banners were torn down," Mr Paterson said. "When I looked around there were three or four guys who I can only assume were Chinese who wanted to fight me. This gang of thugs rolled right through us and we had kids with us. My daughter was still shaking an hour later and is very quiet even now. I don't normally get angry but I am so angry right now.

The police arrested five pro-China demonstrators.

The former Greens senator Bob Brown was there to voice support for Tibetans. "It was highly organised," he said of the pro-China crowd. "Australians will feel a little bit uncomfortable by the fact that communist China came to town and just showed it can buy anything." As a Sinologist from the Hong Kong University of Science and Technology, David Zweig, remarked, "'One World, One Dream' has turned out to be quite a nightmare."

Finally, there's the United Front Work Department, the CCP division that tries to use the Chinese diaspora to do Beijing's bidding . Brady calls it the party's "core subversion organ"; President Xi calls it one of China's "magic weapons". It has no Western equivalent. The United Front has representatives in China's embassies and overseas consulates. It has established hundreds of faux community or friendship or patriotic associations in Australia alone. Some offer support and funding for Australian politicians at all levels. One such group is the Chinese Students and Scholars Association, which rallied the pro-China demonstration during the 2008 torch relay in Canberra. It organises pro-Beijing groups across Australian university campuses, which suppress academics whose teachings are deemed unfriendly to the party's policies and views.

Under Xi, the United Front's activities abroad constitute four key categories. One is to control China's diaspora to make them serve China's foreign policy in their host countries. Another is to co-opt foreigners to aid China's policies. Third is to operate a global communications strategy to promote China's agenda. Fourth is to promote Xi's Belt and Road initiative.

Very interesting, you might think, but do China's agencies conduct assassinations abroad and stage coups in foreign lands?

According to reports in Western media, they are suspected of conducting assassinations in the US in recent years. As for coups, Anne-Marie Brady remarks: "You don't really have to when you have undermined countries from within. The whole point of the United Front is to erode any resistance so you get docile politicians who won't say 'boo' to China." She likens it to water dripping on limestone. A slow, relentless reshaping of a nation's political landscape. And if we don't know what Brady calls the "ABCs" of CCP spy agencies and instruments of influence, we lack the basic literacy to understand the party.

21

DYE AUSTRALIA RED

The *Australian New Express Daily* was set up in 2004, just one of eight Chinese-language newspapers published in Australia, produced six days a week from its offices in the affluent northern Sydney suburb of Chatswood, a favourite area for the Chinese Australian community. The *New Express* was proudly the first to print in the new simplified Chinese characters, a style of writing not much used in Hong Kong or Taiwan but favoured on the Chinese mainland. It was the Australian offshoot of a big Chinese newspaper, Guangzhou's *New Express Daily*.

And the Chinese authorities very much approved of the Australian version. How do we know? Because its owner told us so: "The Chinese government has found this newspaper very commendable because we never have any negative reporting," said the real estate billionaire Chau Chak Wing. "It doesn't deal much about politics, mainly about people's life," Chau said in 2009, in his only media interview in Australia. But an associate professor of Chinese studies at the University of Technology Sydney, Feng Chongyi, saw the paper as very political: "It was previously like the *People's Daily* [the CCP's authoritative mouthpiece]. It lifted many articles straight from the *People's Daily*. It was the main outlet Chau established to curry favour with the Chinese authorities and publish Party propaganda."

The paper was, for a time, edited by Chau's daughter, Winky Chow. And Chau could operate the business because he was an Australian citizen by then. He had also become the most generous overseas-based donor Australian politics had ever seen.

Chau also happened to be a member of Chinese People's Political Consultative Conference (CPPCC) at the local level in the Chinese province of Guangdong. Despite its name, the CPPCC isn't any kind of legislature. It's "a patriotic united front organisation of the Chinese people", according to its former chair, Jia Qinglin, who was a member of the Politburo Standing Committee, the inner sanctum of party power.

And Chau's newspapers went above and beyond their publishing responsibilities to be very helpfully patriotic. In 2008, for instance, when the Olympic torch relay was preparing to run through the streets of Canberra. A problem emerged: not enough Chinese flags to wave. So, as Deborah Snow of *The Sydney Morning Herald* reported at the time, Chau's paper in China, the Guangzhou *New Express Daily*, announced: "'As conscientious patriotic media, and to let more overseas Chinese raise the national flag to support and cheer for the motherland ... and to bless the Olympics and the torch, *New Express* decided to initiate a campaign called "support the torch relay, dye Australia red with the national flag".' It asked manufacturers to supply 1000 flags to be rushed to Sydney. A few days later the newspaper reported that the flags had arrived and that its sister publication, the *Australian New Express Daily*, was distributing hundreds of them to student groups." Very patriotic, no doubt. But in which country's cause?

Professor Feng described the *Australian New Express* coverage with the word "previously" because the paper is now defunct.

Chau shut it down in September 2019, but its website remains. What changed? Australia's parliament passed the law against foreign interference. Specifically, the law against covert interference by a sovereign state or those acting on behalf of a sovereign state. The scaling back at *New Express* and some other Chinese-language media outlets was one of several effects of the new laws. But does it matter what a few Chinese-language websites and newspapers in Australia do? The world is awash with information from every possible viewpoint and in every known language. Pro-Beijing propaganda and news are readily available at the click of a button; likewise, counterviews are just as available. Chinese Australians are perfectly capable of telling the difference and making up their own minds.

It's a public policy matter for two reasons. One is that some of the 1.3 million Chinese Australians rely on Chinese-language media as their only source of news and information. Many have poor literacy in English. The 2016 census found that 820,000 people across all language groups have little or no English. It didn't provide a breakdown by language or ethnicity, but the language most commonly spoken in Australia, after English, is Mandarin Chinese, followed by Arabic and Cantonese. The number of people who reported speaking Mandarin or Cantonese at home was 877,000. We are left to speculate how many of them speak little or no English. Community estimates range up to half. If all the Chinese-language media in Australia are skewed or censored by the party, this group would be living in a propaganda bubble created by an autocratic state opposed to free speech. This is precisely the outcome sought by the CCP. It's the reason it has made a sustained effort to become the monopoly supplier and gatekeeper of ideas and information to the Chinese-speaking community. It hasn't achieved monopoly – the Chinese religious group Falung Gong publishes *Vision Times* and *The Epoch Times* newspapers, for instance. They are the only Chinese-language newspapers in Australia that are opposed to the party's policies and worldview. But Australia's Office of National Intelligence's Open Source Centre analysed twenty months of content from fourteen online Chinese-language news sites and ten popular WeChat sites in 2020. It found that "the most popular online Australian Chinese-language news portals are pro-Beijing and have varying links to the Chinese state via the China News Service, which is controlled by the United Front Work Department", reported *The Age*'s Nick McKenzie. "Australia's most popular news WeChat account is Sydney Today, which is connected to a news website managed by several media figures with connections to United Front groups. Australia's second most popular WeChat account, ABC Media (which has no connection to the national broadcaster) is part of a Sydney-based media group run by a businessman who is also an adviser to the Hunan Provincial Committee of the Chinese People's Political Consultative Conference, a United Front-controlled political body."

Second is that the party's policy towards Australia is now antagonistic. The level of aggression and deception in Beijing's communications intensified in 2020. The advent of the so-called "Wolf Warrior" diplomats is one sign. The fact that one of them, Zhao Lijian, published a concocted image of an Australian soldier murdering an Afghan child is another. This is merely the clearest evidence yet that China's authorities are seeking to provoke and to manipulate Australia. Chinese-language media in Australia can't be considered a "normal" part of the media and information landscape for these reasons. They are heavily influenced by a hostile state that seeks a dominant position by supplying censored and skewed news and information to a part of the Australian community, many of whom are vulnerable to disinformation. To now, Australian officialdom has allowed CCP members and agents to own and operate whatever media they choose in Australia. The party has exploited a country with free speech to create a captive market and inflame social and ethnic division.

Sinologist John Fitzgerald, emeritus professor at Swinburne University of Technology, urges Australia to create more independent Chinese-language sources by stepping up ABC and SBS broadcasting in Mandarin and Cantonese, for instance. Malcolm Turnbull concurs: "There's a big issue with Chinese-language media here. They are so beholden to the Chinese Communist Party." Among the foreign-language media for major immigrant communities in Australia, the Chinese-language media are unique. Says Turnbull: "What are the major languages people speak at home? Number one is Chinese, number two is Arabic and number three is Hindi. There's lots of media in Hindi and lots of media in Arabic but there's no one entity or government controlling it. There are alternative sources of Chinese-language media but it's very important that our national broadcasters are available in multiple languages."

"I can tell you," said ASIO chief Mike Burgess, "the introduction of the FITS [Foreign Influence Transparency Scheme] and EFI [Espionage and Foreign Interference] legislation did have a chilling effect" on the activities of foreign governments and their agents. "And we know that a successful prosecution would have a further chilling effect."

Professor Feng assesses two big changes. First, "Australian society as a whole including the Chinese community is now living in a new structure created after these laws passed in 2018. It was a new framework for dealing with the Chinese authorities." And second, "following the lead of Donald Trump in the US, the whole world has reassessed its relationship with China, and Chinese communities around the world have adjusted accordingly".

The new laws have had an impact by introducing some uncertainty. Previously, hundreds of thousands of people would turn out for the annual Chinese National Day parades in Australia. "But in the last two years all these activities have gone and many of the leaders have deleted their posts and photos supporting the regime of Xi Jinping," said Feng in 2020. "Of course, some are still active, but most have decided to lie down already."

But there are many inert laws on the statute books. Without enforcement, a law is a mere moral exhortation. As one of the instigators of the new laws, John Garnaut, discovered on a sunny summer day in Melbourne. John and his wife, Tara Wilkinson, were in the city, without their kids for a bit, and spontaneously decided to eat lunch outdoors at one of the restaurants in famous Federation Square. John had left government service with the satisfaction of having seen the parliament act on his classified report into covert Chinese government interference, passing two new laws against it, and now worked as a consultant. But when they sat down at a table at Chocolate Buddha, the couple found they couldn't enjoy their lunch. Four people approached, separately, and hovered nearby, uncomfortably close. Men and women, all Asian-looking. They were conspicuous; it was not a very busy time at the restaurant. They said nothing, but would stare at John and Tara until the couple turned to look at them, and then quickly look away. One even sat at the same table, but without ordering, until the waiter asked him to move. He then sat at the nearest corner of the next table. It was unnerving, a deliberate act of intimidation.

"How are you?" John asked one woman in Mandarin. She said nothing and abruptly left. But, oddly, she returned ten minutes later wearing a different-coloured shirt. The group persisted even after John and Tara got up to leave, until Tara started to film them with her phone camera. One man was walking directly towards her until she produced the phone, at which he immediately started walking sideways, crab-style, to avoid having his face recorded.

It wasn't the only act of harassment against Garnaut and his family, but it was a notably overt one. The message was plain: you have displeased the Chinese government and we are going to punish you. We can always find you, we know where you live, we can act with impunity in the middle of Australia's biggest cities. We don't care that you worked for a prime minister. We are not afraid of Australia's authorities. It was 24 January 2019. The foreign influence laws had taken effect six weeks earlier.

Their conduct didn't mark them as professionals. But whoever tipped them off to Garnaut's whereabouts probably was. Federal agencies were vexed about how to respond. In the event, they proved useless. John and Tara took their problem to Victoria Police. The couple sat down with three plainclothes investigators from the Organised Crime Unit at a café in Little Bourke Street in August. As Tara recounted some of her experiences, one of the police officers leaned forward and interrupted: "Do you realise the people behind you are filming us?" The stalkers had helpfully provided firsthand evidence to the police.

These incidents were first reported in my Quarterly Essay *Red Flag: Waking Up to China's Challenge* in November 2019. And further publicised when the *Good Weekend* magazine published an extract from the essay. It was a revelation to most Australians that such state-sponsored harassment was being conducted systematically with impunity. From the moment John and Tara's experience was published, their harassment ceased.

Three conclusions flow. First, the FITS and EFI laws were not being enforced. Second, the federal agencies responsible for enforcing them – the Australian Federal Police and ASIO – failed to act when Garnaut brought his complaint to them. Garnaut had standing and connections and had worked with both agencies, yet they proved useless. Imagine the plight of an ordinary citizen trying to get any action. Third, sunlight achieved the effect that the new laws had failed to. In fact, sunlight or transparency is the main tool of the FITS law. Under the law, the attorney-general's department created a simple online transparency register. The FITS requires that anyone doing the work of a foreign state or political party must put their name on this public register. But that's all. There are no other requirements. It does not constrain a person or company or organisation advancing the interests of a foreign power; it just compels them to say so openly. As ASIO's Mike Burgess said in an interview: "FITS: be open in our country, be very clear that you're lobbying for a foreign government or foreign organisation and we are up for that, we are up for that challenge."

So why wasn't it being enforced? The best defence for this apparent neglect in Garnaut's case is that the law had only recently taken effect, in December 2018. And the revolving door of the Australian prime ministership had spun in between the law's passing and its taking effect. Malcolm Turnbull introduced the law, but it fell to Scott Morrison to enforce it. But if an Australian prime minister announces in parliament that "we will unleash the full force of powerful new laws and defend our values and democratic institutions", and then nothing happens, why would any foreign government take the laws seriously?

One official said that the enforcement budget was inadequate, and for the same reason ASIO has had to concede publicly that it is being "overwhelmed" by the sheer number of foreign espionage and influence activities under way against Australia. Another said that the government was in consultations to clarify details. The *FITS Act* has already been amended several times for clarity. A third said that the problems of enforcing the scheme were being "sorted out". A fourth stated that the government was too busy "chasing terrorists around the desert in Syria", an important activity but not one that excuses allowing foreign government agents to run amok in Australia. Remember that the former ASIO chief Duncan Lewis has described terrorism as a serious problem but foreign government interference as an "existential threat" to the Australian state.

Australia has many fine laws that are being flouted because of a lack of political will. As we've learnt in the last few years, major businesses and famous chefs for years have been systematically underpaying their workers and getting away with it because the Fair Work Commission wasn't enforcing the law. Misconduct by the major banks was rampant because federal agencies lack the staff and the will to investigate. Newly built apartment blocks are uninhabitable because state governments have failed to enforce their building codes. It is a characteristic of Australia today that governments, state and federal, are failing as functional entities. They have allowed vital laws to lapse through inexcusable neglect. They snap into action only when the media expose a vacuum where there is supposed to be an operational core.

The Morrison government eventually got serious. Its first meaningful enforcement was the cancellation of Huang Xiangmo's visa. He was declared persona non grata in early 2019 on character grounds. Huang was identified by ASIO as a covert agent of party influence. He had been a permanent resident, living in Sydney's Mosman in a $12.8-million mansion. Through his generous political donations to both major parties and his philanthropy, he and his property development business, Yuhu Group, established firm political connections. The one that exposed him was his sponsorship of Labor senator Sam Dastyari.

Huang had said in a 2016 interview with the party's *Global Times* that the Chinese Australian community "need to learn ... how to have a more efficient combination between political requests and political donations, and how to use the media to push our political requests". Huang gave $1.8 million to establish the Australia–China Relations Institute at the University of Technology Sydney and said he'd hand-picked former NSW premier Bob Carr to run it. Carr advertised its work as taking "an unabashedly positive and optimistic view of the Australia–China relationship". Huang gave $1 million to the Children's Medical Research Institute at Westmead and $3.5 million for an Australia–China Institute for Arts and Culture at Western Sydney University. He said his $2.7 million in political donations was not to seek favours but to support Australian democracy. Bob Carr left the Australia–China Relations Institute after the foreign interference laws were legislated and before they took effect. In December 2019 the Australian Tax Office won a court order to freeze $140 million worth of Huang's assets against his unpaid tax bill.

The next clear move to enforcement was a pair of appointments in late 2019: the new heads of ASIO, Mike Burgess, and the Australian Federal Police, Reece Kershaw. The former home affairs minister, Peter Dutton, said in an interview in late 2020 that the appointments were "crucial". "That really triggered a forward-leaning response by both agencies. Before then there had been a passive approach to the influence and interference operations of China. The appointment of these two men was for that reason." Asked how he had tasked them, Dutton said: "My riding instruction was that … the threat is real, China is very active and if they found evidence of people breaching the law they should enforce the law and arrest and prosecute, cancel visas or expel people who'd broken the law. Obviously it takes a while but the public is seeing the fruits of that direction." Dutton believes that the government's position is well supported by the electorate: "The public understands the approach to China and the threat to our country. And they do that knowing 10 per cent of the information available to the intelligence community. So their judgment is right. China's behaviour is egregious and it's building."

By the end of 2020, a number of enforcement actions were visible publicly. ASIO and the AFP had joined forces to set up a Counter Foreign Interference taskforce. Even before its formal commencement date of 1 July, the taskforce raided the home, office and car of a Labor MP in the NSW parliament's upper house, Shaoquett Moselmane in June 2020. Moselmane was not well known but he'd attracted some media attention by praising China for its handling of the COVID-19 outbreak and by calling for China to construct "a new world order". He said that he had not been questioned during or after the raids. Media reports said that it was one of Moselmane's staffers, John Zhang, who was the real target of the investigation. Zhang's home and a sunglasses business were also searched by police. When Zhang appealed in the High Court against the constitutional validity of the search warrants, the AFP said that he was suspected of advancing the interests of the Chinese state in league with key apparatus of the party, "including the Ministry of State Security and the United Front Work Department". Zhang, an Australian citizen, first won media attention in September 2019 with the news that he'd completed a CCP propaganda course in 2013.

It later emerged that ASIO conducted a much quieter operation on the same day that Moselmane and Zhang were raided. The agency conducted an entry and search operation that same day against four Chinese journalists. It was only made public when the party-owned *Global Times* revealed the raids on the four journalists nearly three months afterwards, shortly after reporters Bill Birtles and Mike Smith had been harassed out of China. The *Global Times* said the raids on the Chinese journalists were unjustified and unexplained, and exposed Australia's hypocritical attitude to freedom of the press. Ministry of Foreign Affairs spokesman and "Wolf Warrior" diplomat Zhao Lijian said that the searches were "barbaric". When I asked ASIO's chief, Mike Burgess, why they'd been searched and questioned, he obversely replied: "We don't interview journalists for their journalism. If we did we'd be stupidly busy. We only interview journalists for intelligence purposes and if we think they are doing things counter to our ability to protect Australia and Australians from [any] threat to security."

The Australian media later reported that the questioning of the four Chinese journalists, all working for party-owned outlets, was related to the Zhang investigation. The four journalists, plus Zhang and Moselmane, had communicated through a WhatsApp group. The reporters were not suspected of being spies but of operating at the direction of Chinese intelligence services.

One of the Chinese journalists, Yang Jingzhong, who was the Sydney bureau chief for the party's Xinhua News Agency, said Australian authorities raided his home at 6.30 a.m. on 26 June and conducted a seven-hour search, confiscating a number of electronic devices and documents. "I was shocked, but I quickly calmed down because I knew I had not violated any laws. However, my daughter had never experienced such a scene and was very frightened," said Yang. The four quietly returned to China voluntarily soon afterwards.

Birtles and Smith were barred from leaving China during their harassment, as was a former Beijing correspondent for the ABC, Matthew Carney, while Beijing investigated his daughter's apparent visa violation.

In between the ASIO raids on the four Chinese reporters and Beijing's intimidation of Birtles and Smith, Chinese authorities secretly detained Australian CGTN business journalist Cheng Lei on unspecified "national security" grounds. She wasn't formally charged until February 2021. Beijing's moves against these Australian reporters is part of a much larger campaign to quash foreign media reporting in China. Nineteen foreign correspondents from a wide range of countries were forced out of China in the year before Birtles and Smith escaped. And in December 2020 an assistant reporter with Bloomberg News, Haze Fan, was detained on unspecified "national security" grounds. Fan is a Chinese citizen who was working for the US news outlet.

Around the same time as ASIO was knocking on the front doors of the four Chinese journos, two Chinese academics living in Australia had their visas cancelled on unspecified "security" grounds. Chen Hong, quite a well-known researcher and teacher of Australian culture and literature at East China Normal University in Shanghai, was an interpreter for Bob Hawke during a prime ministerial visit to China. As Chen returned to China, he said the visa cancellation was "incredulously stunning". "I have a deep fondness of Australia as a country, a society and a culture. I have done nothing and will do nothing to act as a risk to Australia's security." The second Chinese academic to have his visa cancelled was Li Jianjun, also a specialist in Australian affairs. In the same wave, a Melbourne businessman and prominent Liberal donor had his visa cancelled on security grounds. Huifeng "Haha" Liu had developed relationships with the Morrison government's assistant treasurer, Michael Sukkar, and backbench federal Liberal MP Glady Liu, the ABC reported. When the businessman appealed to the Federal Court against his deportation order, ASIO told the court that he "had engaged, and was at risk of engaging, in activities which constituted 'acts of foreign interference'". ASIO found that the former PLA soldier had lied about the extent of his relationships with Chinese government officials, whereas Liu blamed translation errors. The case was set to be tried in 2021.

In November 2020, the Counter Foreign Interference taskforce laid the first police charges under Turnbull's foreign interference laws. Police arrested a Melbourne businessman, Liberal Party member and former Victorian Liberal party candidate, Di Sanh

Duong, charging him with preparing an act of foreign interference. With interests in building materials, TV sales and gravestones, "Sunny" Duong was president of the Oceania Federation of Chinese Organisations and deputy chairman of the Museum of Chinese Australian History in Melbourne. He was reportedly suspected of a relationship with a foreign intelligence service.

The attorney-general's department, after a near-comical beginning, issued its first serious transparency notices to ask suspected agents of foreign influence why they hadn't put their names on the Transparency Register. The first notice was sent in 2019 to Andrew Cooper, an organiser for a right-wing political outfit who'd invited Tony Abbott to speak at the Conservative Political Action Conference in Sydney. The conference was held in conjunction with the American Conservative Union. The former prime minister wasn't sent a transparency notice, but he was sent a letter advising him of his obligations to disclose any activities that might put him in the thrall of a foreign power. These notifications may well have been issued in all sincerity, as conspicuous acts of punctiliousness and racial neutrality. But it was hard to argue that Abbott was acting covertly. He was the headline act for a widely promoted event. And speaking at a public conference was not a covert act. Abbott is known for many things; subtlety is not among them. He rejected the approach: "Any suggestion that I was a foreign influencer is absurd," he wrote back. But Labor's Kristina Keneally joined the fun regardless: "The FITS law must be applied equally. It can't exempt groups just because you like them. It applies to all potential foreign interference, full stop."

When the department eventually got to dealing with state-sponsored interference in August 2020, it sent a transparency notice to Sydney University over its Confucius Institute. Thirteen Australian universities host these institutes, which are part of a worldwide network established by Hanban, an affiliate of China's Ministry of Education. They teach Chinese culture and language but with CCP characteristics, shaping opinion and extending censorship in accordance with the party's worldview. They've come under increasing scrutiny since 2014 when over 100 academics at the University of Chicago signed a letter challenging the political neutrality of the Confucius Institute on that university's campus. Of the thirteen Australian universities that host Confucius Institutes, four turn out to have given Beijing explicit power to control "teaching quality". This is a surrender of academic freedom in return for foreign government funding.

Australia's ready embrace of these language and culture institutions, funded by the Chinese authorities, is another case of Australia thinking itself close to China when in fact it's been simply uncomprehending. The NSW education department showed a little more vigilance than the universities when it commissioned an independent review of a related program for high schools, the Confucius Classroom agreements. The NSW government's review found that "this arrangement places Chinese government appointees inside a NSW government department", and thus that the program had "appointees of a one-party state that exercises censorship in its own country working in a government department in a democratic system". The NSW government shut down the scheme. It intends to continue the Chinese learning programs but fund them itself.

There have been only three transparency notices issued under Section 46 of the *FITS Act* in the first two years of the register's existence: one to Andrew Cooper, one to Sydney University over its Confucius Institute, and one in 2020 to an undisclosed recipient, which informed sources say was a Chinese company. And yet few of the known organs of the United Front have listed themselves on the Transparency Register. And by the end of 2020, the United Front's marquee organisation – the Australian Council for the Promotion of Peaceful Reunification of China – had not listed itself. According to Professor Feng, the organisation "is explicit that its headquarters are in Beijing and whoever is president is a leader in the Chinese community and enjoys the highest status". Past presidents include Huang Xiangmo. "If they don't register, the others won't register. To deal with the thief, you have to deal with the chief." A former analyst at the Australian Strategic Policy Institute in Canberra, Alex Joske, who specialises in studying China's United Front and other infiltration, says that "you can pull up massive lists of United Front affiliated groups, easily 500 of them" from Chinese-language databases, and over 100 under the Council for the Peaceful Reunification umbrella alone. Some are small and inactive, he says, but many are intact and functioning.

Australia's former attorney-general, Christian Porter, has defended the slowness of the enforcement of the FITS law. Each transparency notice is a test case, he said, as his department issues them to each new category of suspected non-compliance, working through Confucius Institutes, foreign-funded media, United Front "community" associations, and state-controlled companies, for example. "You have to imagine yourself contesting every one in the federal court against the best lawyers," he said in an interview. And when prosecutions eventually emerge under the FITS and EFI laws, "It will be huge – you want to make sure that they're successful." But Alex Joske isn't convinced. "Why have there been no front groups or CCP representatives registering? It really hasn't effectively captured the activity it was designed to. I think there's a lack of resourcing and expertise. I think the enforcement taskforce is not very big and I think they lack linguists and China specialists. I think that's probably why their first big case involved Tony Abbott – there's a culture in government of not going after China-related issues."

Intelligence officials working with the taskforce rejected Joske's criticism: "The taskforce is well resourced in terms of expertise and experience," said one. "It's also important to understand it was deliberately designed so it does not duplicate capabilities that already exist in the AFP or ASIO or elsewhere in the intelligence community." Mike Burgess said that a prosecution under the new laws would "help harden our country" and it would "give a legal basis to our friends to what they can't do in our country which, again, in a democracy is a useful thing – they can never complain they weren't told". But, he said, it would not be "a silver bullet and the government knows that".

The never-ending pursuit of power, the relentlessly expanding influence and the paranoid nature of the Chinese Communist Party means that it will continue to press outwards unless and until it meets resistance. At home and abroad, it imposes one control after another until it is satisfied that it has total control. It is an ideology of authoritarianism animated by a psychology of totalitarianism. For all his satisfaction with progress to date, Burgess doesn't think that the party and its various arms and agents are abandoning their aims: "We've seen foreign countries and espionage services change in response to the legislation. They've modified what they're doing. But that does not mean

they have stopped trying to conduct espionage or foreign interference – we have made it harder for them but they will keep
trying new tricks."

22

CAN WE ENDURE?

If Xi Jinping is serious in telling his party to prepare for an ideological struggle lasting "dozens of generations", the rest of us had better be prepared for a long struggle too. The head of the ANU's National Security College, Rory Medcalf, says: "We cannot take for granted that Australia's liberal democratic system will endure the challenges China and the world throw at us. Australians don't always realise that ours is a great global experiment of a developed, federated and multicultural democracy in the world's most strategically contested region. Our holiday from history is over." Can Australia last the distance?

"The relationship with China has changed," Prime Minister Scott Morrison said in late 2020. But "I don't think Australia has changed over the last ten years. There have been a lot of changes in China over that time. Australia has maintained its positions, but those positions were not as pressed as they are today. This is not the China that John Howard was dealing with." This is true and false. It's true that Australia's essence as a status quo power is constant. It's an exceptionally lucky country and wants nothing more than to enjoy its stability, liberties and prosperity as it sprawls across the continent that it has to itself. Australia has no designs on any other country's territory, bears no historical grudges against its neighbours. China is the revisionist country seeking to reorder the world. It's false that Australia hasn't changed, however.

Reluctantly, Australia has roused itself from the narcotic stupor induced by addictively large amounts of Chinese money. In mid-2018 I asked the secretary of one of Canberra's flagship departments of state whether Australia was going to ban Huawei. We should, replied the mandarin, but I don't think we will. Why not? "I don't think we have the political will. I don't think we're prepared to pay the economic price." But Australia did find the will. It has begun extracting itself from Beijing's fifteen-year-long campaign to buy Australia's quiescence while it subverted Australia's sovereignty. This program to control the country was a formal decision of the Chinese Communist Party's leadership in 2005, as confirmed by defector Chen Yonglin. Through trade, investment, political donations and the promise of a place of favour at the high table of the new empire, Beijing bought and beguiled a continent to the very brink of political and economic submission. But the people, the intelligence agencies, the media, the politicians, then the industrialists and finally even the vice-chancellors started to confront the reality that Xi Jinping's "China Dream" would be Australia's nightmare. As Sun Yat-sen, the leader of the Chinese revolution that overthrew the last emperor, said: "Live in a stupor and die in a dream."

Xi told his party in 2012 after becoming its leader that he was pursuing "dominance" for China. Beijing's idea of dominance turns out to be incompatible with Australia's sovereignty. Australia took China's money gladly, but never took China's strategy seriously until it was hit in the face with it. Sam Dastyari provided the accidental alert to the party's advancing program of subversion through corruption. This overreach confirmed that Xi's plan for domination extends well beyond the South China Sea.

When Australia roused itself, China exposed itself. Xi's regime put aside the pretence of polite diplomacy and mutual respect and set out to break Australia's sovereign will. When two of its embassy officials handed Beijing's fourteen demands to reporter Jonathan Kearsley, with the accompaniment of over $50 billion in trade embargoes, the party's true face was clearly revealed. It was the face of raw power, red in tooth and claw. And when Xi's China became rampant, Donald Trump's America was absent. Australia had long been told that it had to choose between Chinese-funded prosperity and American-sponsored security. In the event, Canberra was abruptly confronted with a different reality: it could rely on neither. The US alliance remained but active assistance was unavailable, and US alliances everywhere became politicised. Trump did confront China but on America's account only, not as part of an alliance. Australia's embassy in Washington spent most of its energies trying not to enlist Trump's help, but to dodge his thunderbolts.

Australia was faced with a moment it had been avoiding for two and a quarter centuries. Dreading, in fact. Standing alone. Forced to feel its own pulse, its breath, to collect its senses and test its resolve against a great power. To merely maintain the status quo of its sovereign independence, Australia needed to change.

Morrison and his ministers, confronted by the onrushing Cyclops, stayed calm while they got busy throughout 2020. There was an exception: the prime minister's reaction to the confected image of an Australian soldier holding a knife to the throat of an Afghan child. It was a provocation and it worked. But he remained sanguine otherwise, even as Beijing piled trade embargo on top of trade embargo: "The relationship still exists, look at trade alone – there have never been bigger volumes. That's a bit of a proof point. When all's said and done, there's still great value in the relationship," he said in an interview in September 2020. "There can be a lot of diplomatic atmospherics but at the end of the day the relationship is still going on."

This claim seems incompatible with the headlines. But the trade statistics to the end of 2020 confirmed the point. Australia's total merchandise exports to China in 2019 were valued at $148.35 billion. Beijing imposed the full range of its trade coercion measures progressively through 2020. The effect? Total merchandise exports to China in 2020 were worth $145.05 billion, according to the Australian Bureau of Statistics. In other words, Australian merchandise sales to China were down by $3.3 billion, or 2.2 per cent. This was real yet modest. The data does not include corresponding figures for trade in services, such as tourism, which is reported later and not available at the time of writing.

So overall, at the macroeconomic level, Xi's campaign to use trade to hurt Australia was failing. Why? Chiefly because of iron ore exports. Chinese demand soared to feed its appetite for steel. Its economic stimulus plan depends on steel-intensive industries. Australia supplies most of China's iron ore; China's second supplier, Brazil, was unable to capitalise because of its own supply constraints. China has no ready alternative. "Forget the sturm und drang," wrote a commodities columnist for *Bloomberg*, David Fickling, in December 2020. "Australia's exports to China, after breaking previous records in each of the past five years, will repeat the trick again in 2021." This was the majority market view as Australia ended the year with its dollar at its highest in over two years and its economy rebounding solidly in spite of the thunderbolts flung from Beijing. The US business magazine *Forbes* ran the headline: "China's Trade Attack on Australia Is Producing Perverse Results."

At the microeconomic level, however, Beijing's trade bans were hurting. Individual companies suffered. Exporters of wine, seafood, meat and timber, for instance, lost sales and profits. But some commodity industries readily found alternative markets. Barley growers managed to divert exports to other countries and lost no export sales overall. The coal industry was able to find other buyers too. After months of avoiding Australian wheat, China abruptly made the biggest monthly purchase of Australian wheat by any one country in history. With shortages at home, Chinese firms bought a record $250 million worth in December 2020. Australia's ability to continue to make large surpluses from its trade with China must "frustrate the hell out of Xi Jinping", suggested the Australian economist Saul Eslake.

This may all change, naturally, but supported Morrison's equanimity to that point.

Did Morrison see China's threats as amounting to something like a lion dance – more dance than lion? "I don't think that's an unfair analysis. It's harder to make [that claim] now than a couple of years ago. I would be very careful to suggest that this is where we want the relationship to be – we would like it to be in a much better place and I think they would like it to be in a much better place." Australia was not for turning, Morrison emphasised: "This is us being who we are, and if that's caused offence, we can only be who we are and pursue our national interests. You have to be even clearer about your lines and hold them and try to build from there."

Research by two Australian think-tanks supports the view that Beijing's coercive trade tactics are more about theatrics than substantial harm at the macroeconomic level. And, of course, theatrics are not just performance. They are psychology and politics, too. Beijing's aim, remember, is to have a political effect. A September 2020 study by the Australian Strategic Policy Institute of 152 cases of Chinese government coercion worldwide over the previous ten years found that China's threats to impose trade sanctions would often not be implemented, or implemented in a fleeting or haphazard way. One main reason was obvious: that cutting trade damages the countries on both sides of the deal. A study a month later by the Australia–China Relations Institute said: "Drawing on the benefit of hindsight, several cases of alleged PRC economic coercion between 2017–2019 [against Australia] turned out to be more bark than bite. It remains too early to tell how much more serious the impact of the latest developments around coal and cotton will be." These two think-tanks have different predispositions to the CCP – with ASPI more sceptical and ACRI more enthusiastic – yet both came to a similar conclusion on this point.

Historically, China's theatrics have borne limited relationship to the underlying stakes. As we've seen, Lord Macartney's 1792 trade mission to Beijing supposedly failed because he refused to kowtow to the emperor, but the Dutch mission shortly afterwards did perform the kowtow yet failed just as miserably to win any trade concession. Similarly, the last British governor of Hong Kong, Chris Patten, found himself subject to insults and noisy threats from the party whenever he expressed a view contrary to Beijing's, but the attacks would suddenly stop when there was something the party wanted from him. "There does not really seem to be any relationship between good political conduct in China's eyes and trade performance," Patten concluded. Australia's confrontation with China is now applying a new test to that observation.

Malcolm Turnbull, the prime minister who first acted to assert Australia's sovereignty against the will of the rampant Xi, says that China's goal is "to make China great again in this region, to be the hegemon, the unrivalled leading power to which other countries will defer. That's clearly its objective." Kevin Rudd, the only Australian with a personal relationship with Xi, simply says that China's policy towards Australia since 2017 has been "hostile". For the first time in half a century of bilateral relations.

Australia has made some serious changes. History demands that it make greater changes yet if it hopes to preserve its sovereignty. First is a quick summary of Australia's most important changes so far, followed by the critical actions that still remain.

The threshold step was Malcolm Turnbull's decision to brace the country for potential trouble. He didn't pretend that all was well as he announced that Australia had "arrived at the beginning of a long program of strengthening our democratic resilience". At the same time, he spoke of the value of the Chinese Australian community. Turnbull alerted Australia rhetorically, and began protecting it legislatively. He put former ASIO chief David Irvine on the board of the Foreign Investment Review Board and upgraded the Critical Infrastructure Centre. As we've seen, Turnbull's government created the foreign interference laws, banned Huawei and ZTE from Australia's 5G network, and moved to ban political donations from foreigners. Critically, the Labor Opposition under Bill Shorten stood with the government on every substantive decision.

Next came Morrison. He, too, tried to prepare the country for hard times ahead: "We have not seen the conflation of global economic and strategic uncertainty now being experienced here in Australia in our region since the existential threat we faced when the global and regional order collapsed in the 1930s and 1940s." When COVID-19 arrived via China, Morrison praised the Chinese Australian community for its responsible behaviour as "model citizens". His government found the political will to start enforcing the foreign interference laws. He allocated the money and personnel to make it happen. A senior official said that there were about 500 known or suspected cases of foreign interference and espionage in Australia in late 2020. The official emphasised the qualifiers "known or suspected". It was possible, in other words, that there were undetected cases, including operations not only from the CCP but also from other countries. Asked for an assessment of ASIO's progress against such a caseload, Mike Burgess said:

> We have a list of what we know about, and we're shrinking that list. We're shrinking that list through those activities – visa cancellations or interviews, that disrupts and reduces harm. In February 2020 I gave a speech where I warned any nation conducting espionage and foreign interference in this country that ASIO and its partners will hunt you down and deal with your activities. Obviously, I cannot go into details but I can confirm that we have made impressive progress. Of course, that does not mean the threats have ended. Foreign intelligence services will still try to steal our secrets and undermine our sovereignty, and they are likely to respond to our successes by using more sophisticated tradecraft and technology in the future.

In his annual public security update, Burgess said that ASIO had dealt with more than thirty cases of foreign interference in 2020, from all countries, while not providing any further detail.

Morrison toughened the foreign investment laws. He declared the Pacific "step-up" policy, offering long-overdue attention and support to Papua New Guinea and the microstates of the Pacific to deflect some of China's advances in the region. His government finally committed to building a strategic oil reserve for Australia. It also created the Critical Minerals Facilitation Office to bring more Australian rare earths into the world supply, helping to break China's near monopoly on elements critical to everything from mobile phones to missile guidance systems. Morrison devised the Foreign Relations Bill, passed by parliament, which prevents states, local governments, universities and others from making deals with Beijing that undercut national policy. Its most conspicuous target was Victoria's Belt and Road agreement. Morrison's government also appointed former chief justice Robert French to draw up a charter of academic freedom for universities. This was to guard against the creeping pressures cowing academics into observing the Chinese Communist Party's definition of allowed speech and inquiry. When only nine out of the nation's forty-two universities had fully embraced the charter by the end of 2020, then education minister Dan Tehan said he was prepared to make signing it a condition of federal funding, which amounts to $14 billion a year.

Morrison's government tore up the three-year-old defence white paper it had inherited and announced a defence strategy update. "The world has changed more quickly than we assessed in 2016," said then defence minister Linda Reynolds. Although it did not increase funding for defence, it did announce the urgent acquisition of long-range missiles. The government also put new effort into its research and development work on hypersonic missiles and a new underwater detection system, among other new technologies. Once again the Labor Opposition, this time led by Anthony Albanese, gave vital bipartisan support for these decisions.

Both Turnbull and Morrison put new energy into improving relationships with other countries concerned about China. Turnbull began with his speech to the Shangri-la Dialogue in Singapore in 2017, calling for like-minded countries to come together to defend the rule of law. The movement reached a threshold in October 2020 when India invited Australia to join its annual Malabar naval exercises. This put Australia's defence forces together with those of the US, Japan and India to create a military manifestation of the "Quad", the Quadrilateral Security Dialogue group of four Indo-Pacific democracies brought closer by China's aggressive tactics. The four hadn't conducted combat manoeuvres jointly for thirteen years.

The Quad graduated to a top-level coalition in March 2021 when US President Joe Biden convened the first summit of its leaders. Their communiqué did not mention China, but it did not really need to. It was as clear as daylight. Biden, Morrison, Japan's Yoshihide Suga and India's Narendra Modi pledged themselves committed to "a shared vision for the free and open Indo-Pacific. We strive for a region that is free, open, inclusive, healthy, anchored by democratic values, and unconstrained by coercion."

It was a clear rejection of the Chinese government's autocratic values and coercive conduct. Three years earlier, China's foreign affairs minister, Wang Yi, had dismissed the fledgling Quad as nothing more than a passing enthusiasm that would "dissipate like the foam on the sea". And a year later, Paul Keating said the Quad was "not taking off". But now the Quad, said Modi, had "come of age – it will now remain an important pillar of stability in the region". Beijing's rising aggression had brought the four leaders together in a classic move to "balance" their combined weight against China's. As the Australian Strategic Policy Institute's director, Peter Jennings, put it: "They are only there because of China. Well done, Beijing."

Was a shared concern about China the reason for this elevation of the Quad? "We discussed China but fundamentally this was not about China – it was really meant to build habits of cooperation and strengthen the ties that bind us," Kurt Campbell, the Biden administration's top Asia adviser and architect of the summit, told me. "I do want to acknowledge that the subtext of all of this, of course, is the challenge that China presents." In short, yes.

That was how Australia changed in the first three years of its awakening. But it's now a new decade, and the Cyclops is looming larger than ever.

23

BRACE

What to do? Australia needs to toughen its protections against China's domineering ways and engage confidently with it for maximum benefit for Australia's people. It needs an energetic engagement, but an armour-plated one, metaphorically speaking. Australia needs to toughen its mindset and its institutions for the hard struggle ahead. Some toughening has begun. Much more remains to be done across the full landscape of Australia's society, governance and economy. In confronting these decisions, Australia should not be tremulous, self-censoring or self-limiting, and ought not to live in fear of Beijing's displeasure. Australia often sees itself through the lens of its vulnerabilities to China, and they are real, but also needs to remember its strengths.

The critical actions that remain? First is to brace ourselves. The Chinese Communist Party is a totalitarian imperial power. We should expect that it will treat us just as it treats anyone over whom it has power. First its own people in their mainland centre, then the peoples on its peripheries of Tibet, Xinjiang and now Hong Kong. The greater its power, the more people it crushes. Its neighbouring states are feeling Beijing's contempt as it seizes their territories, and the more it can seize, the more it will take. This is a simple observation of its behaviour. Australia's challenge won't end if Xi somehow decides to restore trade. That will merely signal a change in tactics. Did China's list of fourteen grievances include any trade complaints? No, it did not. Trade embargoes are Xi's chosen pressure tactic, not the underlying problem. This is about breaking Australia's sovereign will to resist.

Second is to value ourselves and our achievements. This requires a firm mindset, a determination to proudly be ourselves, a distinctive country with our own values and views, our own potential and our own priorities, our own history and our own future, neither Chinese nor American. No country is perfect and Australia has much work to do, notably for Indigenous people. First Nations peoples should not be fated to suffer third-world conditions in a first-world country, but many still do. Yet, overall, Australia has achieved for its people the best living conditions available on planet Earth. It ranks consistently in the top two or three, with Norway and Switzerland, in the United Nations' broad measure of living standards, the Human Development Index. Australia has vaulted ahead of both its great and powerful friends of the last two centuries, Britain and the United States, in quality of life. And in the overall level of freedom for its people, too, according to Freedom House.

Many of the richest Chinese, who can command every luxury and privilege at home, nonetheless prefer to live in Australia. "If the relationship between Canberra and Beijing has seen better days, China's ultra-rich appear to be as enamoured with Australia as ever," the *South China Morning Post* reported in 2018. We are the number one choice for rich Chinese looking to migrate, ahead of the United States, Canada and Switzerland. Indeed, the country with the world's biggest outflow of rich migrants is China, and the country with the biggest inflow is Australia, according to the AfrAsia Bank *Global Wealth Migration Review* published in 2019 and again in 2020. This is a more telling indicator than any amount of nationalist chest-puffing and official propaganda. Capitalism with Australian characteristics is an incomparably better place to live than socialism with Chinese characteristics. We have achieved what people everywhere crave: the highest living standards, the greatest personal liberty, with the most stability and safety available to any people on the planet. In spite of its imperfections, there is nowhere less imperfect. This is an achievement Australians should value and be ready to fight for. There is no individual freedom for anyone in Australia unless everyone's freedom is preserved.

The Australian people seem to be ready for the confrontation. The change in sentiment towards China has been sudden and savage, as measured in the annual Lowy Institute poll of Australians' attitudes to the world. Its 2020 survey found that trust in China had fallen to its lowest level in the sixteen years of the poll's existence. In 2018 a majority – 52 per cent – expressed trust in China. Two years later that had fallen to fewer than a quarter – 23 per cent. And this was before China had moved to impose wide-ranging trade embargoes on Australian exports. For perspective, the countries Australians trust most – New Zealand, Japan, Britain – all registered levels of trust around 80 per cent. The fact that Japan is in that league is telling. Australians are judging countries by their character and their actions, not their race. And Trump's America was trusted by 51 per cent. Beijing has lost the Australian public's support for Belt and Road, too. Eight in ten people said that it was part of China's plan for regional domination. Adds the Lowy's Michael Fullilove: "Almost all Australians would like to see diversification in order to reduce our economic dependence on China, and most would support imposing travel and financial sanctions on Chinese officials associated with human rights abuses."

Has Australia fallen prey to some sort of local Sinophobic hysteria? The Pew Research Center's annual poll of fourteen developed countries' attitudes to China found in October 2020 that across the world "unfavourable opinion has soared over the past year". Pew reported: "A majority in each of the surveyed countries has an unfavourable opinion of China. And in Australia, the United Kingdom, Germany, the Netherlands, Sweden, the United States, South Korea, Spain and Canada, negative views have reached their highest points since the Center began polling on this topic more than a decade ago." Across the fourteen nations, the average percentage of people with an unfavourable view of China was 74 per cent. Australia was higher than average, at 81 per cent, but lower than Sweden's 85 per cent and Japan's 86 per cent. Xi has exposed his character to the world and the world is reacting to what it sees. Australia's people, on this evidence, are neither rabid nor romantic about China. Just realistic.

Then there are the specifics of the task to come.

SOCIETY

Australia has built a Chinese community of 1.3 million people without really understanding it or its consequences. All immigrant communities have strong ties to their home countries. Only one is penetrated by a foreign authoritarian political party with plans to coerce the host country. Australia needs to assist the many Chinese Australians who want to be full participants in the country and deter those who see it as merely a vehicle for serving Beijing's dreams of dominance. To protect and embrace the Chinese Australian community, while confronting the Chinese Communist Party. Australia's ethnic Chinese citizens and residents are the frontline and most vulnerable victims of the party's United Front effort. And they are the first line of protection for all of us, according to former ASIO chief Duncan Lewis. "We need a more prepared community," he says, "but we have a way to go yet. ASIO can't do it by itself. ASIO is very dependent on the community to be alert, but not paranoid." He says that community help has been essential in defeating terrorism in Australia. The Muslim community, in particular, has supplied invaluable warnings to the police and ASIO and has been indispensable to public safety. "The Chinese Australian community could and should be as vital in the work against foreign covert influence, including Beijing's United Front and political corruption." His successor, Mike Burgess, says:

> It is important to understand that ASIO works with – not against – diaspora communities as we seek to help and protect them. I am always at pains to distinguish between diaspora communities on the one hand and the foreign governments and their intelligence services that are conducting foreign interference on the other. I would venture that at least 99.9 per cent of the diaspora community are fine. In fact, it is the diaspora communities that are often the victims of interference. I am an immigrant myself [from England with his family when aged seven]. I understand that fondness for the country of your birth does not mean you are disloyal to Australia, and it certainly does not mean you are a security threat.

Modern Australian multiculturalism has no difficulty with the international attachments of immigrants. A Hawke government immigration minister, Robert Ray, liked to quip with various ethnic communities that while he fully expected the first-generation immigrants to cheer for the sports teams from their country of origin, their Australian-born kids should be screaming for the Aussie teams. In other words, we understand that you have ties of sentiment and bonds of kinship to other countries, and we're unconcerned. We know it takes time to put down roots in new social soil. This is a part of democratic pluralism and it's an enrichment of a society. But it cannot tolerate acts to advance a foreign political movement with hostile intentions. While the authorities seek to isolate malign agents of party influence, and then deport or prosecute them, the rest of us have a responsibility to embrace the Chinese Australian community and oppose racism.

The Chinese Australian community needs help. Andy Chen's story illustrates the way that the official divergences between political systems can divide a mother and her son. "My mother and I arrived in Australia from China on the same day three decades ago", in the post-Tiananmen wave of immigrants, says Chen, whose name I've changed to protect his identity. Today, Chen does expert policy work for the federal government; his mother has been a prominent voice in a local Chinese community and is suspected of having links to the CCP's influence activities in Australia. They haven't spoken in years.

> This divergence in the worldviews held by my mother and
> I can be traced back to the moment my parents separated.
> My father raised me by inculcating in me a strong belief
> in liberal democratic principles, and a commitment to our

adopted country. My mother, on the other hand, rode the wave of China's economic rise and prospered from business ties to China. While I distinguish a love for my culture and heritage from my views towards the party-state, my mother – like so many other first-generation migrants – fails to draw such a distinction. My family's story is but one of many stories from the "4 June 1989" generation of Chinese Australian migrants. It is a story of how when two countries [get] rich together, but later fall inexorably apart as a result of differences in values and political systems, it ruptures family ties, even between a mother and her son.

Many first-generation immigrants understandably feel a strong sense of attachment to China, but the party's successful fusion with Chinese culture and identity, both in China and here in Australia, has made it all the more difficult for many Chinese Australians to see a distinction between a criticism of the party-state and an attack on their own identity.

He points out that the CCP uses Australia's White Australia history to inveigle the Chinese Australian community into believing that the federal government's policies on China are purely motivated by a racist resentment of China's rise. "It's a narrative that many Chinese Australians subscribe to," Chen tells me. Why? "It's more comforting to interpret the government's policies and our public commentary as motivated by racism, than to confront the painful reality of the government of our ancestry committing abhorrent crimes against an ethnic minority and working against the interests of our adopted country."

So Australia must, he explains, "[reassure] Chinese Australians that we belong to and are respected in this country while continuing to discuss these complex issues". He says that it's important for Australia's national interest to keep talking about "the party's efforts to sway the loyalty of Chinese Australians. We must not self-censor for fear of offending some within the community."

The COVID-19 crisis seemed to energise racists against the community. "Asians have been called dogs, spat at and told to eat bat soup," said Griffith University historian Natalie Fong. Ghosts of the White Australia policy era appeared: "There are references to the same language and racist cartoons [of the White Australia period]. That legacy raises its head from time to time." An example of the ghosts of racism past was Senator Eric Abetz's effort in October 2020 to pose as the Aussie reincarnation of Senator Joe McCarthy. In 1950s America McCarthy was so successful at scaremongering and witch-hunting over the threat of Soviet communism that the genre is now named after him – McCarthyism is synonymous with hysterical allegations of disloyalty and insinuations of treason. During an Australian Senate committee hearing into community relations, the Liberal senator from Tasmania attempted to apply a loyalty test to three Chinese Australians who'd come to help inform the committee. He asked each if they were "unconditionally willing to condemn the Chinese Communist Party dictatorship". One of the three, Yun Jiang, responded by condemning the human rights abuses of the Chinese government, but said it was unfair to demand that Chinese Australians be asked to state their political positions publicly. Another, Osmond Chiu, a research fellow at the Per Capita think-tank, later remarked: "It felt a bit surreal. The best comparison I can think of the top of my head is it like an inquisition or show trial. I think it says a lot if Chinese Australians can't even appear before a Senate committee without their loyalty being questioned." Some in the Chinese Australian community sided with Abetz. Jimmy Cheng from the Australian Values Alliance said that if the three "have no courage or conscience, they must not be allowed to participate in politics in Australia. They will betray Australia's interests." Which displayed some of the strong feelings and divergent views within the Australian Chinese community. But Abetz's approach was a use of position and parliament to divide, not to unify. Australia's Race Discrimination Commissioner, Chin Tan, immediately stated the core principles at stake: "No Australian should have their loyalty to this country questioned or undermined because of their ethnic origin, nor should they be required to prove their loyalty. Treating people prejudicially based on race or ethnicity is contrary to Australian democratic values of equality, and to our fundamental human rights." Kevin Rudd suggests that "we need to have better resources for the full and effective implementation of Australia's racial discrimination laws. All Australians of different ethnicities should be protected to the full extent of the law and by authoritative statements on a continuing basis by the prime minister of the day. You do not challenge any individuals' Australianness as a result of ethnicity."

Happily, Abetz's is not the approach championed by his leader. Scott Morrison routinely follows this advice from Rudd – he has condemned racism and worked to unify. "I'm very enthusiastic about the patriotism of the Chinese community. The best way for immigrant communities is to encourage them to be enthusiastic about what moved them to want to move to Australia in the first place. One reason Australia has been successful as a multicultural nation is because we are quite good at blending patriotism with traditional cultures. It's important to continue to bolster a sense of civic pride and patriotism. That's the best defence. Whether it's the Chinese Australian community or the Italian Australian community or any other." In the 1980s, John Howard as opposition leader notoriously called for Asian immigration to be "slowed down a little". He has since regretted saying this. Howard is noted for his strong allergy to admitting error. Yet, in 2001, on the twenty-fifth anniversary of assuming the prime ministership, he conceded that "it was one of my mistaken contributions to the debate". This may be evidence of Howard's growth in maturity. It would be gratifying to think it is evidence of a growing Australian maturity.

The purposeful enforcement of the foreign interference laws would help. The immigrants who are here because they want to be here, living as Australians, would be freed from pressure from those who do not. As Professor Feng Chongyi puts it, "When I came to Australia in 1995, the United Front groups were much less aggressive, but now they aggressively promote this very toxic nationalistic ideology and authoritarian ideology. They force everyone in the Chinese community to take a position – you are our friend or you are our enemy." It's time for Australia to put the same question to the United Front organisers and agents who abuse Australia's democratic freedoms to covertly choke off those freedoms for others.

A review of the immigration mix is timely, too. The composition of the pre-pandemic intake of 160,000 foreigners who are accepted each year to settle in Australia is under constant, quiet review by the immigration department. China has been one of the top two source countries in recent years. Post-pandemic, the department should continue to admit large numbers of ethnic Chinese immigrants. Over Australia's history, most Chinese immigrants have proved to be first-class settlers and citizens. It was Australia's loss to expel them during the White Australia era and the country should never repeat that costly mistake.

Australia has never recovered from the economic consequences. By driving out all "coloured races", the White Australia policy expelled the greatest force for the development of the northern part of the continent. For example, while Europeans took up the land titles in tropical North Queensland granted after 1876, it was the Chinese settlers who did the arduous work of clearing the heavy tropical jungle so that it could be farmed. They pioneered the banana industry and planted sugar, as well as organising the transport and shipping to get the produce to the cities to the south. It was the Chinese community of North Queensland that provided the capital as well as the labour for regional development, as historian Henry Reynolds documented in his book *North of Capricorn*. And it was the Chinese who operated the thriving fishing industry of the Cairns region. Years after the Chinese and other "coloureds" had been driven out, it was admitted in the Queensland state parliament in 1913 that "the North would be a perfect wilderness today if it had not been for the Chinese opening it up".

The wealthy Chinese merchants in the region were respected local community leaders and important contributors to local life. It was the Chinese immigrants who drove the economy of Darwin, too. "Little or no life appeared" in the European parts of Darwin, while Chinatown was "a welter of life and activity", as a Norwegian scientist, Knut Dahl, observed from a visit in the 1890s. He described the flourishing Chinese families as a "happy" community enjoying life to the full, while the Europeans "very often" sat lonely in their houses or drinking in the public houses, "deploring the fate that had left them stranded on this barren coast".

To this day, northern Australia's underdevelopment is a national frustration, with Canberra trying to engineer activity through the Northern Australia Infrastructure Facility and various subsidies to keep the Northern Territory viable more than a century after vandalising Australia's far north by expelling its dynamic Chinese, Japanese, Pacific Islander, Malay, Filipino and other populations.

When the White Australia laws were under debate in the new national parliament, their sharpest critic, Bruce Smith, member for Parkes, described them as unnecessary, hysterical and racist. And he left this timeless diagnosis of the mainstream mindset: "Honourable members do not differentiate between acts which may be prevented by legislation, and qualities which are inherent in another people, and on that account make them such great opponents." Australia today must confront through legislation and other measures the harms exported by the Chinese Communist Party while embracing the remarkable qualities of the Chinese people. Generations of Chinese immigrants have proved to be great contributors to the full spectrum of modern Australia's success. But we have to question the immigration department's success in assessing applicants in recent years. The flourishing United Front activities in Australia are evidence that too many of its organisers and agents are finding a welcome rather than a searching scrutiny. Australia has to protect itself from further easy penetration by people hostile to our democracy. Two protective measures stand out. First is that immigration needs to involve better-qualified officials from ASIO and Australian diplomatic staff much more closely in assessing immigrants. This already occurs in some cases. The evidence is that it needs to occur in many more. While the federal government develops the skills and knowledge to winkle out the subversive from the sincere, it should also consider changing the composition in favour of Chinese immigrants from places other than mainland China (while still judging all applicants according to the same criteria). Screening must still apply, of course, but prima facie ethnic Chinese immigrants from Taiwan or Hong Kong are more likely to value Australian liberties. This is not an absolute answer, but it is a way to improve the balance of risks, at least until the government is capable of competent screening of people seeking permanent residency and citizenship.

Australia doesn't operate immigration as an act of charity, except in the refugee category. In the main it is operated as a tool of hard-headed national interest. It seeks to admit people most suited to the country's needs. Preference should not only be given to immigrants with the most suitable work skills but also those with the most compatible values. Immigrants committed to liberal democratic principles should always be given priority over those who are not.

News media and community communication is a key area in need of attention. In the 2020 budget the government allocated $23.6 million over four years for "social cohesion strategic communications". According to a senior official, the point is to get accurate information from the government directly to the Chinese Australian community in their own languages. This would be a good start, but no more than that. And with the advent of

COVID-19, even some of this modest sum was reallocated to government information campaigns about the pandemic. The federal government needs to revisit this and take communication with the Chinese Australian community more seriously. This is the single most important field of struggle, according to Xi, because the human mind is the ultimate strategic space that the party seeks to dominate. In a speech in August 2013 to the party cadres responsible for ideology and propaganda, Xi said that schools, the media, the internet, and people's thoughts are "*zhendi*". Which translates to "battlegrounds". "If we do not occupy the *zhendi*, other people will do so." Each individual's mind is a battleground that the party must occupy. Xi classes all thoughts as red, black or grey. Red thoughts are ones approved by the party. Black thoughts or knowledge are tainted by the West: "We must be bold enough to lay siege to black terrain and gradually implement a change of colours." Grey thoughts need to be converted to red.

The Chinese-language media, including social media, in Australia have been flooded with red thoughts, with the aim of drowning all others. Because these thoughts are in Chinese, it's a zone that's invisible to the mainstream Australian community. A report by the Australian Strategic Policy Institute in December 2020 illuminated the problem. The ASPI researchers, led by the Chinese-speaking Alex Joske, examined the twenty-four Chinese-language media outlets in Australia and "found that 17 had attended the United Front's forum for overseas Chinese media, 12 had executives who were members of United Front groups, and at least four appear to have received funding or support from the CCP. Anti-CCP media outlets such as *The Epoch Times* and *Vision Times*, which both count members of the Falun

Gong religious group among their staff, face coercion. Their advertisers are pressured by the Chinese government, and businesses distributing their papers are intimidated."

But it was the dominant Chinese-language social media forum, WeChat, that most alarmed Joske and his three colleagues: "WeChat may be driving the most substantial and harmful changes ever observed in our Chinese-language media sector. The app is particularly important to Chinese Australians and helps people stay connected to friends and family in China. It's used by as many as 3 million users in Australia for a range of purposes including instant messaging." Research by RMIT's Haiqing Yu and UTS's Wanning Sun found that it's also the most popular way for Chinese Australians to get news.

WeChat is based in mainland China and controlled by Beijing. When Scott Morrison tried to use WeChat to respond to the Chinese foreign ministry's publication of an invented image of a child-murdering Australian digger, he found himself censored. So, the Chinese government has free use of Twitter and all the other big US-based social media outlets, and total control over WeChat and all other entry points to Chinese audiences. The party can penetrate anywhere, but no one can penetrate it.

"WeChat's record of censorship, information control and surveillance, which align with Beijing's objectives, is deeply troubling," the ASPI researchers wrote.

Media outlets on WeChat face tight restrictions that facilitate CCP influence by pushing the vast majority of news accounts targeting Australian audiences to register in China. Australian-registered WeChat accounts for media can post only four times a month, while ones registered in China can post daily but are subject to even greater censorship and must be registered through a Chinese company or individual. Even Morrison's official WeChat account has been shaped by the restrictions – it's registered to an unidentified Chinese man from Fujian Province. Networks and information sharing within the app are opaque, contributing to the spread of disinformation. Messages between users, even outside of China, are monitored for content that might unsettle the CCP.

Joske and his colleagues drew the obvious contrast. The party was dominant in Australian Chinese-language media and Australia was absent. The report recommended three domestic actions and one international one. At home, that party-led media need to disclose themselves as agents of foreign influence on the Transparency Register; that the government do more to support Chinese-language media, "such as by expanding ABC and SBS offerings and establishing scholarships for Chinese-speaking journalism students"; and that it hold WeChat to the same standards of transparency, privacy and freedom of speech that Australia is asking other social media to observe. And abroad, that it work with like-minded countries to "push for an end to WeChat's unfair and illiberal settings by threatening penalties such as a ban if it refuses to meet these standards".

DEMOCRACY

Australia's democracy is a precious asset, yet it's wide open to manipulation. What is the use of all of Australia's defence force personnel and all its ships and planes if the decision-making system has already been taken over by Beijing? If a foreign power were to command the allegiance of enough key members of

Australia's federal political system, Australia's sovereignty would already be lost. Invasion becomes redundant, the ADF impotent. And Sun Tzu's famous dictum realised: "The supreme art of war is to subdue the enemy without fighting."

When the chief of the defence force, Angus Campbell, was asked to speak in 2019 about the nature of war in 2025, it was telling that he didn't mention physical combat. He devoted his entire speech to political warfare. Authoritarian states, he said, "see war in much broader terms" than democratic ones. "Its reach extends from what we would see as 'peace' right through to nuclear war. In other words, it's a constant of life. For these states, the strategic landscape requires a never-ending struggle. It's a struggle that has been maintained throughout history, and it's a struggle that's happening right now" in the grey zones of political warfare, said Campbell. The first phase of such war is conducted in information campaigns and political activity. Australian governments – federal, state and local – as well as local councils, schools, universities and community groups, could do much more to educate immigrants and the wider community alike on the value of democracy and the responsibilities of citizens.

Second are political parties. "I do worry about the issue of financing political parties," says former ASIO boss Duncan Lewis. "We need a mechanism that maintains parties free of foreign influence." Astonishingly, until 2019 it was legal for foreigners to donate to Australian political parties. The law now forbids foreign donations, but it's still only the barest beginning of fixing Australia's ramshackle political funding system. There have been multiple reports written and recommendations made. Unfortunately, we rely on politicians to make laws to fix the problems of donations to their own parties.

At a minimum, the system needs to be tightened by these steps. One, ban all cash donations; credit cards and bank transfers can be traced, cash cannot. Two, require immediate disclosure of all donations and the identity of the donors on public registers; there is no argument for allowing long reporting lags to remain. Three, impose caps to limit donations to "retail" size of maybe a few thousand dollars or so, rather than permit "wholesale"-sized donors buying outsize influence. Four, enlarge and empower the federal money-tracking agency, AUSTRAC, to enforce the laws and to monitor the sources of funds, to prevent organised crime and foreign sources penetrating the system. Five, create a national integrity commission, or "federal ICAC", to investigate corruption. This last step is now agreed in principle by the Coalition, Labor and the Greens, but they have failed to settle on the terms of such a commission. Every day they dally, they allow the CCP to make inroads by a country mile.

Third are MPs and senators. At the moment, there is no systematic scrutiny of politicians to block covert agents of foreign influence from taking seats in parliament. Without due care it can happen and has happened. A former intelligence officer for the Chinese government sat in New Zealand's parliament. He didn't disclose the salient fact that he'd worked in a Chinese spy agency for fifteen years before running for office. In Australia, Sam Dastyari was operating as a political asset for Huang Xiangmo while a sitting senator. Serious questions about a former member of the NSW parliament, Ernest Wong, were probed by the NSW ICAC in 2019.

Australia relies on chance at the moment: the chance that the media might notice a covert agent of influence; the chance that ASIO might be tipped off; the chance that, if ASIO is tipped off in time, its advice will be heeded. Lewis warned the political parties about Huang and others in personal briefings with the party leaders, but they continued to accept their money regardless. This haphazard approach must be replaced with a systemic one. All MPs and senators should be required to submit to a formal security clearance. Most Australians assume that this already occurs as a matter of course, given that non-politicians are required to get a clearance if they want to work on sensitive contracts for companies or government departments. They're shocked to learn that lawmakers require no vetting. The former foreign affairs minister Julie Bishop said: "I always found it extraordinary that I as foreign minister had no need for a security clearance, but my staff had to go through the most rigorous security clearances to ensure that I had top level [clearance] but no politician is ever subjected to that." A reporter put this to Morrison in 2019 as an idea for increasing public confidence in MPs and senators. His reply was that politicians' backgrounds were too diverse. This is an excuse, not a reason. ASIO currently screens thousands of federal public servants and, informally, some politicians too. However, Duncan Lewis has said that ASIO shouldn't vet MPs and senators for fear of being seen to be intruding into politics. He's right. Because it would make the domestic intelligence agency the gatekeeper of Australia's democracy. Yet this already happens informally and selectively. The better way is to create an independent parliamentary office to run security checks on new MPs and senators, and to do so at the candidate stage. Set up as a parliamentary agency, it would be accountable to the parliament itself. We have precedents, though in different realms of expertise. The Parliamentary Budget Office, for instance, was created in 2012 to provide expert, non-partisan costings of the political parties' budget proposals. Why did we need this? Because we'd learnt that we couldn't trust politicians to be honest about the true cost of their election promises. This problem had dogged every election campaign for decades and confused the electorate. The Parliamentary Budget Office, well regarded by all political parties, solved the problem. Other independent agencies exist within the parliament too. Sick of endless rorting of politicians' expenses, the Turnbull government established the Independent Parliamentary Expenses Authority in 2017. These new agencies have performed well, solved issues and improved Australia's democracy. We should set up an independent, non-partisan parliamentary agency along the same lines to examine the backgrounds of candidates standing for parliament. Surveyors of the history of democracy – including John Keane in his work *The Life and Death of Democracy* and Francis Fukuyama in *The Origins of Political Order* and *Political Order and Political Decay* – observe that democracies either innovate or die. It's time to innovate a little more.

Fourth is, where possible, bipartisanship. It can be very tempting for an Opposition to make trouble for a government that's struggling to cope with foreign coercion or intrusion. For instance, in Canada the conservatives have been demanding that Prime Minister Justin Trudeau impose trade sanctions on China in retaliation for Beijing's coercion of Canada. This politicises the issue, undercuts national unity and makes it easier for Beijing to manipulate Canada's political system.

Until now, Australia has been fortunate that the two main parties have been in broad agreement on the need to defeat foreign interference and coercion, and on the means for doing so. It's not been perfect – it would have been better that Labor not tolerate Huang's annexing of its NSW branch, for example. And it would have been better that Morrison not label legitimate scrutiny of new Liberal MP Gladys Liu as racist. But, by and large, the parties have cooperated. One indication: the foreign interference laws passed with bipartisan support. Another: Labor supported the government decision to ban Huawei from the 5G network. A third: when it emerged that China was imposing multiple trade embargoes on Australian products, the Opposition could have chosen to blame Morrison for mismanaging the relationship. It would have created a mighty political stink, divided the country and thrilled Xi Jinping to be able to divide and conquer so easily. But Labor, under Anthony Albanese, took the responsible course in the national interest. However, the onus to maintain bipartisanship shouldn't fall only on the Opposition. The government needs to make an effort to sustain a bipartisan front in the national interest. Indeed, the main onus is on the government. Why? The clue is in the word "government". Morrison and his ministers need to realise that they are entering a historic confrontation with a nuclear-armed great power. The Coalition has been lucky to have Labor's support to date. It needs to take bigger steps to achieve as much cooperation as possible in the national interest.

Labor's foreign affairs spokesperson, Penny Wong, has repeatedly approached the foreign affairs minister, Marise Payne, to propose a more structured bipartisanship on China. Payne has refused the offer every time. This is political vanity and partisan neurosis. Payne needs to think about the country; she should accept the offer and work with Wong. As the Labor leader in the Senate told the ABC's David Speers in late 2020: "It is good practice on these issues where you are dealing with an assertive, at times aggressive, great power – which is China – for there to be stronger engagement with the Opposition. I think that would be helpful. Regrettably that doesn't happen much, and I do recall many occasions on which Ms [Julie] Bishop – and we had a fair few ding-dong battles – but she would call me and we would talk through how we would talk through particular issues. I regret that doesn't happen now."

Labor's deputy leader, Richard Marles, has suggested taking bipartisanship on China to another level. In an interview in 2019, Marles, the shadow defence minister, proposed a new structure, perhaps called a strategic council, including relevant members from both main political parties. It would meet and attempt to construct "settled bipartisan positions" on China policy, as Marles put it, "that almost look like doctrine, so our departments can have confidence of our position not over the next three years but the next thirty years". A strategic council would not be "just some pollies in the members' dining room", he said, but something like a bipartisan cabinet. Its membership would be public, but its proceedings private. It would be properly resourced by the government, with the benefit of full briefings from the public service. "So that we can reconcile the bipolar view that exists in Australia on China – the economic opportunity that China represents, versus the security anxiety that many people feel." Marles said that while the government would have to lead in creating such a mechanism, "I've never felt the need so acutely to get some bipartisanship on this".

Is this undemocratic? Bipartisanship already operates in many areas of Australian policy. The main parties broadly agree on defence, immigration, foreign affairs and intelligence, for example. Marles is proposing a formalisation of the bipartisan approach in one particular area. It would be neither binding nor permanent. It's a good idea, but can the leadership set tribalism aside long enough to do it? As the ANU's Rory Medcalf says: "One of the difficulties we have had to come to terms with on the China issue is our inability to come to a consensus." In a two-party system, it takes two to consent.

ECONOMY

"Australia calls itself a civilized country, but its behaviour is confusing," wrote the *Global Times*, the most bellicose of Beijing's mouthpieces, in 2017. "While it is economically dependent on China, it shows little gratitude." Australian governments and businesses had long rejoiced in the simple-minded idea that trade is trade, conducted for profit and mutual advantage. But no. The Chinese Communist Party sees trade as merely one element of its all-encompassing projection of power. Beijing expects its trade to generate gratitude from its trading partners. And if it doesn't? The *Global Times* gave the answer three years later: "If Australia provokes China more, China will fight it to the end to protect its core interests. Australian education, mining and agriculture all desire improved ties with China." This unsubtle threat was being put into practice heading into 2021. In response, there are some orthodox solutions and some less orthodox ones.

The best form of insurance against such risk is the ancient principle of diversification. Before the strategic trade embargoes imposed on Australia in 2020, this old lesson had been rediscovered by some Australian businesses, which had put most of their eggs in the China basket only to find China giving the basket a sudden jolt. The milk companies A2 and Bellamy's, for instance, soared on booming Chinese demand and then were hammered when Beijing abruptly decided to restrict imports to encourage local production. By contrast, diversity saved Australia's thermal coal industry from any serious pain from Beijing's go-slow on Australian imports in early 2019. While some shipments were caught in Chinese harbours and piled up on docks as Beijing sought to discipline Canberra, most were simply diverted to other markets. But the thermal coal market is highly diversified globally; other industries will have a harder time.

Australian companies and industries have generally failed to learn from these experiences. Beijing is now forcing upon them the diversification they failed to find themselves when they had the opportunity. It's a costly lesson. The companies that escaped Beijing's sanctions in 2020–21 should not consider themselves safe from future Chinese embargoes. Even those within the supposedly immune iron ore trade. China relied on Australia for some 60 per cent of its iron ore in 2020. It bought another 20 per cent from Brazil, and dug up the rest domestically. This Australian trade was considered sanctions-proof because China could not replace the volume, quality or reliability of Australian ore. But to draw on this as any source of comfort or complacency would be another error of historic proportions by Australia.

Why? The world has two enormous sources of iron ore: Australia and Brazil. Chinese state-owned companies are about to bring a third on line. They are pouring billions into the vast Simandou iron ore deposits of West Africa's Guinea. The Simandou prospect has a troubled past but a prospective future. China's state-owned enterprises, supported by Beijing's Belt and Road billions and together with Singaporean investors and Rio

Tinto, intend to bring the ore into the world market. "Under all scenarios Simandou will be developed, with or without Rio Tinto," Rio's then boss Jean-Sebastien Jacques said in July 2020. Simandou is so big that it's sometimes called the "Pilbara killer". Australia and Brazil have some time: to get the Simandou ore to a port requires that a 700-kilometre rail track be built. Guinea's government signed a deal in November 2020 with a China-backed consortium to build the railway and a deep-water port that would start shipping ore by 2025. "We finally have hope of realising this old dream for the country," Guinea's mines minister Abdoulaye Magassouba said. In the first phase it is planned to produce 150 million tonnes of iron ore a year, adding 7 per cent to global capacity. Although the US$14 billion project could run into trouble, it would be imprudent to bet Australia's national export revenue on this. Australia has been warned. It has four years to find better ways of earning an income than rock-scraping. Within this time, Simandou could very well be shipping major quantities of iron ore and Australia will have lost its comfortable dominance and price premium. Australian national strategy should be premised on the strong possibility that its rock-based luck is on its last gasp.

For the Australian firms suffering immediately from China's strategic sanctions, the Morrison government was developing some plans to offer transitional support to the targeted companies, without actually reimbursing them for losses. Direct subsidies would likely contravene the rules of the World Trade Organization, but other mechanisms could include substantial extra government funding for trade promotion or industry marketing arrangements, and help with finding new markets. For companies and industries in deep difficulty, structural adjustment plans and support are another option. The government has no intention of fully compensating businesses because it would introduce "moral hazard", encouraging companies to take even greater risks by expecting government-guaranteed protection against loss.

A better use of government energy is diversifying the export markets where Australia sells its wares. To the Morrison government's credit, it was already deep in negotiations to widen trade opportunities with a range of countries before Beijing's sanctions. The free trade agreement with Indonesia took effect in 2020. Canberra was in free trade talks with the European Union and negotiations for a broad Asian regional free trade deal known as RCEP, the Regional Comprehensive Economic Partnership. This is led by the ten ASEAN nations and embraces China, South Korea, India, Japan, Australia, Indonesia and New Zealand. An initial RCEP agreement was signed in November 2020. If ratified, the RCEP and EU deals are highly prospective, continent-sized opportunities. Negotiations for a deal with a post-BREXIT Britain was another, smaller prospect, but launched with larger razzle dazzle courtesy of Boris Johnson: "I want a world in which we send you Marmite, you send us Vegemite. We send you Penguins and you send us, with reduced tariffs, these wonderful Arnott's Tim Tams. How long can the British people be deprived of the opportunity to have Arnott's Tim Tams at a reasonable price?" Britain levied an 8 per cent tariff on Tim Tams at the time. So the answer is, even with full tariff elimination, probably forever. Tim Tams are not cheap. Britain offers Australia a better lesson through recent history rather than through a glittering possibility in its future.

When the United Kingdom dumped Australia to join the European Common Market in 1973, it was a profound shock.

London cut Australia's longstanding preferential access to the British market and switched all its preferences to Europe instead. In Australia it was widely considered a bitter political betrayal. "In two world wars, New Zealand, Australia and Canada – with India, South Africa and other members of the then Empire – sent thousands upon thousands of troops, airmen and sailors to help save Britain from the Germans," Alexander Downer wrote in London's *Telegraph* in 2016. "Despite this sacrifice, the attitude of the Heath government in the seventies was 'So what?' ... Doug Anthony, the then deputy prime minister, was so incensed that he abandoned his lifelong support for the Queen in Australia and joined the republican movement." Downer's father, then Australia's high commissioner to London, was devastated. Australia's apple exports fell by 70 per cent, its butter exports by 90 per cent. Any Australian forty-eight years old or older lived through the consequences, whether they understood them or not.

Australia didn't just survive. It thrived. Ultimately, by forcing us to compete and survive in the wider world, Britain did Australia a favour. "Australia's abandonment by Britain was the salutary shock that this country needed," economist Oliver Hartwich wrote a few years ago. "Britain may have sought to profit from its turn to Europe, but it was Australia that gained most from it." In his 2017 Lowy Lecture, Boris Johnson reflected that Australia's fate in being forced to embrace Asian trade in the 1970s led to a better outcome than Britain's decision to throw in its lot with Europe.

The pressure of China's trade truculence also inspired some unorthodox responses. Peter Dutton proposed to the prime minister in mid-2020 that Canberra talk to the other three Quad countries – the US, Japan and India – about creating a democratic buyers' club to coordinate trade to defeat China's coercive tactics. So if China boycotted a commodity from one country, the other three would look to buy more to share the pain. Morrison didn't develop the proposal. But this idea, or similar ones, was under discussion in a number of capitals at the end of 2020, including in Washington. *The Wall Street Journal* reported that the Trump administration was weighing such a plan in its final months; a former national security adviser to Joe Biden in his vice-presidency, Danny Russel, said that such an idea, which he described as a "victims' fund", could be achievable under a Biden administration: "Yes, the sky's the limit with creative options." Much will depend on the Biden presidency.

An overarching aim of the CCP is to fuse China's civilian economy with its military economy. This is its "military-civil fusion" development policy to create an integrated national strategic system. This includes requiring civilian infrastructure – including telecommunications – to meet military needs, and treating scientific research as a unified civil-military whole. It's integral to Xi's "China Dream" of the "great rejuvenation of the Chinese nation". Australia needs to adjust its entire research, science, university, computing, communications and manufacturing sectors to this reality. "In practice", says the Pentagon's annual report to Congress on China for 2020, military-civil fusion "means there is not a clear line between the PRC's civilian and military economies, raising due diligence costs for US and global entities that do not desire to contribute to the PRC's military modernisation".

All of these are defensive considerations, to protect what Australia already enjoys. But we know that even pre-pandemic the Australian economy was running on the fumes of the 1980s and '90s reforms. If Australia hopes to enjoy future long-term growth, it needs new vigour. For that it must look within. And that demands a serious reform program. Before the pandemic, the Morrison government was in denial about this, because reform is hard and likely to be unpopular, as Hawke and Keating and Howard and Costello found. But it's the essence of political leadership to do what's needed rather than what's convenient. The Reserve Bank governor, Philip Lowe, put it elegantly in an interview: "The best option" for Australia is "creating an environment where firms want to innovate, invest, expand and hire people. I think that's the best option. I'm sure at the analytical level the government would agree. The challenge they have is to develop a program to do that." Anything else is talking points.

DEFENCE

Ten years ago, very few Australians would have foreseen the political and economic hostility Beijing is openly showing Australia today. What sort of hostility need we prepare for over the next ten years, or more? Trying to predict the exact state of mind of the party's leadership a decade or two or three from now is impossible. But we can have an informed look at its developing capability. Intent can change abruptly; capability builds over years. So that's the first key variable Australia needs to have a stab at.

The good news is that China's out of practice. It hasn't fought in serious combat since its war with Vietnam in 1979. The party's media refer to this as the military's "peace disease". Xi's constant refrain to his troops on his perpetual circuit of visits to China's military bases is to "be ready to fight and win". The two most common slogans in its military newspapers and journals in Xi's

years, however, expose the party's anxieties. One is the "two ina-
bilities". This expresses the concern that the People's Liberation
Army lacks the ability to wage modern war, and that its officers lack the ability to command modern war. The other slogan
is the "five incapables". These are the incapability of some officers to judge situations, understand superiors' intentions, make
operational decisions, deploy troops, or deal with the unexpected.
These slogans together suggest deep top-level concern at the
PLA's ability in the very fundamentals of warfighting. These slogans are aired so often – more than 100 times in the *PLA Daily*
in 2018 alone, according to Harvard's Alastair Iain Johnston –
because Xi wants them fixed. He is intent on his goal to build a
"world-class military" by 2049, the centenary of the founding of
the People's Republic.

The bad news for China's rivals and potential enemies is that
it is making tremendous progress. It is plain for all to see that
the central US strategic policy in the Indo-Pacific – deterrence –
is failing to deter or prevent China from pursuing its carefully
relentless expansion. And in its annual report to Congress on
China for 2020, the US defence department said that "China
has already achieved parity with – or even exceeded – the US in
several military modernisation areas". The Pentagon emphasised
three in particular. First was shipbuilding: "The PRC has the
largest navy in the world, with an overall battle force of approximately 350 ships and submarines including over 130 major
surface combatants. In comparison, the US Navy's battle force is
approximately 293 ships as of early 2020. China is the top ship-
producing nation in the world by tonnage and is increasing its
shipbuilding capacity and capability for all naval classes." Second was land-based conventional ballistic and cruise missiles, of

which China has 1250 with ranges of 500 to 5500 kilometres. Third was its integrated air defence systems, which the Pentagon described as "robust and redundant".

It's self-evidently a good idea for Australia to have the capacity to defend itself. A full-scale continental invasion is highly unlikely today, but a country doesn't need to be invaded to be coerced or incapacitated. Australia needs to be able to defend its interests, including the vital commercial lifeline of its maritime trade, against any threat of interruption, embargo or blockade. Australia's naval power has grown considerably in the last decade, and its air force is progressively taking delivery of its F-35 stealth fighters. But the most effective weapon for defending an island continent and for keeping international waterways open is the submarine. Silent, lethal, almost invisible.

According to China's 2019 defence white paper, its navy is accelerating the transition of its tasks from "defence on the near seas" to "protection missions on the far seas". In the past twenty-five years, China has built thirty conventional submarines and twelve nuclear submarines. Together with the subs it has bought from Russia, the People's Liberation Army Navy currently has seventy-four submarines in service in total. The US has a total of sixty-six. Of China's twelve nuclear submarines, four are capable of launching nuclear-tipped ballistic missiles. The Pentagon expects that China will build another twenty-five conventional subs by 2025. On average, that's one new submarine entering the water every two months. As well as four more state-of-the-art nuclear-powered, nuclear-armed submarines over the next ten years.

Australia awoke from a deep torpor to step up its traditional hard power defences, announcing a strategic update in 2020. It only woke after a series of debacles. Perhaps the greatest bungle was the replacement of the submarine fleet. It's the sort of fiasco that reveals a country deeply complacent about its security. The net results are that the first of Australia's twelve new submarines will be operational in the mid-2030s and the last won't be in service till 2050. And that's if everything runs on time and to plan. The defence department has assessed that a three-year delay in this project would create a "capability gap" – in other words, Australia's six ageing Collins-class submarines would be out of service before the new ones started arriving. No submarines. The history of major defence acquisitions suggests that a three-year delay in such a big and complex program is more likely than not.

So China has seventy-four submarines now and is upgrading its fleet. Australia has six, increasing to twelve over the next thirty years, and possibly a gap of unknown duration when it has as few as zero subs. Australia's complacency and flip-flopping incompetence was based on two assumptions. First was that China was not a hostile power, and that it wouldn't be able to credibly threaten Australia for decades even if it became hostile. Second was that America would take care of everything. In plain language, Australia could fumble around, pretending to run a defence force, while being nice to China and obliging to America, and everything would be fine. Even if something went awry in the region, the US has sixty-six submarines and a world-class nuclear capability. What could possibly go wrong?

Two things: China and America. The Xi regime revealed itself to be undeniably hostile to Australia while building submarine capability and the world's biggest navy at breakneck speed. And not only did America lose much of its military advantage over China, but Donald Trump politicised US alliances so that they've become less reliable. "To re-establish credible deterrence of China," wrote a US military strategist who was the top policy-thinker in the Pentagon during the Obama administration, Michèle Flournoy, "US policymakers need to start thinking more creatively about how to shape Beijing's calculus. For example, if the US military had the capability to credibly threaten to sink all of China's military vessels, submarines, and merchant ships in the South China Sea within 72 hours, Chinese leaders might think twice before, say, launching a blockade or invasion of Taiwan; they would have to wonder whether it was worth putting their entire fleet at risk." Even if China were to lose much of its navy at the same time, by this logic the overwhelming American nuclear advantage would guarantee that the US would prevail.

China has been working on this, too. For decades Beijing's stockpile of nuclear warheads was stable at fifty or fewer, according to Pentagon estimates – the actual number is a state secret. From 2006 or so it started expanding its nuclear arsenal and continues to do so: "Over the next decade, China's nuclear warhead stockpile – currently estimated to be in the low-200s – is projected to at least double in size as China expands and modernises its nuclear forces," according to the Pentagon's 2020 China report. The Federation of American Scientists estimates that China has more, around 320. Beijing plans to be able to deliver nuclear-tipped missiles from air, land and sea – the same ability that America has. Compared to US or Russian nuclear arsenals, China's is small. The Americans have 6185 warheads, of which 1750 are deployed. The Russians have similar numbers. Could China catch up? It has the capacity to add about 2000 new nuclear warheads a year, according to Michael Mazza of the American Enterprise Institute and Henry Sokolski of the Nonproliferation Policy Education Center. They argue that China could achieve nuclear parity with the US in five to ten years.

Australia, of course, has no nuclear weapons. Australia relies on the United States to protect it under the US nuclear umbrella, otherwise known as the doctrine of extended nuclear deterrence. Australia is not alone – many US allies, including Japan and South Korea, shelter under the same umbrella. It simply means that if an enemy were to attack a US ally with nuclear weapons, the US would retaliate by attacking the aggressor with its nukes. That requires an enormous amount of faith in America. The US would have to be willing to engage in nuclear war – risking its own cities and its own peoples' lives – to defend one of its allies.

The question for Australia now is whether that is going to remain a credible deterrent to China over the decades to come. Hugh White, former defence department chief strategist and ANU professor emeritus, considered the question of a Chinese nuclear threat to Australia: "But how real is this risk? Is there really any possibility that China, India or anyone else would launch a nuclear attack on Australia? The answer is almost certainly no, but that is not much help, because an actual nuclear attack is not the main problem we need to deal with," he wrote in his 2019 book *How to Defend Australia*. The main problem was nuclear blackmail: "A far more realistic possibility is that China could use *the threat of a nuclear attack* to force us to capitulate in a conventional war." One scenario would be a Chinese naval blockade of Australia to force Canberra to bend to Beijing's will and yield its sovereignty. Could Australia use its military to attack China's navy and break the blockade? Not if it thought that Beijing would escalate to a nuclear attack in return.

"Unless we were certain they were bluffing, it is hard to see how we would not do as China demanded," wrote White. Australia's conventional forces would be useless "if China could simply trump them with nuclear threats. The only clear way to avoid this appears to be to counter China's nuclear threat with a nuclear threat of our own". The conflict could continue at the level of conventional forces. This is the policy of minimum deterrent that both Britain and France maintain. Mao Zedong understood the concept perfectly: "We need the atom bomb. If our nation does not want to be intimidated, we have to have this thing." It was the beginning of China's nuclear weapons program.

Australia can avoid this unpalatable calculus if it is satisfied that it can rely on American extended nuclear deterrence. Can it? It is difficult to imagine that Donald Trump would have decided that any US allies were worth the risk of nuclear war. Even as Joe Biden signals a return to a more conventional US strategy, America's allies now know that the country that is capable of electing a Trump-type nativist leader is capable of electing another.

Even if the US moved in all good faith to defend its allies, there are ever-rising doubts about its ability to keep its technological edge against China. "US forces wouldn't even know if Beijing had decrypted all of their protected weapons systems, and read their most highly classified communications going back years," a retired US admiral and former national security adviser to Bill Clinton, Joe Sestak, wrote in late 2020, assuming Beijing reached its aim to master quantum computing decryption by 2030. "Until, without warning, one day its entire, now-defenceless digital systems are rendered completely useless." This should also be an omen and advice to Australia to put as great a priority on cutting-edge cyber capability as China does. China's doctrine puts increasing weight on "system destruction" warfare. Australia's non-government cyber experts say that Canberra is years behind both Beijing and Washington in cyber exploitation and defence.

In the 1960s, Australia under John Gorton started work on the infrastructure for a nuclear bomb capability. But Australia changed course, trusted America to do the dirty work, and became a leader of the non-proliferation movement and signed the Nuclear Non-Proliferation treaty in 1973. But Hugh White is not the only strategist to break the longstanding Australian taboo on the issue. He is one of three former occupants of the same post – chief strategist for the defence department – to raise the question over the past year or so. Indicating how much Australia's situation has changed, Paul Dibb and Richard Brabin-Smith have also put it on the table. If the real experts tell us that we need to consider nuclear capability, we should probably consider it.

In *How to Defend Australia*, White said that his "preliminary conclusion" is that nuclear forces could be justified if there were no alternatives, but that Australia was not likely to be in that position. He did, however, advocate a major step-up in Australian conventional forces, including at least a doubling of the number of Australian submarines. He suggested that Australia's defence spending increase from the current annual 2 per cent of GDP equivalent to at least 3.5 per cent to adequately stand against Chinese aggression.

What does the federal government think? Australia's *2020 Defence Strategic Update* dropped a longstanding reference in Australia's white papers to the importance of US extended nuclear deterrence. It was "horribly absent" and "suggests a loss of faith" in the credibility of American deterrence, interpreted Rod Lyon, a senior fellow at the Australian Strategic Policy Institute. When I asked Scott Morrison whether he thought Australia needed to revisit the nuclear weapons question, he replied that "it's a function of another debate, and you know where that debate is at". He meant that an Australian nuclear weapons capability needs an Australian nuclear energy industry to support it. And the Howard government legislated against nuclear reactors, other than the small reactor for producing medical isotopes in Sydney's Lucas Heights. Morrison's energy minister, Angus Taylor, has said that the government is open to revisiting the question of nuclear power if the economics supports the argument. With solar energy the cheapest source of new power, they do not. Asking the prime minister the same question a different way, I asked Morrison whether Australia today could have full faith in the credibility of US extended nuclear deterrence? "I don't have any doubts about US reliability."

But reality is on the side of reassessment. For Australia to go from the status quo to joining the ranks of the world's nine nuclear weapons powers would take ten to fifteen years; it would need to put in place the nuclear fuel cycle and infrastructure to support a nuclear industry, for starters. There is a powerful case for moving towards readiness. A hostile China is expanding all elements of its nuclear and conventional forces. America under Obama lost its will to war – Syria trampled all over Obama's "red line" on chemical weapons, and China simply ignored his demands that it cease its territorial expansion in the South China Sea. And America under Trump lost interest in its allies while embracing some of its enemies. Trump was happy to leave Australia alone on the front line of confronting China over the

Huawei ban while he thought he could cut a trade deal with Xi, as his national security adviser John Bolton attested. Beijing is malign and Washington under Trump was truant. Can Australia endure as a vibrant democracy? Not if its survival rests in the hands of either of these great powers.

The man Bob Hawke turned to thirty years ago to spur Australia's engagement with a rising China today describes the logical consequence now that China is risen: "There was always going to be systemic competition between a rich China and the US-led West," says Ross Garnaut. "The pull of each of the pole stars depends on how attractive each turns out to be for its own citizens and for people everywhere." Unfortunately, the US-led West isn't looking its best at the moment, and that's a liability for the democratic world. "History," says Garnaut, "has weighted the scales against democracy at the critical time. The systemic competition is coming to a head when the US and the democratic West are less attractive than they have been for many generations."

After the success of his 1964 work *The Lucky Country*, Donald Horne wrote his 1976 follow-up, *Death of the Lucky Country*. He wrote: "In the lucky style we have never 'earned' our democracy. We simply went along with some British habits." This isn't quite right. Australia joined alliances and fought wars to defend democracy against fascism. In World War II against fascist Japan and Germany and Italy, and again in the coalition to defeat the modern Islamist fascists of Daesh, the so-called Islamic State. Australia today finds itself forced to protect itself against the aims of the Chinese Communist Party. It now must earn its democracy or lose it.

Ultimately, Australia would be most successful by having a cooperative working relationship with China to deal with shared problems of disease and destabilisation, climate and crime, trade and trafficking. But Australia must be able to set the terms of its engagement, to exercise its sovereignty and keep it intact for generations to come. Ross Garnaut's counsel: "The most important thing that we can do is make our own democracy work for all Australians. That means unshackling policy from foreign and vested interests, to allow government in the public interest." He says that the result of his son's handiwork is just a starting point: "The anti-interference legislation, which was not directed only against China, was an important step. It has to be taken much further."

Australia needs to concentrate on strengthening itself, making itself armour-plated against foreign subversion and domination, so that it can engage confidently with China and the world, because it cannot count on anyone else. Australia is best served when democracy is thriving everywhere, but with a global democratic recession now entering its fifteenth year, we have to be prepared to face a world where it is in retreat everywhere. Australia has to be prepared to go it alone if necessary. History is forcing us out of our complacency. Whenever Australia is asked to choose between China and America, the ultimate answer must be that we choose Australia.

The world does not yet have a coherent response to Beijing's domineering, and it might never create one, but informal gatherings of countries are beginning to happen out of concern for a common cause – disparate countries including India and France, Britain and Vietnam, Australia and America, but also among them Japan and Germany, whose leaders recognise an authoritarian threat when they see it. German defence minister Annegret Kramp-Karrenbauer told *The Sydney Morning Herald* that Germany aimed to join naval patrols in the Pacific in 2021: "We share the same values, principles and interests. As a consequence, we stand united against those who challenge us. I am convinced territorial disputes, violations of international law and China's ambitions for global supremacy can only be approached multilaterally." Beijing is increasingly recognised as a threat not only to the Indo-Pacific but to national sovereignty and human liberty everywhere. The stronger Australia stands, the more inclined other countries will be to stand with it. How much another country is willing to help you is partly dependent on how much you might be able to help it. No nation wants a feeble ally.

In Homer's *The Odyssey*, Ulysses and his men ultimately prevail against the giant Cyclops. How? Though trapped in his cave, they keep their nerve. They don't let size define them or their foe. They remain united; they beguile him with apparent friendship, plying him with wine; they try not to slay him but to blind him in an act of what today would be called asymmetrical war, driving a sharpened pole into his single eye as he sleeps; they cleverly keep the Cyclops isolated from the other giants; and they turn his exports to their advantage, clinging to the underside of his rams as they leave his cave to go to pasture while the blind giant feels only the rams' backs. Neither the lure of the Land of the Lotus-eaters nor the violence of the Cyclops could rob Ulysses and his crew of their freedom. But then again, *The Odyssey* is just a story. Australia must write its own.

ACKNOWLEDGEMENTS

Speaking and writing honestly about the China of Xi Jinping is not risk-free. I want to thank each member of my family for their support and fortitude in this cause. My greatest debt in all my work is to my chief collaborator, my secret weapon, my wife, Mindanao.

Free speech and searching analysis are not automatic or inevitable. They are hard-won rights denied to most of the world's population.

These rights exist in Australia only because of the principles and institutions of our free society, defended by brave men and women over generations. There are fewer free societies on earth with each passing year.

I thank and acknowledge my employer, Nine, publisher of *The Sydney Morning Herald* and *The Age*, for its steadfast defence of the principles of fearless and independent journalism.

I thank Black Inc. for its courage in publishing this book and its forerunner, the Quarterly Essay *Red Flag*. As we have seen in recent years, not all publishing houses are committed to the very principles that allow them to exist. Chris Feik deserves particular acknowledgement for both inspiring the idea for the book and for forbearing with its author.

I pay tribute to the frontline news reporters in Australia's media and worldwide who do the daily work of informing all of us about the realities of our nation and our world. Without their work, our freedoms would inevitably be drowned by deceit, ignorance and public relations.

The journalists and writers who bear the greatest risks are the ones closest to Xi Jinping's grasp. China is "the world's worst jailer of journalists", according to the Committee to Protect Journalists' 2020 report. At the time of writing, two Australian writers are in detention in China's system of political "justice": blogger Yang Hengjun was detained in 2019, and broadcaster Cheng Lei in 2020.

I acknowledge their suffering, a reminder of George Orwell's insight: "In a time of deceit, telling the truth is a revolutionary act."

INDEX

3G network 17
4G network 16–17, 19
5G network 15–24, 37–8, 42, 220, 222, 242–3, 250, 296, 321 *see also A Comprehensive Guide to 5G Security*; Ericsson; Huawei telecommunications; Internet of Things; Nokia; ZTE
2008 Beijing Olympic Games torch relay 266–9, 272 *see also* People's Armed Police (PAP); 'Sacred Torch Guard Team'; Sebastian Coe; *The Sydney Morning Herald*; Tibet protestors; Yolaine De La Bigne
2020 *Defence Strategic Update* 336

A Comprehensive Guide to 5G Security 18
A2 milk company 323–4
Abbott, Tony (Australian fmr prime minister) 166, 285, 288
ABC (Australian Broadcasting Corporation) 10, 104, 124, 228, 275, 284, 316
ABC Media 274 *see also* Hunan Provincial Committee of the Chinese People's Consultative Conference
Abe, Shinzo (Japan's fmr prime minister) 131–2, 189
Abetz, Eric (Liberal senator) 308–9
Afghanistan 191, 253
AfrAsiaBank (*Global Wealth Migration Review*) 302–3
Ai Weiwei (Chinese artist) 6–7
AIS (automatic identification system) 185
Al Jazeera 103
Albanese, Anthony (Labor Opposition leader) 237, 299, 321
Alipay (mobile payments app) 135–6

All-China Federation of Industry and Commerce 141
Amazon 133
AMC (US cinema chain) 137
American Civil War 171–2
American Conservative Union 285
American Drug Enforcement Administration 204
American Enterprise Institute 227, 236, 333
AMP Society 40–1
An Anatomy of Chinese (Link Perry) 111
Anbang Insurance Group 138 *see also* Wu Xiaohui
Andrews, Daniel (Victoria Labor premier) 116, 120
Ant Group 135 *see also* Jack Ma (Ant Group)
Anthony, Doug (Australian fmr deputy prime minister) 327
Anxiety Disorders Foundation 82
Anzac Day (Australia) 171
Apple Pay 135
Arts Centre Melbourne's Asia-Topa Festival 2017 116–18 *see also The Red Detachment of Women*
Ashe, John (UN General Assembly president) 4, 85–6
Asia Maritime Transparency Initiative 185
Asia-Pacific 72, 252, 260
Asia-Pacific Economic Cooperation (APEC) 50
Asia Society Policy Institute 107
Asian Australian Alliance 32
ASIO *see under* Australian Security Intelligence Organisation (ASIO)
Association of Southeast Asian Nations (ASEAN) 181–2, 198, 233, 326

Atlas of Shame 172
Atlas of the Century of National Humiliation in Modern China 172
AuMake 46
aussietheatre.com.au 116
AUSTRAC federal money-tracking agency 318
Australia 2–3, 15–24, 36–9, 41–2, 58–63, 67, 69, 71, 73, 76, 79, 81, 97, 112, 116–18, 165, 171, 183, 210, 240, 267, 276, 296, 303, 309–10, 313, 316–17, 319–21, 328–29 *see also* Chinese Australian community; Chinese-language media in Australia
    Australia–China relations 49, 74–9, 123–9, 239–40, 263, 280, 301, 338–9
    Australian citizens kidnapped 5, 98–9, 263–4
    Australian First Nations people 302
    Belt and Road Initiative (BRI) 190, 194, 244, 298
    and Britain 2, 45, 238, 326–7
    Chinese immigration 309–13
    COVID-19 international inquiry 26, 33–4, 36, 99–100, 120, 127–8, 227–32, 237, 243
    and *daigou* 46
    drug trafficking to 205
    economic dependence on China 4–5, 8–9, 13, 43–5, 48, 51–2, 114, 120–1, 215, 239, 323
    the fourteen demands by China 242–8, 302
    and multiculturalism 306
    the Muslim community 305
    racial discrimination 31–2, 35, 308
    racial discrimination laws in Australia 31
    racial discrimination slurs on Australia 26–9, 35, 36, 245, 307–8
    and South China Sea 119, 240, 244
    supply of resources 45–7, 50, 73, 79, 238–40, 324
    suppression of the Australian press 9–11, 245
    thermal coal exports to China 45–6, 96, 221–2, 224–5, 235, 324
    trade sanctions imposed by China 33–4, 95–6, 99, 212, 221–2, 227, 229, 233–6, 242, 247, 293, 295, 321, 323–4, 326, 327–8

    universities and Chinese students 8, 26–7, 72, 100, 240, 243
Australia and militarisation 20, 41, 76–7, 80–1, 240, 276, 288–9, 297, 331–2, 334–7, 340
    2020 *Defence Strategic Update* 331, 336
    Australian Defence Force (ADF) 317
    countering espionage 20, 41, 76–7, 80–1, 240, 276, 281, 284, 288–9, 297
    the doctrine of extended nuclear deterrence 334–7
    and nuclear weapons 336–7
    the Quadrilateral Security Dialogue 299
Australia and parliament 67, 82–4, 92–3, 262, 278–80 *see also* Foreign Influence Transparency Scheme Bill 2018 (FITS); National Security Legislation Amendment (Espionage and Foreign Interference) Bill 2018 (EFI); Parliamentary Joint Committee on Intelligence and Security (PJCIS)
    and bipartisanship 12, 69, 82–3, 90–2, 237, 290, 320–3
    Critical Minerals Facilitation Office 298
    defence strategy update 298–9
    Fair Work Commission 279
    FITS Act Transparency Register 285–8, 316
    foreign interference laws 10–12, 20, 35, 37, 67, 69, 77, 80–4, 87, 91, 93, 124, 225, 240, 243, 273, 277–81, 284, 289, 310, 318, 321, 339
    Foreign Relations Bill 298
    Independent Parliamentary Expenses Authority 2017 320
    Northern Australia Infrastructure Facility 312
    Nuclear Non-Proliferation treaty 336
    the Pacific 'step-up' policy 298
    Parliamentary Budget Office 319–20
    and political donations 52–6, 65, 81, 87, 89, 296, 317–18
    and strategic oil reserve 298
Australia and the Northeast Asian Ascendancy (Garnaut Report) 71–4
Australia China Business Council 232
Australia First Nations people 302

Australia–China Joint Agricultural
Commission 95
Australia–China Relations Institute
(ACRI) 280, 295
Australia–Chinese Institute for Arts and
Culture 280
Australian Associated Press 124, 268
Australian Bureau of Statistics 293
Australian Council for the Promotion of
Peaceful Reunification of China 61,
287
Australian Cyber Security Centre 97
Australian Defence Force (ADF) 317
Australian Federal Police (AFP) 10, 70,
266, 278, 281–2, 288
Australian Foreign Affairs 262
Australian Greens party 318
Australian Guangdong Chamber of
Commerce 61
Australian Industry Group 233
Australian Labor Party 9, 35, 52, 54–5,
67–9, 71, 79, 82–4, 87–8, 90–1, 226,
318, 320–1
Australian Liberal Party 9, 21–2, 68–9,
79, 84, 87, 89, 226 *see also* Coalition
Australian National University (ANU)
8, 71, 104, 181 *see also* National Security
College (ANU)
Australian New Express Daily 271–3
Australian Security Intelligence
Organisation (ASIO) 9–10, 41–2,
53, 55, 64, 69–70, 76–7, 79–81, 87–8,
240, 261–2, 278–84, 288, 297–8, 305,
313, 318–19 *see also* Counter Foreign
Interference taskforce
Australian Security Intelligence Service
(ASIS) 261
Australian Signals Directorate (ASD)
16–19, 261
Australian Strategic Policy Institute
(ASPI) 104, 208, 287, 295, 300,
314–16, 337
Australian Tax Office (ATO) 280–1
Australian Values Alliance 62, 117, 309
Austria 194
Austria-Hungary 170
authoritarianism 94, 99, 110, 119, 210,
230, 288, 310, 339

Bagshaw, Eryk (*The Age*) 10
Bangladesh 199
Bannon, Steve (US election campaign
chief executive) 78

Baogang Guo (Dalton State College) 109
Barmé, Geremie (Australian Sinologist)
99, 126–7, 130, 154–5, 207
BBC (British Broadcasting Corporation)
10, 38, 98
Beidou global positioning system (GPS)
199–200
Beijing Yeshi Enterprise Group Ltd. 141
Bellamy's Organic 323–4
Belt and Road Initiative (BRI) 3, 105,
131, 141, 177, 179, 189–91, 193–200,
207, 211, 244, 269, 298, 303, 324
Belt and Road News Network, The 104–5
Biden, Joe (US president) 145, 159, 248,
258–9, 299, 328, 335
Bigne, Yolaine De La 268
bin Laden, Osama 253
Birmingham, Simon (Australian Liberal
senator) 96, 221
Birnes, William (American publisher)
257
Birtles, Bill (Australian media
correspondent) 9–11, 282–3
Bishop, Bill (Sinologist) 137
Bishop, Julie (Australian fmr foreign
affairs minister) 319, 322
Blanchette, Jude (China adviser) 210
Bloomberg News 283–4, 293
Bo Xilai (fmr commerce minister) 107–8,
110
Bolton, John (US fmr national security
adviser) 16, 37, 338
Boon, Maxim (*Daily Review*) 117–18,
120 *see also The Age*; *The Red Detachment
of Women*
Boxer Rebellion 1900 170
Brabin-Smith, Richard 336
Brady, Professor Anne-Marie (NZ
Sinologist) 2, 38, 89, 208, 262–3, 265,
269 *see also Australian Foreign Affairs*;
'Party Faithful' essay; University of
Canterbury
Brazil, Matthew (*Chinese Communist
Espionage: An Intelligence Primer*) 262
Britain 7, 170, 173, 189, 201, 212, 214,
225, 233, 238, 302–3, 326–7, 335, 339
Britain and MI5 (domestic secret service)
261
Britain and MI6 (secret service) 261
British East India Company 7, 202–3
British House of Commons 214
Brookings Institution 204
Brooks, Mel (*The Producers*) 117

Brown, Bob (Greens fmr senator) 269
Brown, Kerry (English Sinologist) 150–1
Brunei 183, 227
Burgess, Mike (ASIO director-general of security) 16, 19, 20, 275, 278, 281–2, 288–9, 297–8, 305
Byrne, Anthony (Australian Labor senator) 67–9, 82–3, 88, 90–3

Caixin (business news magazine) 136
Callahan, William (international studies professor) 172, 174
Camdessus, Michel (IMF French head) 202
Cameron, David (British fmr prime minister) 214
Campbell, Angus (Australian defence force chief) 317
Campbell, Kurt (US top Asia adviser) 300
Canada 31, 212, 219–20, 224, 302, 304, 320
Cantonese 275
capitalism 303
Carney, Matthew (ABC correspondent) 10–11, 283
Carouso, James (US chargé d'affaires) 88
Carr, Bob (foreign affairs minister) 9–10, 84, 280
Carter, Sir Nick (British Army chief of defence staff) 249
CBC 10
CCP (Chinese Communist Party) 2, 4–6, 8, 12, 23–6, 28, 33–5, 38–9, 44, 51–3, 55, 59, 66–9, 74, 77–8, 80–1, 85–6, 94–5, 99, 108, 110, 117–18, 125–6, 130, 144–6, 166, 171, 175, 178, 192–3, 210, 212, 226, 236, 238–9, 241, 257, 261–2, 267, 274–5, 295, 297–8, 301, 305–8, 312, 318, 323, 338 see also Belt and Road Initiative (BRI); China Daily; Global Times; People's Daily; People's Republic of China (PRC); United Front Work Department; Xinhua News Agency
  1928 Sixth Party Congress 167
  2017 Nineteenth National Congress 106, 231
  2017 party constitution 24–5
  advancing foreign policy 211
  aim of long-term political dominance 159–60
  being a 'friend of China' 89, 180–1
  the cadres 75–6, 147, 160, 314

control of foreign world waishi 208–9, 220
control of press and social media 11, 101–4, 132–3, 141–2, 159, 162–4, 228, 315–16
control of religion and groups 158–9
control of the market economy 134–41
control of the private market 24, 140–1, 210–11
the extradition treaties 56–8
the 'foreign elite capture' policy 2–3
the National Intelligence Law of 2017 24
and 'official talk' 111–12
the one-party state 107, 162, 286
and party leadership 109, 155–6, 291
power checks and balances 157–8
and propaganda 27, 36, 75, 97, 102–5, 112, 116, 120–1, 129, 134, 154, 220, 271, 273, 282, 303, 314
'reform and opening' 48
the reification campaigns 126–7
rewriting history 163–4
the rule by politics 57
suppression of Western press 10–11, 282–3
and yishixingtai (ideology and thought) 102–3
CCP Central Committee of the Chinese Communist Party 104
CCP Central Leading Group on Internet Security and Informatisation 133
CCP Central Military Commission 266
CCP Central National Security Commission 142
CCP Central Party School 147
CCP General Office of the Central Committee of the Communist Party of China 157
CCP International Liaison Department (ILD) 265
CCP Ministry of Commerce 22–3
CCP Ministry of Culture and Tourism 26–7
CCP Ministry of Education 26–7
CCP Ministry of Foreign Affairs 22, 26–7
CCP Politburo 39, 56
CCP Politburo Standing Committee 63, 170, 272
Center for Strategic and International Studies 139, 185

Central Political and Legal Affairs
   Commission 58
Chan, Anson (Hong Kong fmr chief
   secretary) 240–1
Channel 7 124
Charles Koch Institute (YouGov 2020
   poll) 260
Chau Chak Wing (real estate billionaire)
   64–6, 75–6, 84, 85–8, 271–2 *see also*
   Kingold Group
Chen, Andy 306–7
Chen Hong (director of Australian
   Studies) 78–9, 222, 284
Chen Yixin (secretary-general of political
   and legal commission) 155
Chen Yonglin (first secretary for political
   affairs) 4, 263
Cheng, Jimmy (Australian Values
   Alliance) 309
Cheng Jingye (Chinese ambassador to
   Australia) 33–4, 84, 227–30, 291
Cheng Lei (Australian business journalist)
   98–9, 283
Cheng Yonglin (Chinese diplomat) 261
Children's Medical Research Institute
   (Westmead) 280
Chin Tan (Australia's Race
   Discrimination Commissioner) 31, 309
China 4–5, 9–10, 15–18, 21, 29–30,
   35, 71–4, 78, 84, 114, 164–5, 180–1,
   189, 192, 227, 230, 238, 273, 283,
   301–4, 306–07, 339 *see also* Cantonese;
   Mandarin Chinese; PRC (People's
   Republic of China); Republic of China
   the Atlas of Shame 172
   the *Atlas of the Century of National
      Humiliation in Modern China* 172
   the 'century of humiliation' 169–71,
      173–4, 178, 203
   and debt-trap diplomacy 195–6, 201
   Defence Education Day (National
      Humiliation Day) 171–2
   and economic growth 44–5, 47–8,
      73, 130, 175–6
   the extradition treaties 205
   and the Han people 29–31, 166, 192–3
   and human rights 8, 32, 36, 160, 240,
      247, 308
   the Hurun Report 139
   leader in technology and
      communications 130, 176–7
   and nationalism 29, 59–60, 155, 169,
      174–5
   and non-Han ethnic groups 29
   Opioid War 2013–2018 203–6
   racial discrimination 30–2, 59
   the Republic of China 165
   and rule of law 105–6
   the symbol of the dragon 29–30
   a wealthy market economy 134–9
   and *xiaokang* (small comforts) 175
China and history 49, 122–3, 162, 164–7,
   170–3, 190
   All-Under-Heaven (*tianxia*) 207
   the *Book of Rites* (*Liji*) 172–3
   Boxer Rebellion 1900 170
   China's Civil War (1920s and 1930s)
      117
   Da Ming Ren (people of the Great
      Ming) 165
   Emperor Qianlong 1792 122–3
   First Sino-Japanese War 167
   the Great Canal 177, 190–1
   the Great Wall 177, 190
   Han dynasty 190
   Hong Xiuquan (Taiping Heavenly
      King) 173
   the Manchu 166, 173
   the Mandate of Heaven 207
   Marco Polo (*Marvels of the World*)
      190
   Ming dynasty 162, 165
   New Territories 99-year lease 202
   Opium Wars 170, 202–3
   Qin dynasty 165
   Qing dynasty 49, 162, 166, 172–3,
      180, 202–3
   the Rape of Nanjing 1937 171
   the Roman ancient organisation
      200–1
   the Silk Road 190–1
   Taiping Heavenly Kingdom 173
   Taiping Rebellion (1850–1864)
      172–3
   Tokyo's Twenty-One Demands 1915
      171
   the Yellow Emperor (Huang Di)
      29–30, 166
   and *Zhongguo* (colloquial name) 166
   and *Zhonghua* (Middle Kingdom or
      Central Kingdom) 165, 176
   and *Zhonghua Renmin Gongheguo*
      (People's Republic of China) 165
China and militarisation 36, 80, 88,
   182–3, 215, 257, 328–30, 332–4
   2019 defence white paper 331

China and militarisation *cont.*
 Beidou global positioning system
 (GPS) 199–200
 and cyber technology 41–3, 97, 245,
 335–6
 global positioning system (GPS)
 199–200
 and 'grey zone' political warfare 69,
 97, 185–7, 189, 191–2, 195–7,
 207–9, 240, 317
 H-6K strategic bombers 119
 nuclear weapons power 337
 the 'string of pearls' (international
 chain of ports) 199
 the 'zero-sum' doctrine 188, 210, 228
China and technology 177, 180, 208,
 249–50 *see also* 5G network; Huawei
 telecommunications; Tencent (video
 game company); ZTE
China Central Television (CCTV) 27,
 101–3
China Daily 23
China Daily Mail 186
China Dashboard project 107
China Development Bank 227
China Global Television Network
 (CGTN) 98, 103–4, 283
China Institute for International Strategic
 Studies 265 *see also* Joint Staff
 Department Intelligence Bureau (JSD)
China Institutes of Contemporary
 International Relations 263
*China Matters: Getting It Right for
 Australia* (Linda Jakobson and Bates
 Gill) 211
China Radio International 104
China Southern airline 51
China United Front Course Book 59–60
China–Australia Entrepreneurs
 Association 61
China–Australia Free Trade Agreement
 (ChAFTA) 242
Chinese Australian community 36,
 58–62, 81, 116–19, 236–7, 271, 273,
 280, 296–7, 304–15
Chinese Australian Forum 236
*Chinese Communist Espionage: An
 Intelligence Primer* (Peter Mattis and
 Matthew Brazil) 262
Chinese Communist Party (CCP) *see
 under* CCP (Chinese Communist Party)
Chinese Embassy (Australia) 267
Chinese National Day 276

Chinese Nationalists Kuomintang 117,
 146, 167–8, 215 *see also* Sun Yat-sen;
 Taiwan
Chinese People's Political Consultative
 Conference (CPPCC) Guangdong 272
Chinese Students and Scholars
 Association 61, 267, 269
Chinese University of Hong Kong 102,
 273–5
Chinese-language media in Australia
 314–16 *see also* ABC Media; *Australian
 New Express Daily*; Hunan Provincial
 Committee of the Chinese People's
 Consultative Conference; WeChat
Chiu, Osmond (Per Capita think-tank
 fellow) 308–9
Chow, Winky (Chau Chak Wing's
 daughter) 272 *see also Australian New
 Express Daily*
Chubais, Anatoly (Yeltsin's economic
 affairs deputy) 139–40
CNBC (US financial news channel) 98
Coal & Allied 52 *see also* Rio Tinto;
 Yancoal
Coalition 9, 226, 237, 318, 321 *see also*
 Australian Liberal Party
Coe, Sebastian (2012 London Games
 chairman) 268
Cold War 77, 88, 262
Colvin, Andrew (Australian Federal
 Police fmr head) 70
Commonwealth Parliamentary Offices
 (Melbourne) 56
Communist Youth League 149–51
Confucius Classes and Institutes 103,
 174, 285, 287
Confucius Institute (University of
 Chicago) 286
Confucius Institute (University of
 Sydney) 286–7
Conroy, Stephen (Australian Labor
 senator) 52–3, 55
Conservative Political Action Conference
 285
Cooper, Andrew 285, 287
Cooper, Zack 227, 236
Costello, Peter (Australian fmr treasurer)
 71, 329
Counter Foreign Interference taskforce
 281, 284, 288
'Countering China's Influence Activities:
 Lessons from Australia' (Dr Amy
 Searight) 36–7

COVID-19 international inquiry 26, 33–4, 36, 99–100, 120, 127–8, 227–31
COVID-19 pandemic 26, 32–3, 71, 100, 105, 110, 120–1, 125, 164, 219, 228, 232, 235, 244, 281, 297, 308, 310–11, 314, 328–9
Coward, Noël 132
Critical Infrastructure Centre 296
Critical Minerals Facilitation Office (Australia) 298
Crumpton Group (US-based geopolitical advisory business) 210
Cultural Revolution 60–1, 107, 114, 127, 144, 146–9, 152, 154, 156, 223
Curtin, John (Labor prime minister) 68, 93
cyber technology 41–3, 97, 245, 335–6
Czech Republic 23

Da Ming Ren (people of the Great Ming) 165
Dahl, Knut (Norwegian scientist) 311–12
daigou 46
Daily Review 117–18
Dalai Lama 151–2, 212, 214–15, 224–5
Dalgaard, Carl-Johan (Danish researcher) 200–1
Dalian Wanda Group 137–8
Dalton State College 109
Danby, Michael (Australian Labor senator) 88
Dastyari, Sam (Australian Labor senator) 8–9, 54–5, 82, 87, 89, 280, 291, 318
Davidson, Admiral Philip (US Indo-Pacific Command) 183
Death of the Lucky Country (Donald Horne) 338
debt-trap diplomacy 195–6, 201
Defence Education Day (National Humiliation Day) 171–2
Delury, John (Wealth and Power: China's Long March to the Twenty-First Century) 48–9, 169, 174–5, 207 see also Orville Schell
democracy 49, 69, 73, 99, 108, 114, 157, 161, 210, 310, 313, 316–17, 319–20, 338–9
Dempsey, Martin (US Joint Chiefs of Staff chairman) 251–2, 254
Deng Xiaoping 3, 12, 48–9, 80, 106–7, 138, 145, 152, 175, 178
Deng Yuwen (Communist newspaper fmr editor) 110

Denmark 23
Department of Foreign Affairs and Trade 96, 221
Der Spiegel (Germany) 10
Di Sanh 'Sunny' Duong (Liberal party candidate) 284–5
Dibb, Paul 336
Dictionary of Ideas (Brockhampton) 113
Dikötter, Frank (professor of history) 30
Djibouti (Africa) 80, 195
doctrine of realism 39
Document No. 9 (Communique on the Current State of the Ideological Sphere) 157–61
Dorfman, Zach (US journal Foreign Policy) 5, 263 see also 'The Disappeared' 2018 report
Doshi, Rush (director of China strategy) 247–8
Downer, Alexander (Australian fmr foreign affairs minister) 9–10, 65, 327
Dreyfus, Mark (Labor Party senator) 87–8, 92–3
Duterte, Rodrigo (Philippines' president) 214, 225
Dutton, Peter (Australian fmr home affairs minister) 20–3, 25, 70, 86, 281, 327–8

Field Research 46
Fitzgerald, John (Australian Sinologist and emeritus professor) 27–8, 275
Five Eyes Allies (intelligence-sharing alliance) 220
Flournoy, Michèle (US Undersecretary of Defense for Policy) 256–7, 333
Fong, Natalie (Griffith University historian) 308
Forbes (US business magazine) 130, 132, 135, 294
Forbidden City (Beijing) 30
Forde, Matt (British satirist) 131–2
Foreign Affairs 77–8, 256–7
Foreign Influence Transparency Scheme Bill 2018 (FITS) Australia 67, 69, 76, 81, 93, 275, 278–9, 285–8 see also FITS Act Transparency Register
Foreign Investment Review Board 42, 239, 296
Foreign Policy (US journal) 5, 263
Forrest, Andrew 'Twiggy (Fortescue Metals founder) 229–33 see also Minderoo charitable foundation (Walk Free)

Fortescue Metals Group 229, 232
Four Corners (ABC) 55
Fox Hunt campaign 264
Foxtel cable TV service 104
France 170, 202, 212, 225, 335, 339
Freedom House (US-based independent watchdog operation) 177, 302
French, Robert (fmr chief justice) 298
Fu Zhengyuan (scholar) 106
Fukuyama, Francis 190, 320 *see also Political Order and Political Decay*; *The Origins of Political Order*
Fullilove, Michael (Lowy Institute) 303–4

Galileo global positioning system (GPS) 200
Gandhi, Mohandas 'Mahatma' 7
Gang of Four 107 *see also* Jiang Qing
Gao Yu 160
Gaoshan, the 29
Garnaut, John (fmr Beijing correspondent) 64–6, 70, 73–8, 80, 85, 276–9 *see also Foreign Affairs*; *The Age*; *The Sydney Morning Herald*
Garnaut, Ross (economics professor ANU) 71–4, 79, 338, 339
Garnaut Report (*Australia and the Northeast Asian Ascendancy*) 71–4
Gehry, Frank (architect) 65
Gekko, Gordon 44
General Office of the Central Committee of the Communist Party of China 157
George Washington University 103
Germany 162–3, 170, 189, 201–2, 304, 338–40
Gill, Bates (*China Matters: Getting It Right for Australia*) 211
Gillard, Julia (Australian fmr prime minister) 16, 42–3
global financial crisis 50
global geopolitics 25
global positioning system (GPS) 199–200
Global Risk Insights (London) 131
Global Times 23, 27, 34, 127, 280, 282, 323
Global Wealth Migration Review (AfrAsiaBank) 302–3
globalisation 191
Good Weekend magazine 278
Google 133
Gorton, John (Australian fmr prime minister) 336

Gottliebsen, Robert (business commentator) 48
Great Canal 177
Great Hall of the People 152
Great Leap Forward 60, 111, 114, 146, 154, 235
Great Wall 177
'Greater East Asia Co-Prosperity Sphere' 189
Green, Celia (English philosopher) 69
'grey zone' political warfare 69, 97, 185, 186–87
Griffith University 308
Grossman, Derek (US RAND analyst) 198
Gu Su (professor of political philosophy) 102
Guangdong 152, 272
Guangzhou 64, 202–3
Guangzhou *New Express Daily* 271–3
Guizhou Province 175

H-6K strategic bombers 119
Hainan Island (South China Sea) 118, 188
Haiqing Yu (RMIT University) 315
Han Changfu (agriculture minister) 95
Han dynasty 190
Han people 29–31, 166, 192–3
Hangzhou 204
Harris, Admiral Harry (US Pacific Command commander) 78
Hartcher, Peter (*Red Flag: Waking Up to China's Challenge*) 278 *see also Good Weekend* magazine; *Quarterly Essay*
Hartwich, Oliver (economist) 327
Harvard University 258, 330
Hastie, Andrew (Liberal senator) 82, 84–90
Hawke, Bob (Australian fmr prime minister) 70–9, 284, 329, 338
Hayton, Bill (BBC journalist) 38, 162–7 *see also The Invention of China*; UK Chatham House think-tank
Heydarian, Richard Javad 195
History of the Peloponnesian War (Thucydides) 39
Ho Chi Minh City University of Law 181
Hockey, Joe (Australian fmr treasurer) 50–2
Hoffman, Samantha (Australian Strategic Policy Institute) 208

Homeland Dream 2019 game 177
Homer (*The Odyssey*) 1, 3, 12–13, 226, 229,
    236, 292, 300, 340
Hong Kong 57, 145, 170, 215, 239,
    240–1, 243, 265–6, 271, 295, 301, 313
    see also New Territories 99-year lease
Hong Kong Basic Law 241
Hong Kong exchange 136
Hong Kong 'One Country, Two Systems'
    177–8
Hong Kong University 30
Hong Kong University of Science and
    Technology 29, 269
Hong Xiuquan (Taiping Heavenly King)
    173
Horne, Donald 338 *see also Death of the
    Lucky Country; The Lucky Country*
How to Defend Australia (Hugh White)
    334–6
Howard, John (Australian fmr prime
    minister) 71, 290, 310, 329, 337
Hoyts (Australian cinema chain) 137
Hu Jintao 102, 106
Hu Xijin (*Global Times* editor) 127
Hu Xingdou (Beijing-based political
    economist) 235
Hu Yaobang (CCP general secretary) 152
Hua Chunying (CCP foreign affairs
    ministry) 26
Huang Di (Yellow Emperor) *see* Yellow
    Emperor (Huang Di)
Huang Xiangmo (property tycoon) 9–10,
    53–5, 64, 76, 82, 89, 280, 287, 318–19,
    321 *see also* Yuhu Group
Huawei telecommunications 10, 15–19,
    20–4, 35, 37–8, 41–3, 68, 124, 219, 220,
    222, 225, 228, 242, 291, 296, 321, 338
    see also 5G network
Hugh, John (Australian Values Alliance)
    62
Huifeng 'Haha' Lui (fmr PLA soldier)
    284
human rights 4, 8, 32, 36, 73, 220, 309
Human Rights Watch 32
Hunan Provincial Committee of
    the Chinese People's Consultative
    Conference 274
Hunt, Greg (Australian health minister)
    231–2
Hurun Report 2020 139

Imaging Intelligence Division 265
Imperial Twilight (Stephen Platt) 123

Independent Commission Against
    Corruption (ICAC) NSW 52–3, 318
India 7, 23–4, 145, 199, 227, 233, 299,
    328
Indian Ocean 199
Indonesia 5, 196–8, 201–2, 221, 227
Indonesia EEZ 187–8 *see also* Natuna Sea
Inglis, Lucy (*Milk of Paradise*) 203
Instagram 133
Institute for International Finance (IIF)
    193–5
International Cultural Exchange
    Association 61
International Memorial Day for Comfort
    Women 171
International Monetary Fund (IMF) 105,
    195, 202
Internet of Things 15, 250 *see also* 5G
    network
Iraq invasion 253
Irvine, David (ASIO fmr director-general
    of security) 40–2, 296
iShares 135
Islamic State (Islamic fascists of Daesh)
    338
Israeli Mossad 261
Italy 170, 194, 201, 338

Jacques, Jean-Sebastien (Rio Tinto fmr
    boss) 325
Jakobson, Linda (*China Matters: Getting It
    Right for Australia*) 211
Jamestown Foundation 103
Japan 6, 23–4, 44, 68, 71, 145, 170–1, 173,
    176, 180, 185, 189, 212–14, 217–18,
    225, 227, 240, 252, 303, 328, 334,
    338–9 *see also* Tokyo's Twenty-One
    Demands 1915
Jardine, William (merchant) 203
Jennings, Peter (Australian Strategic
    Policy Institute ASPI director) 300
Jia Qinglin (CCP Politburo Standing
    Committee member) 272
Jiang Qing 116
Jiang Zemin 106
Johnson, Boris (UK prime minister) 326–7
Johnston, Alastair Iain (Harvard
    University) 330
Joint Staff Department Intelligence
    Bureau (JSD) 265 *see also* China
    Institute for International Strategic
    Studies; PLA Institute of International
    Relations

Joko Widodo (Indonesian president)
187–8
Jones, Lee (Queen Mary University
academic) 198
Joske, Alex (China analyst and linguist)
63, 104, 287, 288, 314–16
Joyce, Rob (US National Security Agency
cybersecurity adviser) 254–5
JPMorgan Chase 135

Kadeer, Rebiya (leading voice of the free
Uighurs) 31, 192–3
Keane, John (*The Life and Death of
Democracy*) 320
Kearsley, Jonathon (reporter) 125, 241–2,
292
Keating, Paul (Australian fmr prime
minister) 71, 84, 226–7, 300, 329
Keneally, Kristina (Labor senator) 285
Kennedy, Paul 174
Kennedy, Scott (Chinese business expert)
139
Kershaw, Reece (Australian Federal Police
head) 281
King George III 122
Kingold Group 64 *see also* Chau Chak
Wing
King's College (London) 150
Kiribati 218
Kishi, Nobusuke (Shinzo Abe's
grandfather) 189
Kovrig, Michael (Canadian fmr diplomat)
219
Kramp-Karrenbauer, Annegret (German
defence minister) 339–40
Kyrgyzstan 195

Lam, Willy Wo-Lap (Chinese University
of Hong Kong) 102, 107–9, 114–15,
133, 142
Lam Min Yat (Hong Kong columnist) 30
Laos 195
Latin America 233
Le Monde (France) 10
Lee-Jackson Day (United States) 171
Lenin, Vladimir 229–30, 237
Lewis, Duncan (ASIO fmr head and
national security adviser) 9, 42, 55, 70,
76–7, 80, 88, 240, 279, 305, 317, 319
Li, the 29
Li Jianjun (academic) 284
Li Keqiang (China's premier) 176
Li Wenliang, Dr 164

Liang Qichao (nineteenth-century
intellectual and politician) 165
Liangjiahe (Shaanxi province) 148–9
liberal democracy 145, 158, 160, 248, 262,
290, 313
liberal democratic freedom 105
Library of Chrysanthemum Fragrance
146
Link, Perry (Chinese linguistics expert)
111, 223 *see also An Anatomy of Chinese*
Little Red Book 116
Littleproud, David (Australian agriculture
minister) 95–6
Liu, Gladys (Liberal MP) 284, 321
Liu Xiaobo (Chinese writer and
democracy advocate) 214
London School of Economics 172
Long March 146
Lord Macartney (British envoy to China
1792) 122–3, 295
Lou Jiwei (finance minister of China)
50–2
Lowe, Philip (Reserve Bank of Australia
governor) 47, 209–10, 329
Lowy Institute 8, 32, 36, 226, 303, 327
Lynas Corporation (Australian rare earth
company) 213
Lyon, Rod (Australian Strategic Policy
Institute) 336–7

Ma, Jack (Ant Group) 135–7 *see also*
Alipay (mobile payments app)
MacDonald, Claude 202
Macron, Emmanuel (French president)
212
Magassouba, Abdoulaye (West Africa's
Guinea mines minister) 325
Mahathir Mohamad (Malaysia fmr prime
minister) 196
Malaita Province (Solomon Islands) 4
Malaysia 5, 175, 183, 187, 227
Malaysia East Coast Rail Link 196
Maldives 195, 199
Manchu invaders 166
Manchuria 162, 180
Mandarin Chinese 272, 275, 277
Mao Zedong 3, 11, 60–3, 107, 111,
113–14, 117–19, 126–7, 130, 144–7,
152–6, 158, 163, 172, 175–6, 235, 335
see also Cultural Revolution; Great
Leap Forward; Jiang Qing; Library of
Chrysanthemum Fragrance; Little Red
Book; Red Detachment; Red Guards

forced integration of people 180, 192–3, 207, 301
founding of modern China 1949 176, 208
his ideology 113–14
the 'model dramas' of the revolution 116
the propagandist 150–1
the 'Yan'an rectification campaign' 1942–1945 155
Marles, Richard (Labor deputy leader in the Senate) 56, 322
Marsudi, Retno (Indonesia's foreign affairs minister) 188
Marx, Karl (*The Communist Manifesto*) 7, 44
Marxism 142
Marxist-Leninist system 128, 208
Mason, Peter (Australian businessman) 40–2
Mastercard 135
Mattis, Peter (former CIA analyst) 63, 103, 259, 262 *see also Chinese Communist Espionage: An Intelligence Primer*, Jamestown Foundation
Mazza, Michael (American Enterprise Institute) 333
McCarthyism 308
McDougall, Gay (UN Committee on the Elimination of Racial Discrimination) 31
McKenzie, Nick 55, 274 *see also The Age*; *The Sydney Morning Herald*
Medcalf, Rory (National Security College ANU) 8–9, 12, 69, 290, 323
Meiji Restoration (Japan) 173, 180
Melbourne Crown Casino 54–5
Melbourne Town Hall 60–1
Meng Jianzhu (CCP Politburo member) 56, 58–60
Meng Wanzhou (Huawei chief financial officer) 219
Merkel, Angela (German Chancellor) 162–3
Middle East 233, 259
Milne, A.A. (*Christopher Robin*) 131
Minderoo charitable foundation (Walk Free) 233
Ming dynasty 162, 165
Modi, Narendra (India's prime minister) 299–300
Monash University 151
Mongolia 162, 180, 212, 215–16, 225

Mongols, the 29
Moon Jae-in (South Korean president) 216
Morrison, Scott (Australian prime minister) 12, 23, 25, 36, 79, 93, 97, 99, 127–8, 230–2, 239, 290, 292, 294, 296–7, 299, 315–16, 321, 328, 337
Morrison government 33, 100, 221, 228, 280, 325–6, 329
Moselmane, Shaoquett (Labor MP) 281–3
Murnain, Kaila (NSW Labor Party general secretary) 52–3
Museum of Chinese Australian History (Melbourne) 285
Myanmar 199

Nakazawa, Katsuji (*Nikkei* newspaper) 150
Nanjing University 102
Nansha (Spratly Island) 183
National Ballet Company of China 116–19 *see also The Red Detachment of Women* 2017
National Broadband Network (NBN) 16, 42–3
National Chengchi University Taiwan 195
National Farmers' Federation 233–4
National Humiliation Day (Defence Education Day) 171–2
National Intelligence Law of 2017 24
National Museum of China (Beijing) 170, 174
National Press Club 53, 94, 97–8, 100, 105, 110, 192, 247
National Security College (ANU) 8, 290
National Security Committee (Australia) 20–4
National Security Legislation Amendment (Espionage and Foreign Interference) Bill 2018 (EFI) 67, 69, 76, 81, 93, 275–6, 278, 287–8
Natuna Sea 187–88
neoliberalism 159
Netherlands 31, 304
New Territories 99-year lease 202
New York Times 104
New Zealand 23–4, 303, 318
News Corp 124
Nikkei newspaper 10, 150
Nine-Dash Lines 182, 188
Nine News 125

Nobel Peace Prize 214
Nokia (Finland) 19
Non Proliferation Policy Education
Center 333–4
non-Han ethnic groups 29 *see also* the
Gaoshan; the Koreans; the Li; the
Mongols; Tibetans
North Africa 201
North Korea 77, 118
Northern Australia Infrastructure Facility
312
Norway 23–4, 212, 214, 225, 302
NSW Department of Education 286
Nuclear Non-Proliferation treaty 335–6
Nye, Joseph (Harvard political scientist)
258

Obama, Barack (US fmr president) 5,
131, 178, 183, 203–4, 259, 337
Oceania Federation of Chinese
Organisations 285
Ochmanek, David (US RAND analyst)
255
Office of National Intelligence's Open
Source Centre (Australia) 274
Oldfield, Stewart (Field Research) 46–7
Olsson, David (Australia China Business
Council national president) 232
One Belt, One Road 189–90
Opioid War 2013–2018 203–6
Opium Wars 170, 202–3
Organisation of Islamic Cooperation 5
Orwell, George (*Animal Farm*) 102, 111
O'Toole, Erin (Canada's opposition
leader) 220
Overseas Chinese Affairs Office 63
Oxford Dictionary of Political Quotations
237

Packer, James 65
Pakistan 5, 199, 200
Palau (South Pacific micro-state) 212,
217–18, 224–5 *see also* 'Compact of Free
Association'; United States
Papua New Guinea 298
Paracel Islands (South China Sea) 88,
119, 183–4, 187
Park Geun-hye (South Korean fmr
president) 216
Parliamentary Budget Office 319–20
Parliamentary Joint Committee on
Intelligence and Security (PJCIS)
82–5, 92

'Party Faithful' essay (Professor Anne-
Marie Brady) 263
Patten, Chris (British fmr governor of
Hong Kong) 295–6
Pax Americana 252 *see also* US Seventh
Fleet
Payne, Marise (Australian foreign affairs
minister) 53, 96, 98–9, 228, 231, 321
PayPal 135–6
Peard, Anne-Marie (aussietheatre.com.
au) 116
Pearson, Elaine (Human Rights Watch
Australian director) 32, 35
Pence, Mike (US fmr vice-president)
21–2
Peng Liyuan 30
People's Armed Police (PAP) 266–8
People's Daily CCP 12, 28, 101, 105, 271
see also Zhong Sheng 'Voice of the
Centre'
People's Liberation Army (PLA) *see under*
PLA (People's Liberation Army)
People's Republic of China (PRC) *see
under* PRC (People's Republic of
China)
Per Capita think-tank 308
Permanent Court of Arbitration in The
Hague 80
Pew Research Center poll 304
Philippines 182–6, 212, 214, 225, 227
PLA (People's Liberation Army) 75,
103, 106, 116, 152, 265–6, 330 *see also*
People's Armed Police (PAP)
PLA (People's Liberation Army) Air
Force 119, 191
PLA (People's Liberation Army) Navy
184, 186, 331
PLA and intelligence 261–3, 265–6 *see
also* CCP Ministry of State Security;
Joint Staff Department Intelligence
Bureau (JSD); PLA Strategic Support
Force
PLA Daily 330
PLA Institute of International Relations
265
PLA Literature and Arts Publishing
House 251–2
PLA National Defence University 186
PLA Strategic Support Force 265
PLA The Second Bureau of the General
Staff's Third Department 252
PLA Unit 61398 252
Platt, Stephen (*Imperial Twilight*) 123

Platts commodity industry newsletter 221
Poland 23
Poling, Gregory (Asia Maritime
　Transparency Initiative) 185
Political Order and Political Decay (Francis
　Fukuyama) 320
Polo, Marco (*Marvels of the World*) 190
Pompeo, Mike (US fmr secretary of state)
　262
Port of Darwin 8, 202
Porter, Christian (Australian fmr
　attorney-general) 68, 83, 86, 92, 287
PRC (People's Republic of China) 2,
　10, 19, 22–3, 26–7, 57–8, 60, 101, 111,
　139, 146, 163, 165, 172, 180, 208, 223,
　230, 263, 328, 330 *see also* Cultural
　Revolution; Great Leap Forward;
　Mao Zedong
　　2019 seventieth anniversary 177
　　economic coercion and trade
　　　sanctions 210–25, 227–8, 230,
　　　233–6, 240, 295, 320
　　Zhonghua Renmin Gongheguo 165
PRC Central Political and Legal Affairs
　Commission 58
PRC Ministry of Commerce 22–3, 27
PRC Ministry of Culture and Tourism
　26–7
PRC Ministry of Education 26–7, 286
PRC Ministry of Foreign Affairs 22,
　26–7, 216, 242, 282, 315
PRC Ministry of Public Security MPS
　(*Gonganbu*) 10, 265
PRC Ministry of State Security MSS
　(*Guoanbu*) 155, 263–5, 282 *see also*
　China Institutes of Contemporary
　International Relations; Enterprises
　Division; External Security and
　Anti-Reconnaissance Division; Fox
　Hunt campaign; Imaging Intelligence
　Division; Skynet campaign
PRC National People's Congress 139, 192
PRC State Council 146, 194
Putin, Vladimir (Russian president) 140,
　253–4, 261

Qantas 51
Qi Quao-qiao (Xi Jinping's sister) 110
Qian Qichen (China foreign affairs
　minister) 6
Qiao Liang (Chinese military theorist and
　former general) 191, 250–2
Qin dynasty 165

Qing dynasty 49, 167, 172–3, 175, 180,
　202
Quadrilateral Security Dialogue 299–300,
　328
Quarterly Essay 278
Queen Mary University London 198

Raby, Geoff (diplomat) 84
Rape of Nanjing 1937 171
Ray, Robert (Australian fmr immigration
　minister) 306
Red Detachment 117
Red Flag: Waking Up to China's Challenge
　(Peter Hartcher) 278
Red Guards 147
Red Songs concerts (2016) 60–1, 63, 117
Refinitiv (US financial data supplier) 193
Regional Comprehensive Economic
　Partnership (RCEP) 326
Reilly, James (University of Sydney) 211
Reklai, Leilani (Palau tourism association
　president) 218
Remengesau, Tommy Jr (Palau fmr
　president) 218–19
Ren Zhiqiang (billionaire real estate
　tycoon) 110
Republic of China 165
Reserve Bank of Australia 47–8, 209, 329
Reuters newsagency 221, 267
Reynolds, Henry (*North of Capricorn*) 311
Reynolds, Linda (Australian fmr defence
　minister) 97, 298
Rigby, Richard (ANU) 181
Rio Tinto 50, 52, 324–5 *see also* Coal &
　Allied; Yancoal
Riordan, Primrose (*The Australian*) 58
RMIT University 315
Robb, Andrew (Liberal party senator) 84
Rogers, Admiral Mike (US National
　Security Agency and US Cyber
　Command head) 37
Roman ancient organisation 200–1
Rosen, Dan (US Rhodium Group) 107
Rubbery Figures (TV show) 132
Rudd, Kevin (Australian fmr prime
　minister) 11, 42, 50, 65, 107, 128, 145,
　239–40, 296, 309
Russel, Danny (US fmr senior Asia
　adviser) 184, 328
Russia 77, 139–40, 170, 175, 199, 221,
　333 *see also* Soviet Union
Russia Federal Security Service (FSB) 261
Ryckmans, Pierre (Sinologist) 6

'Sacred Torch Guard Team' 267–8
Sangay, Lobsang (Tibet's exiled president) 192
Sarkozy, Nicolas (French fmr president) 212
Saudi Arabia 5
Sautman, Barry (political science professor) 29, 30
SBS (Special Broadcasting Service) 275, 316
Scarborough Shoal (Huangyan Island) 186
Schell, Orville (*Wealth and Power: China's Long March to the Twenty-First Century*) 48–9, 169, 174–5, 207
School of the Air 82
Schriver, Randy (Pentagon Asia policy official) 37
Searight, Dr Amy ('Countering China's Influence Activities: Lessons from Australia') 36–37
Senkaku Islands (Diaoyu) 185, 213
Sestak, Joe (US admiral and fmr national security adviser) 335
Shambaugh, David (US Sinologist) 103
Shanghai exchange 136
Shangri-La Dialogue 2017 299
Shantou 152
Shenzhen 152
Shirk, Susan (University of California Sinologist) 106
Shorten, Bill (fmr Labor party leader) 56, 84, 87–8, 90, 296
Silk Road 190
Simandou iron ore (West Africa's Guinea) 324–5
Simington, Rory (principal analyst) 221
Simpson, Fiona (National Farmers' Federation president) 233–4
Singapore 23–24
Singtel (Optus parent company) 40
Skynet campaign 264
Smith, Bruce (Australian MP) 312
Smith, Graeme (Australian National University) 104
Smith, Mike (Australian media correspondent) 9–11, 282–3
Snow, Deborah (*The Sydney Morning Herald*) 272
social media 133, 274, 315–16 *see also* Amazon; Facebook; fintech platforms; Google; Instagram; Mark Zuckerberg; Twitter; WeChat; WhatsApp

socialism 12, 105–6, 134, 154, 159, 303
Sokolski, Henry (Nonproliferation Policy Education Center) 333–4
Solomon Islands 218
South China Morning Post 302
South China Sea 7, 35, 53–5, 63–4, 80, 88, 118–20, 181–5, 187, 195, 214, 225, 240, 292, 333, 337 *see also* Hainan Island; Nansha (Spratly Island); Paracel Islands; Spratly Islands
South East Asia 227
South Korea 71, 78, 171, 212, 216–18, 225, 304, 334
Soviet Communist Party 115, 178, 229–30
Soviet Union 44, 77, 89, 103, 115, 118, 126, 249, 261, 308
Soviet Union KGB 261, 263
Spain 304
Spavor, Michael (Canadian businessman) 219
Speers, David 321 *see also* ABC (Australian Broadcasting Corporation)
Spence, Michael (University of Sydney vice chancellor) 84
Spratly Islands (South China Sea) 88, 119, 183–4, 187 *see also* Nansha (Spratly Islands)
Sri Lanka 199
Sri Lanka Hambantota port 196, 202
State Administration for Religious Affairs 63
State Ethnic Affairs Commission 63
Stockholm International Peace Research Institute 255
Stokes, Kerry (billionaire founder of Seven West Media) 120–1, 232 *see also* *The West Australian*
Suga, Yoshihide (Japan's prime minister) 299
Suharto (Indonesia fmr president) 202
Suidani, Daniel (Malaita Province Solomon Islands governor) 4
Sukkar, Michael (Morrison government assistant treasurer) 284
Sullivan, Jake (Biden national security adviser) 259
Sun, Warren (historian) 151
Sun Tzu (ancient Chinese strategist) 252–3, 317
Sun Yat-sen 165, 167–9, 291 *see also* Kuomintang Nationalists; Republic of China

Sweden 302, 304
Sweden Post and Telecom Authority 24
Swinburne University of Technology 27,
   275
Switzerland 302
Sydney 4
Sydney Opera House Trust 40
Sydney Today 274
Sydney Town Hall 60–1

Taiping Heavenly Kingdom 173
Taiping Rebellion (1850 to 1864) 172–3
Taiwan 4, 23, 71, 162, 167–68, 177, 212,
   214–15, 217–18, 224–5, 243–4, 271,
   313
Tajikistan 195
Taylor, Angus (Australian energy
   minister) 337
Taylor, Brendan (ANU) 181
Tehan, Dan (Australian fmr education
   minister) 298
Telegraph (London) 327
Tencent (video game company) 177 see
   also Homeland Dream 2019
Terminal High Altitude Area Defense
   (THAAD) 216–17
Terrill, Ross (Australian Harvard
   Sinologist) 142, 180
Thailand 200
The Age 10, 55, 62, 64, 74, 85, 118
The Atlantic 267
The Australian 53, 58, 124
The Australian Financial Review (AFR)
   33, 43, 46–7, 124, 227
The Daily Telegraph (News Corp) 28, 124
The Diplomat 181
'The Disappeared' 2018 report in Foreign
   Policy (Zach Dorfman) 263
The Epoch Times 104, 274, 314
The Financial Times 177
The Governance of China 2014 (Xi Jinping)
   134
The Guardian 124, 221
The Hague 80, 88, 182, 225
The Invention of China (Bill Hayton) 162,
   164
The Lucky Country (Donald Horne) 338
The New York Times 10
The Origins of Political Order (Francis
   Fukuyama) 320
The Red Detachment of Women 116–19,
   121 see also Arts Centre Melbourne's
   Asia-Topa Festival 2017; National

Ballet Company of China
The Strategist 27
The Sydney Morning Herald 55, 62, 64, 74,
   85, 124, 268, 272, 339
The Wall Street Journal 10, 130, 136, 253
The Washington Post 148–49, 266
The West Australian 120
Thucydides (History of the Peloponnesian
   War) 39
Tiananmen Square 49, 62, 72, 114,
   133–4, 152–3, 163–4, 266, 306
Tibet 162, 180, 192–3, 212, 214, 301
Tibet protestors 64, 266–9
Tibetan Buddhism 216
Tibetans 29, 35, 151, 153, 192–3
Tillett, Andrew (The Australian Financial
   Review) 33, 227
Time magazine 268
Timor-Leste 195
Tojo, General Hideki 189 see also 'Greater
   East Asia Co-Prosperity Sphere'
Tokyo's Twenty-One Demands 1915 171
totalitarianism 108, 111, 144, 301
Trudeau, Justin (Canadian prime
   minister) 219–20, 320
Trump, Donald (US fmr president) 16,
   22, 30, 37, 78, 132, 154, 159, 191,
   204–6, 222, 258–9, 276, 292, 303, 328,
   332, 335, 337
Trump, Melania 30
T.S. Lombard research house 196
Tsai Ing-wen (Taiwan Democratic
   Progressive Party president) 214–15,
   218
Tunzelmann, Alex Von (Oxford historian)
   7
Turkic people 180
Turnbull, Malcolm (Australian fmr prime
   minister) 9, 11–12, 15–24, 35, 37–9,
   66, 68, 70, 73, 76–7, 79–84, 86–7, 90–3,
   127–8, 226, 228, 232–3, 250, 275, 279,
   296, 299, 320 see also A Bigger Picture;
   Foreign Influence Transparency
   Scheme Bill 2018 (FITS); Huawei
   telecommunications; Independent
   Parliamentary Expenses Authority
   2017; National Security Committee;
   National Security Legislation
   Amendment (Espionage and Foreign
   Interference) Bill 2018 (EFI); Shangri-
   La Dialogue 2017; ZTE
Turnbull government 9, 42, 53, 228
Twitter 133, 154, 315

Uhlmann, Chris (ABC presenter) 55
Uighur Muslims (Xinjiang Province) 4–5, 8, 31, 35, 145, 151, 153, 158–9, 180, 192–3, 233, 243
UK Chatham House think-tank 38
UN Committee on the Elimination of Racial Discrimination 31
UN Convention of the Law of the Sea (UNCLOS) 182–4, 187–8, 225, 244
UN Convention on Human Rights 35
UN General Assembly 4, 160
United Arab Emirates 5
United Front Work Department 24–5, 39, 59–63, 81, 86, 166, 262, 269–70, 274, 282, 287, 305, 310, 312–14
United Kingdom 16, 23 *see also* Britain
United Nations 84–5, 106, 158
United Nations' Human Development Index 302
United States 23–4, 31, 36–7, 47, 49, 68, 73, 78, 84–5, 98, 130–1, 170, 176, 191, 199, 203–5, 213–14, 217–18, 184, 222, 224, 227, 240, 302, 304, 328, 330–1, 339
the 9/11 attacks ·253, 262
and Afghanistan 191, 253, 259
the American Civil War 171–2
'Compact of Free Association' with Palau 217
the doctrine of extended nuclear deterrence 334–7
the global positioning system (GPS) 199–200
Iraq invasion 253
Lee-Jackson Day 171
and the military 330–5
November 2020 presidential election 230
the Opioid War 2013–2018 (fentanyl) 203–6
and the South China Sea 183–4
and Terminal High Altitude Area Defense (THAAD) 216
trade sanctions imposed on China 205–6, 211
United States Attorney's Office (New York's southern district) 85, 87
United States Center for Disease Control and Prevention 204
United States Center for Strategic and International Studies report 36–7
United States CIA 85, 103, 261, 262
United States Congress on China 2020 328, 330, 333

United States Cyber Command 37
United States FBI 85, 87–8, 261
United States Joint Chiefs of Staff 251
United States Marshall Plan 193
United States National Security Agency 16, 37, 248, 254–5, 261
United States Navy 330 *see also* US Seventh Fleet
United States Pacific Command 78
United States Pentagon 328, 330–1, 333
University of Canterbury 38
University of Melbourne 118
University of New South Wales 56
University of Queensland 221
University of Sydney 65, 84, 211
University of Technology Sydney (UTS) 9–10, 60, 65, 271, 280, 295, 315
Unrestricted Warfare (Qiao Liang and Wang Xiangsui) 250–2, 257
US RAND Corporation 198, 255–6
US Seventh Fleet 252, 254 *see also* Japan; Pax Americana
USS *Blue Ridge* (US Seventh Fleet) 252

Vantage Australia 236
Varghese, Peter 221–3 *see also* Department of Foreign Affairs and Trade; University of Queensland
Varieties of Democracy (Gothenburg University Sweden) 105
Venezuelan crisis 1902 201
Venmo 135
Victoria Police Organise Crime Unit 277–8
Viet Hoang (expert on law of the sea) 181
Vietnam 23–4, 183, 187, 198, 227, 339
Vision Times 104, 274, 314

Waldorf Astoria (New York) 138
Wall Street Journal 328
Wang, Christina (chief executive) 61
Wang Jianlin (Dalian Wanda Group) 137–8
Wang Qishan (China's vice-president) 137
Wang Xiangsui (Chinese fmr colonel) 250–2
Wang Xining (PRC deputy ambassador) 94–8, 99–101, 105–10, 112, 245
Wang Yi (China foreign affairs minister) 96, 181, 299
Wanning Sun (University of Technology Sydney) 315

Washington Post 45
Wealth and Power: China's Long March to the Twenty-First Century Wealth and Power (John Delury and Orville Schell) 48–9, 207
WeChat 274, 315–16
Wei Fenghe, Lieutenant General (China's defence minister) 163–4
Weiku.com 204
Wen, Philip (Beijing correspondent) 62, 64
Wen Jiabao (China's fmr premier) 212
Western Sydney University 280
WhatsApp 283
Whipps Jr, Surangel (Palau president) 219
White, Hugh (Australian fmr defence department strategist and ANU emeritus professor) 334–36 *see also How to Defend Australia*
White Australia Policy 29, 306–8, 311–12
Wikileaks 150
Wilde, Oscar 189
Wilkinson, Tara 276–8
Willox, Innes (Australian Industry Group chief executive) 233
Wolf Warrior movies 263
Wong, Ernest (NSW Labor MP) 318
Wong, Penny (Labor leader in the Senate) 35, 56, 91, 321–2
Wood Mackenzie global energy consultant 221
World Bank 45, 195
World Health Assembly 34, 230–1
World Health Organization 230–1
World Trade Organization 44, 48, 213, 223, 325
World War I 172
World War II 44, 68–9, 77, 146, 258, 338
Wu Xiaohui (Anbang Insurance Group) 138
Wu Zuxiang (fiction author and literature professor) 111
Wuhan 100, 120, 164

Xi Jinping 4, 6–8, 11–12, 15–16, 24–5, 28, 30, 33–4, 36, 49, 64–5, 84, 88, 94–5, 103–4, 106, 109, 126, 136–7, 164, 169–70, 178, 180–1, 210, 214, 223, 225, 228, 239, 266, 296, 301–2, 304, 321, 329–30 *see also* Liangjiahe (Shaanxi province); Peng Liyuan

anti-corruption campaign to catch 'tigers and flies' 57, 109–10, 151, 155
censoring of criticism 131–3
the 'clean plate' campaign 234–6
the Communist Youth League 149–51
'community of common destiny' 180–1, 188–9, 207, 209
the concept of 'mega-security' 142
growing up in Cultural Revolution 144–50, 154
his book *The Governance of China 2014* 134
his 'China Dream' 157, 171, 174–5, 179, 191, 291–2, 328
his conservatism 114–15
and Document 9 (Communique on the Current State of the Ideological Sphere) 157–9
and Maoist ideology 113–14, 148, 151, 153–4, 156
mass arrests and demotions 108, 155
a 'president for life' 130, 178, 198
president China Central Television (CCTV) 101–2
the 'rectification program' 155
the regime 99, 101, 104–5, 107, 134–40, 155, 181, 228, 246, 248, 276, 292, 332
and 'striving to achieve' 3, 80, 178
Thoughts on Socialism with Chinese Characteristics for a New Era 140–1
the 'three magic weapons' 62–3, 113, 269
'Xi Jinping Thought' 130
and '*zhendi*' 314
Xi Zhongxun (Xi Jinping's father) 145–53 *see also* Cultural Revolution; People's Republic of China National People's Congress; People's Republic of China State Council; Zhongnanhai leadership compound
Xia Yeliang (Peking University Professor) 142
Xinhua News Agency 101, 235, 283
Xinjiang Province 4, 8, 31, 35, 162, 180, 192–3, 243–5, 301

Yan, Sheri 85
Yancoal 52 *see also* Coal & Allied; Rio Tinto
Yang Hengjun, Dr 'Henry' 98–99

Yang Jiechi (China foreign affairs minister and CCP Politburo member) 39
Yang Jingzhong (journalist) 283
Yat-sen Li, Jason 236
Ye Qing 141
Yellow Emperor (Huang Di) 29–30, 166
Yellow Emperor worship ceremony 166
Yeltsin, Boris (Russian post-Soviet president) 139–40
Yeo, George (Singapore fmr foreign affairs minister) 39
YouGov 2020 poll (Charles Koch Institute) 260
Yue Su (Economist Intelligence Unit) 141
Yuhu Group 280
Yun Jiang 308

Zhang, John (Australian Labor staffer) 282–3
Zhang Binglin (classical scholar) 166
Zhang Rongan (Chinese Students and Scholars Association head) 267
Zhang Zhaozhong, Major General (military theorist) 186–7

Zhao Lijian (China's foreign affairs ministry) 164, 274, 282
Zhao Ziyang 49
Zhong Shan (trade minister) 96
Zhong Sheng 'Voice of the Centre' (*People's Daily*) 28
Zhongguo 166
Zhonghua 165
Zhonghua Renmin Gongheguo 165
Zhongnanhai leadership compound 146
Zhou Enlai (Chinese fmr premier) 150
Zhou Long (China's consul-general to Victoria) 232
Zhou Xiaochuan (China central bank chief) 47
Zhu Rongji (first Vice Premier of China) 44, 45, 48–9, 210
Zhuhai 152
ZTE 21–2, 24, 37, 42, 222, 242, 296
Zuckerberg, Mark 133–4
Zweig, David (Sinologist Hong Kong University of Science and Technology) 269